THE TRAGEDY OF THE MIDDLE EAST

The Middle East goes through a seemingly endless cycle of conflict and violence as it falls behind the rest of the world in democratic and economic development. Dictatorship remains the main form of government; demagoguery often dominates intellectual and civic life. A serious reevaluation of whether to change these structures ended with the defeat of the moderate forces favoring reform. *The Tragedy of the Middle East* tries to explain why and how this region is different from other parts of the world. A key factor is the strength of regimes that have learned how to stay in power by using "trump issues," including antagonism toward the West, to defeat criticism. Even the radical Islamist opposition is integrated into the system, since many of its ideas reinforce the status quo, while its threat makes many citizens look to their rulers to protect them from revolutionary change. This book provides a comprehensive analysis of the region's issues and why they remain unresolved.

Barry Rubin is Director of the Global Research in International Affairs (GLORIA) Center of the Interdisciplinary Center in Herzliya, Israel, and is editor of the *Middle East Review of International Affairs*. He is the author of fifteen and editor of eighteen books on international affairs, including *Revolution Until Victory? The Politics and History of the PLO* (1999) and *The Israel–Arab Reader*, sixth edition (2002).

THE TRAGEDY OF THE MIDDLE EAST

BARRY RUBIN

CAMBRIDGE
UNIVERSITY PRESS

PUBLISHED BY THE PRESS SYNDICATE OF THE UNIVERSITY OF CAMBRIDGE
The Pitt Building, Trumpington Street, Cambridge, United Kingdom

CAMBRIDGE UNIVERSITY PRESS
The Edinburgh Building, Cambridge CB2 2RU, UK
40 West 20th Street, New York, NY 10011–4211, USA
477 Williamstown Road, Port Melbourne, VIC 3207, Australia
Ruiz de Alarcón 13, 28014 Madrid, Spain
Dock House, The Waterfront, Cape Town 8001, South Africa

http://www. cambridge.org

First published 2002

Printed in the United States of America

Typeface Sabon 10.25/13.5 pt.   *System* QuarkXPress™ [TB]

A catalog record for this book is available from the British Library.

Library of Congress Cataloging in Publication data
Rubin, Barry M.
The tragedy of the Middle East / Barry Rubin.
p. cm.
Includes bibliographical references and index.
ISBN 0-521-80623-2
1. Middle East – Politics and government – 1945–   I. Title.
DS63.1.R835 2002
956.04–dc21   2002023794

ISBN 0 521 80623 2 hardback

*This book is dedicated to those who
struggle for real freedom and democracy
in the Arab world and Iran.*

Only when I traveled to Europe, a couple of decades ago, did I discover that, contrary to what my teachers taught me, George Orwell was not a villain.

> Issam Mirzu, Syrian dissident, at a civil society meeting in Damascus, January 12, 2001

Often, some people astonish me when they refrain from conducting an analysis and tend to improvise positions that are, usually, verbal and sentimental, are not based on the developments, and do not solve the problems.

> President Bashar al-Asad of Syria, July 16, 2001

Benefit from your own lessons lest you should be burdened with the accumulated price you pay for them and then you will get drowned.

> President Saddam Hussein of Iraq, August 8, 2001

CONTENTS

PREFACE

The Middle East is the world's most controversial region. Yet despite all the attention focused on the area, many longer-term and vitally important issues and trends often seem to be overlooked in the immediate and crisis-oriented focus. This book is an attempt to get beyond that barrier in order to deal with important points that, although generally neglected, help to explain the rush of events and developments.

While it uses printed primary sources, it should be stressed that this book also tries to bring to light the behind-the-scenes dialogue that goes on concerning the region. It is based on hundreds of conversations over several decades with Arabs and Iranians trying to understand and explain their region. The gap between official and published discourse and what people really think, but often cannot say, is central to the analysis presented here.

A note on transliteration: I would have preferred to have a consistent transliteration of Arabic names; the problem is that sources used often employ a different spelling from what I would prefer. To alter all of the spellings from the translations and other materials would lead to even greater confusion. Consequently, aside from some basic standardization, I have left the spellings as they appear in the source footnotes, though I would have preferred to do otherwise.

I would like to thank the Global Research in International Affairs (GLORIA) Center of the Lauder School of Government, Interdisciplinary Center, for its help, and to thank especially Cameron Brown, Lawrence Joffe, Joy Pincus, Elisheva Rosman, and Caroline Taillandier for their help. The greatest thanks of all go to Judith Colp Rubin, my best friend and favorite editor, whose advice and help, as always, were invaluable.

I

THE TRIUMPH OF THE
"OLD MIDDLE EAST"

It was the end of an era for a young century. Lasting peace, rising prosperity, and expanding democracy had seemed inevitable. A return to
the past of irrational conflict, the triumph of forces opposing progress,
had seemed impossible. Yet in August 1914, these dreams were being
shattered for Europe. British Foreign Secretary Sir Edward Grey, looking out his window as twilight fell in London, said mournfully, "The
lamps are going out all over Europe. We shall not see them lit again in
our lifetime."[1]

In European cities, towns, and villages, crowds cheered the advent of
war as a relief from everyday life's boredom and disappointments, mani-
festating the all-too-human desire to leap over difficulties and to solve the
myriad problems of individuals and societies in a single bound. Once
again, from this moment and for many decades thereafter, Europe was
engulfed in turmoil – including three major international conflicts – as
factions battled over democracy versus despotism and over which political, economic, and social system would dominate the modern world.

During this era of about seventy-five years, from World War One's
beginning to the Cold War's end, prospects for stability and peaceful
progress were repeatedly disrupted by national hatreds, unresolved ethnic conflicts, economic depressions, and ideological struggles. Attempts
by a single leader, idea, or country to dominate the continent would destroy cities and pile up mountains of corpses. Only near that terrible
twentieth century's close did Europe evolve beyond that phase to
achieve a basic consensus on key issues that made possible real peace
and cooperation.

1 On Sir Edward Grey see, for example, http://www.firstworldwar.com/bio.grey.htm.

To start a book on the contemporary Middle East by referring to a past European era of crisis may seem strange. Yet there are many parallels between the year 2000 for the Middle East and Europe's critical turning point in the year 1914. What was unique about the Middle East was not the existence there of turbulence and dictatorship but the inability to transcend these factors. Instead, at the very moment when the Arab world appeared able to escape the treadmill of a half-century of tragic history, it suddenly reverted to the old patterns. A new Middle East had seemed to beckon, a land of milk and honey just over the next hill. Now as this vision was torn apart the old, familiar, and ugly landscape of war, strife, and hatred reappeared instead.

Not only did the Middle East turn back to its well-worn ways in the year 2000, which was bad enough, but this outcome was greeted in the Arab world with enthusiasm, and a remarkable minimum of debate over the alternatives. Like the joyous marching off to battle that Europe had experienced at the start of World War One, it was almost as if there was a visible sense of relief that history and ideas were returning to their proper course.

On the surface, this defeat for better times and hope seemed to reflect the downfall of the Israeli-Palestinian peace process as it appeared to approach its moment of triumph. Many observers argued that this failure resulted from the nearest of misses, the historical equivalent of a wrong word or gesture. In fact, though, these events reflected profound, powerful, and well-rooted forces – the mass and not the margins of the substantive issues shaping Middle Eastern politics and doctrines.

Almost exactly a year after the peace process collapsed so completely, a terrible terrorist attack struck at American territory, far from the Middle East, on September 11, 2001, killing more than 3,000 Americans. The assault was carried out by a small group of what seemed the most extreme and deviant of Islamist radicals. Yet while the attack itself was the act of a few individuals, the sympathy and justification it received among Arabs and Muslims in the region also revealed far wider and deeper forces.

A question of tremendous importance faced the Middle East at the onset of a new century that – itself a revealing fact – was determined by a Christian chronology powerful enough to define the world's sense of time. Why did the region have such a troubled history that was so hard for it to escape? Given this question's overriding significance – not only within the Middle East but throughout a world so affected by it – there was surprisingly little reflection on how such a remarkable thing had happened. Some took it for granted; others were overwhelmed by specific events; still others accepted the view that the area's problems all had little to do with its own ideas and ways but were merely the product of Western misunderstanding, interference, domination, and imposed injustice. Sadly, this dominant approach only obfuscated the true causes of the crisis. Tragically, such an approach will make it harder to solve them and will contribute to even more bloodshed and suffering in the region.

This crisis actually began at a time when the Arab-Israeli conflict was closer to resolution than ever before. It intensified in reaction to U.S. and Israeli proposals that would have given Syria the Golan Heights and created an independent Palestinian state, with its capital in East Jerusalem on a quantity of territory equivalent to the West Bank and Gaza. Similarly, Israel's withdrawal from southern Lebanon a few months earlier was not taken in the Arab world as a step toward peace but as a signal to intensify violent struggle. At any rate, to blame Israeli or American "intransigence" or lack of effort for this regression – at a time when the most significant concessions in history were being offered – makes it impossible to understand what actually did happen and its meaning for the region's history.

Indeed, these circumstances suggest the Middle East's great leap backward took place not because of a failure to find a solution to the problem but for exactly the opposite reason – that is, because of the apparent proximity of a negotiated agreement that would have satisfied most Arab grievances. Instead, Arab leaders and opinion makers made a choice to "let" public opinion press for renewed radicalism, after so many years of not trying to shift that opinion in a moderate direction or heeding it on any other issue.

Whatever disagreements remained about precise borders, the implementation of an agreement, refugees, and other details, why did this long-awaited imminent breakthrough coincide with an explosion of violence, hatred, and intensified hard-line stands in the Arab world? The answer must be that the very prospect of peace, along with the need for making compromises in order to move forward, appeared so threatening to Arab leaders and intellectuals and to the masses as to promote a reaction that was exactly the reverse of what most Western observers had anticipated. In political and ideological terms, peace with Israel was perceived as being more threatening than a continuation of conflict with Israel.

At first, this might seem paradoxical, yet it was actually an eminently rational calculation. Most of the Arab world – and Iran as well – is ruled by regimes that cannot or will not provide democracy, civic freedom, human rights, and economic progress. An end to the conflict with Israel would produce a huge increase in demands for reform and change, threatening these regimes' very existence. Apart from often being apologists for their political leaders, much of the Arab intelligentsia – or the party men who, Soviet style, act that role as the rulers' servants – have staked their careers and passions on ideologies that could not accept, or perhaps would not survive, such a transition.

This is not to ignore the fact that these stands were ostensibly, perhaps even genuinely, motivated by such virtuous concepts as solidarity, supporting the underdog, demanding justice, claiming one's rights, gallantly refusing to surrender a cause, preserving identity, and dreaming of an ideal society. Bad policies can always be justified by good excuses, and solving problems can be made to seem very crass in comparison to defending noble ideals. Yet those who preach hatred and dispatch suicide bombers on their missions reap the benefits of power while rarely suffering for the damage they inflict on other people's lives. As Hazem Saghia, a Lebanese writer living in London, suggests, "For the regimes and elites, [these are] deliberate policies to benefit themselves. But the peoples are also responsible for it . . . and [ultimately] they pay the price."[2]

The masses, though, had been fed continually for many years – with little or no alternative available – on the same basic ideas from Arab nationalist rulers, their salaried intellectuals, and radical Islamist movements. Rather than offering truly competing visions, rulers and radical oppositionists competed to prove themselves more militant in the systematic cultivation of hatred, anger, and xenophobia, rejecting the West and excoriating Israel.

Blaming the foreigner for all difficulties and shortcomings is an old political tool found everywhere in the world and throughout its history. Nowhere, however, has it assumed such paralyzing and obsessive

---

2 Hazem Saghia, in *al-Hayat*, February 28, 2001. Translation in Middle East Media Research Institute (MEMRI) No. 198, March 27, 2001.

proportions as in the contemporary Middle East. The information available to most people in the Arab world is extremely limited and often quite inaccurate. In the resulting dialectic, leaders manipulate the masses but then become to some degree prisoners of the very public opinion they have labored to produce or sustain.

Outside observers should not be bound by the same illusions, however. They should not fail to understand how these officially approved grievances preserve Middle Eastern countries and politics from the kind of scrutiny and expectations that apply to other parts of the world. What should instead be at the center of concern and evaluation is the fact that the twenty-first century's onset showed an Arab world that had missed many opportunities to move toward democracy, human rights, economic development, and social progress on a wide variety of fronts. Leaders extolled as embodying great hopes for reform proved themselves little or no improvement over those they had replaced.

The real question for the Middle East during the 1990s was which of two paradigms would triumph. On one hand, there were powerful forces seeking to find some new version of the ideas that had dominated the region during the previous half-century: that the West was an enemy of the Arabs and Muslims, that Israel must be eliminated, that statist economies and dictatorial regimes were the proper systems for the Arabs, and that either Arab nationalist or radical Islamist ideas should guide these nations.

The alternative paradigm would bring the region more into line with what was happening elsewhere in the world. If Arabs, and Iranians as well, wanted to achieve peace, progress, stability, and better lives, then they should adopt such ideas as privatization, democratization, a strong civil society independent of government control, open debate, Western methods adapted to their own cultures, peace with Israel, and a better relationship with the United States.

For reasons involving the interests of those groups already holding power, however, the forces advocating the status quo defeated proposals for change. On the political level, the global rethinking that followed the collapse of the Soviet bloc and communism almost totally bypassed the Arab world. There was remarkably little development of civil society, despite ample publicity for even the tiniest apparent progress on that front, much of which was quickly rolled back. As

Saghia has pointed out, "[We in] the Middle East are under the illusion that the world waits for us and will wait for us forever."[3]

It would not be inaccurate to say that the Arab world after the year 2000 is still governed largely in the same way – and often by the same people – as it had been during the 1970s and 1980s. At best, democracy exists in a formal structure of elections and parliaments that ensure that incumbents always win and legislatures never have much influence. The scope of permissible debate is remarkably narrow. The media, schools, and other institutions remain overwhelmingly in government hands and in the service of the official political line. Each crisis has seemed to reinforce rather than to undermine this system.

In Algeria, the attempt to open the system through freer elections showed the rulers that such a strategy would result in an Islamist takeover. The military suppressed the voting, and a bloody civil war resulted. The lesson taken was that democracy was extremely dangerous.

In Syria, the death of President Hafiz al-Asad brought his son, Bashar, to power. The junior Asad, despite being touted as a reformer, quickly quashed any steps toward change. In Iran, the popularly elected President Muhammad Khatami was stymied by hard-liners who continued to control the country, block his reforms, and arrest his supporters. The conclusion drawn from these instances was that change was very dangerous and could destroy any regime that was too soft or flexible.

In Iraq, President Saddam Hussein survived his aggression against Kuwait, broke all of his commitments to the West made in 1991, and still managed to keep the offensive in weakening international sanctions against him. The lesson derived from this experience was that since the West would not really punish extremist behavior, the radicals should keep acting in this way while moderates, unable to rely on Western protection, must appease extremists in order to survive.

On the economic level, the Middle East was slipping behind the rest of the world. In the midst of rapid population increases, regimes were unable to create jobs, improve infrastructure, or provide necessary services. Of course, petroleum and natural gas resources provided riches to some countries, yet in real terms their spending and populations rose as their income remained level. Saudi Arabia's debt

3 Ibid.

reached alarming proportions. Even in the richest states, higher expectations, public demands, and social change intensified the potential for an explosion. Other Arab countries with far larger populations remained poor. Everywhere, government domination of economies created inefficient sectors, limited invigorating competition, and made innovation extremely rare. Subsidies designed to ensure the regime's popularity damaged prospects for growth and productivity. Violence, turmoil, and hostility to the West discouraged foreign investment.

Many international studies confirm this poor performance and relative lack of progress compared to the West and even to other Third World regions.[4] The United Nations Development Program's *Human Development Report 2000*, for example, placed all Arab states "low" on its index of life expectancy, adult literacy, school enrollment, per capita GDP, and similar factors. Between 1990 and 2000, most Arab countries showed virtually no improvement. Excluding the oil-rich Gulf Arab states and Libya, average GDP per capita in the rest of the Arab world stood at just $1,398 (less than $4 per day). By comparison, Turkey's GDP per capita was $3,167, and Israel's stood at $15,978.[5]

On the social level, increasingly large proportions of young people have found that existing regimes cannot provide jobs or a better life. Urbanization and education produces people who are less passive and readier to question the system, including a growing proportion of women dissatisfied with their traditional social status and ready to play a public role for the first time in history. Most of all, there is a tidal wave of younger people who want jobs and housing, are less inclined to be passive, and have less respect for the existing system. Demands for a greater say in decision-making are coupled with the search for some set of ideas that will explain the Arab world's problems and provide solutions to them.

When considering their substantial problems, Arab leaders and intellectuals have found themselves looking into an abyss. Yet this is not the same chasm perceived by Western observers. To those in the West – and also for a small group of liberal critics within the Arab world – the threats are conflict, economic backwardness, and social

---

4 See Chapter 2 of this volume.
5 Amy Hawthorne, "The Arab World and the Millennium Summit: Avoiding the Globalization Challenge," Washington Institute for Near East Policy, *Policy Watch* No. 485, September 13, 2000.

stagnation. To the Arab and Iranian ruling elites, the real threats are instability, loss of power and wealth, destruction of tradition, the triumph of Western influence, the subversion of Islam and Arabism by globalization, and the treasonous betrayal of their most passionately held ideological tenets.

In this context, it is easy to understand why so many fear reform. At any rate, change has terrors of its own. It could bring anarchy, instability, and intensified suffering. Even with all the risk and struggle required, progress might not bring the rewards it promised. The most difficult of situations can easily be considered preferable to the unknown. For Arab and Iranian leaders, the Soviet bloc's downfall was not a call to freedom and democracy but a threat that they would face the same fate as had befallen the communist elites. The West thought that the rational interest of the Arab world and Iran lay with conflict resolution, liberal capitalism, and democracy. Yet those who ruled and enjoyed privileges in those countries viewed such an outcome as a disaster, as threatening the destruction of their way of life and even the loss of their own lives.

To preserve the status quo without altering it required finding some way to revitalize the old ideologies and causes, some way to keep their people enthusiastic supporters of the government and system. Such ideas had to tap into the masses' deepest passions in order to persuade them to set aside aspirations for a better life, accept their current government with all its faults, and make them want to fight anyone challenging it. These dominant forces wanted not to resolve grievances – at least by anything short of total victory – but to inflame them even further. Rather than face very real, serious, and difficult domestic problems, then, it was far easier to reignite an ideological mobilization against external enemies who allegedly wanted to humiliate their people, trample their honor, kill their women and children, and destroy their religion. The targets against which they focused grievances were the very people, institutions, and ideas that represented the alternative system they rejected.

All these ideas were familiar and, however repackaged, precisely the same ones that had failed the Arab world – but also preserved the regimes – for so many decades. Once again it was argued that Israel is too evil to make peace possible, but still could be destroyed if Arabs and Muslims united and devoted their resources to the effort. The United States was to be hated as arrogant and ruthless, but could nonetheless be chased out of the region. Violence was claimed to be a tool that

8

could be profitably exploited at low risk, terrorism an instrument that might be deployed while denied, and war a vengeance that could be threatened without any costly consequences. Revolution and militancy could go hand in hand with economic development, and indeed were portrayed as prerequisites for such progress. Democracy was said to be not a foundation for peace and domestic prosperity, but rather a Western trick to despoil the Arabs and drain Islam of its meaning, a luxury that could not be afforded in a time of confrontation.

According to this doctrine, the way to victory was not pragmatic adjustment to reality but rather having a correct political line. Speeches, articles, and sermons taught the people a set of basic principles to which all must adhere: You can get everything you want without compromise, and to demand all with no concessions is simply a matter of justice. The true hero is not he who achieves material improvements and benefits for his people but the one who does not bend no matter what the cost. The most radical ideology or state can be allowed to define others' political choices without inevitably threatening their survival.

Governments believed that they could inflame the masses in order to win cheap popularity and then channel to their benefit the tidal wave of anger and hatred they had unleashed, like the otherwise destructive roaring flood of water directed through sluice gates to generate electricity. At any rate, with rulers, writers, clerics, generals, and professors swearing that real peace, moderation, and reform would destroy religion and betray the Arab and Muslim people, delivering God and nation to demonic enemies, who could persuade the people otherwise? And if everyone who disagreed was branded a traitor and enemy agent, how many would dare to dissent from this chorus?

While these forces opposing change were well entrenched, those favoring reform were extremely weak. Even the most moderate among them knew that they must be cautious if they were to avoid an unpleasant fate – which in some places meant death or imprisonment, in others the loss of reputation and livelihood. The forces of liberal democratic opposition were only tiny groups of intellectuals and businesspeople lacking an organized base of support and far outnumbered by radical Islamists. Many of their best minds had exiled themselves to the West. Even the most courageous among those who remained had only limited access to the media and other state-controlled institutions.

On top of all these handicaps, the reformers were constantly on the defensive, accused of being Zionist puppets and American agents who were disloyal to the Arab cause and heretics against Islam. Westerners might think that change was rational and inevitable, but their views counted for nothing in the Middle East. On the contrary, if these foreigners favored something, all the more reason to be suspicious. Whatever gestures Arab or Iranian leaders made to U.S. and European viewpoints in their English-language statements, this rhetoric often had little or no relationship to what they said and did at home.

What was taking place in the Middle East, then, was not so much a confrontation of civilizations as something far simpler and quite common in world history: the determination of elites and systems to survive, oppositionists' efforts to seize power for themselves, and reactionary hatred and fear of what others called "progress." In European history, similar circumstances had called forth communism, fascism, Nazism, reactionary religious movements, extreme nationalism, and a wide range of retrograde ideas. Why should it be surprising that the Middle East would experience a parallel pattern when faced with a similar set of challenges?

The difference, however, is that in the Middle East – in contrast to all other parts of the world – the reactionary, anti-modernization forces won. Was this outcome inevitable? Obviously, there were powerful tides – deep and long-term factors – pushing in that direction. The underlying real issues were hidden under a seemingly endless avalanche of dramatic events: wars, threats, declarations, issues, crises, negotiations, peace plans, debates, terrorist attacks, conferences, and summits.

So dense was this veil that the real questions were hardly ever asked, much less answered. In Saghia's words, "While the modern world is engaged in an unprecedented technological and communications revolution we are busy with questions and concerns that belong to the [past]. . . . Rarely does someone talk about the need to achieve investment . . . about educating the youth to have the qualifications demanded by the global economy, about the development of regional water resources, about freedom, about the status of women, etc."[6]

One central issue for consideration is why the Arabs selected a strategy so objectively harmful to their own interests and prospects. It is a

---

6 Saghia in *al-Hayat*.

question often asked by Arab intellectuals themselves, albeit more often in private than in public. Yet there is no big mystery here. No matter how much damage these decisions did to the masses' lives or to the countries' resources, they were still in the ruling elites' interest. And if this interest was a short-term, short-sighted one, this is hardly unusual in the world, either now or in the past. In discussing the prevalence of dictatorship and lust for power in Arab states, a Palestinian writer remarked, "Most of all this is human nature."[7] That assessment is quite true, but the question remains: Why can humans get away with more in some places than in others?

Perhaps the main reason in this case is the way in which solutions to the main problems were defined. The questions shaping the Arab and Islamic debate included: Why are we behind the West in terms of wealth, power, influence, and development? How can we catch up with it or even surpass it? Does the West have some secret of success that we can adapt or copy, be it military organization, technology, economic system, constitutionalism, nationalism, socialism, the role of women, secularism, or something else? What should we accept and what must we reject from Western society in order to find a balance between solving our problems and keeping our own distinctive ways? Or is it better to fight and resist the West, to view it as an enemy that seeks to subordinate the Arabs and to destroy Islam?

Being behind the West in terms of power, prestige, and progress was especially galling to Arab and Muslim societies that viewed themselves as superior in civilizational and theological terms. They felt themselves heirs to a proud heritage characterized by great empires that had once dominated the Middle East and that had surpassed Europe culturally. They also believed that their religion's precepts more closely approximated God's preferences. Clearly, the world was somehow wrong and must be set right, by whatever means were necessary.

At the same time, though, this overweening confidence in their superiority was blended with a debilitating inferiority complex, a feeling of being helpless, doomed to be subdued by more powerful outside forces. The fear that the West might actually be superior enhanced the bitterness, anger, and cynicism so common in the region. Perhaps some

---

7 Fuad Abu Hijla, *al-Hayat al-Jadida*, June 13, 2000. Translation in MEMRI No. 102, June 16, 2000.

intrinsic flaw meant that the Arabs would never be worthy of development or democracy. These attitudes also reconciled people to dictatorship and failure. And if the glittering prizes of this world were out of reach, at least honor and principle could be preserved by maintaining doctrinal rigidity.

The ideal response to the problems of Arabs and Muslims had to take into account all these factors. Yes, Arabs and Muslims were the best of peoples and should defend their splendid heritage. Yes, the West was so powerful that its domination would be assured if current conditions remained unchanged. Yet the temptation to adapt to this world order must be resisted. Through unity and ideology, suspicion and sacrifice, the battle could yet be won, or at least not lost. There were three types of responses to the challenge of the West and modernity, but only two of them met this test.

Sadly, the option that would have been most effective was least acceptable. The liberal response, ultimately strongest everywhere else in the Third World, was weakest in the Arab world. This approach saw the West's success as based on the invention of new techniques that could be copied or adapted by other communities. These principles included pragmatism, economic development through private enterprise, secularism, parliamentary democracy, the individual nation-state inspiring its own patriotism while pursuing its own interests, and the creation of strong civil societies. In this view, the West was a potential ally, a "club" well worth joining. Both Jews (through Zionism) and Turks (through Kemalism) adapted such a liberal European interpretation of progress, relative secularism, and nationalism within the region.

But most Arabs rejected this approach, deeming it a failure when it had been to some extent tried by them during the 1930s and 1940s.[8] Like the views of those who came to power in Russia in 1917, in Germany in 1933, China in 1949, and Iran in 1979, the dominant view in the Arab world was that dramatic political and economic progress required rebellion against the prevailing Western model. The 1990s saw some revival of the notion that imitating those who had succeeded made sense, but this remained the worldview of a very distinct minority, even among intellectuals, and failed to transform a single state. Indeed, it was precisely against this model – and the West's alleged attempt to impose

8 See Albert Hourani, *Arabic Thought in the Liberal Age, 1798–1939* (New York, 1970).

it on the Middle East – that nationalist and Islamist movements and regimes were struggling with such determination.

The second option, the Pan-Arab nationalist approach, insisted that the Arabs were behind only because the West was oppressing them and holding them back. The answer was for Arabs to unite into a single nation-state (or at least to cooperate very closely) and expel Western influence from the Middle East, a program that included Israel's destruction. The best political system would be a one-party state led by a populist dictator. For economic development, the system was state socialism on the Soviet model. This was the dominant ideology and guide to action for Arab leaders from the 1950s to the 1990s and beyond.

The third alternative, the Islamist political view, agreed with Arab nationalism that revolution was necessary and that the West was the source of Arab and Iranian difficulties. By contrast, though, it argued that Arabs and Muslims had so far failed to overcome this subordination because they had abandoned their own religious tradition. Only a return to Islam would make possible the defeat of Western political and cultural oppression, along with rapid development and social justice. Borrowing from the West should be carefully limited to certain technological tools. This ideology became the motive force behind Iran's revolution and the Afghan struggle against the Soviets, and was the doctrine of most opposition movements in the Arab world from the early 1980s onward.

Given the triumph of the Arab nationalist and Islamist responses over the liberal model, the second half of the twentieth century in the Middle East can be called the Era of Radical Expectations. It began with the decline of European domination in the late 1940s, the 1948 Arab-Israeli war, and the ensuing wave of radical nationalist coups. It was characterized by the hegemony of Pan-Arab nationalism, radical dictatorships eager to intimidate moderate neighbors, moderate states imprisoned by this doctrine's constraints, regional instability, extensive violence of all types, a verbal obsession with the Arab-Israeli conflict, and the alliance of key Arab states with the USSR. During the 1970s, two new aspects were added: the wealth of oil-producing states, and revolutionary Islamist movements.

As a result, the Middle East's history between the 1950s and 1990s largely revolved around attempts to implement the Pan-Arab or revolutionary Islamist models. During that period, most Arabs professed to believe that some leader, country, or revolutionary movement would conquer and unite the region, transforming it virtually overnight through some magical political and economic formula. If total justice and total victory were so close to realization, there was no need to compromise. These doctrines promised that the Middle East would not have to adjust to the world and to the unfavorable balance of forces. Instead, others would have to adjust to the Middle East's desires.

Each of these efforts failed, and yet none of them was really discredited. If they didn't work, there would just have to be greater effort, for a longer period and with even more sacrifice. The underlying premises were never really reexamined.

At first, Arab nationalists put the highest priority on overthrowing the monarchies or ineffective republican regimes ruling their countries. Egyptian President Gamal Abdel Nasser made the classic statement of this philosophy in his autobiography. While he was fighting against Israel during the 1948 war, Nasser recounted:

"One day Kamal ed-Din Hussein [another Egyptian officer] was sitting near me . . . looking distracted, with nervous, darting eyes. 'Do you know what Ahmed Abdul Aziz said to me before he was killed [in battle]?' he said.

"'What did he say?'" I asked.

"He replied with a sob in his voice and a deep look in his eyes, 'He said to me, 'Listen, Kamal, the biggest battlefield is in Egypt.'"

Nasser added, "I used often to say to myself: 'Here we are in these foxholes, surrounded, and thrust treacherously into a battle for which we were not ready,'" because Egypt's government had betrayed them. His thoughts returned to Egypt, which was "besieged by difficulties and enemies," betrayed from within and disarmed against its foes.[9] The task was to overthrow the corrupt and incompetent regime at home, to build up the country, and then from this basis of strength to confront the Arabs' external enemies.

Yet things did not work out quite that way. True, four years later Nasser seized power in Egypt, and counterpart nationalist officers did the same elsewhere. But these new governments were unable to work together effectively. The rulers of Egypt, Syria, Iraq, and later Libya all proclaimed their superiority and their right to lead the Arab world. In

9 Gamal Abdul Nasser, *Egypt's Liberation: The Philosophy of the Revolution* (Washington, DC, 1955), pp. 22–3.

other places, the revolution failed to appear or to succeed. By the 1960s, the Palestinians and other groups had borrowed from Third World revolutionary doctrines to argue that their guerrilla struggles would provide the vanguard for a regionwide upheaval. Saudi Arabia and other traditionalist states professed to join the Arab nationalist parade, while defensively raising the shield of Islam and loyalty to their monarchies against the radical doctrines.

As the Arab nationalists discovered the difficulty of achieving power and governing well, they increasingly turned their eyes outward again, seeking to fight Israel and to oppose the West, often in alliance with the USSR. But in these confrontations, and in facing the challenges of economic development, rhetoric could not overcome problems. Both domestically and internationally, the regimes managed very badly, losing the foreign wars and the domestic battle for progress.

Decades of such struggle, division, and mismanagement left the Arabs weak, deeply divided, and even further behind the West. The preferred solutions actually worsened the Arab dilemma. It seemed, as one Arab writer put it, as if the Arabs were engaged in "a race to suicide."[10] Only cumulatively did these programs' failures and the disasters they brought gradually begin to push them into an agonizing reappraisal that could mean the abandonment or revision of their most basic political beliefs. Yet, in the end, the old vision continued to prevail.

With Arab nationalism bringing disappointment when it did not take power, and disenchantment when it succeeded, radical Islamists put forward their candidacy for leadership. The Iranian revolution of 1979 opened a new era of Islamist radicalism, just as Nasser's 1952 coup had begun the wave of Arab nationalist revolt. It inspired a plethora of client or independent groups seeking to take over Lebanon, Algeria, Egypt, and Saudi Arabia, as well as among the Palestinians and everywhere else in the region.

Like the nationalists, the Islamists provoked disappointment when they gained power – in Iran, Sudan, and Afghanistan – and demoralization when they were defeated. Also like the nationalists, their shortcomings as revolutionaries and rulers pushed them into putting even more emphasis on combating alleged external enemies. Just as Saddam Hussein's defiance of the West and invasion of Kuwait had represented

10 Cited in *Middle East Mirror*, May 27, 1994.

a second stage of Arab nationalism, Usama bin Ladin's attacks on America and a new wave of Islamist ideology focusing on jihad against non-Muslims brought a second stage for Islamism.

Nevertheless, the new anti-foreigner jihadist Islam proved more attractive for Islamists and more beneficial for regimes than was the old anti-regime revolutionary Islamism. Just as Arab nationalists had shifted from failed domestic reform to foreign adventures, radical Islamists now made the same change. Since their previous efforts had failed to overthrow any Arab state, bin Ladin and his allies shifted to a struggle against foreign non-Muslims instead. Thus, bin Ladin's two main innovations were to define all Christians as well as Jews as Islam's enemies, and to justify killing as many Americans as possible wherever they could be found. Broadening the circle of enemies made the struggle more difficult but also offered his audiences the deep satisfaction and powerful emotional impetus that arise from the most extreme ideas and challenges.

Still, whatever popularity or influence they achieved, both Arab nationalists and Islamists failed to achieve their goals, despite trying virtually every possible tactic. They used conventional war, subversion of neighbors, propaganda, assassination, terrorism, military coups, guerrilla warfare, grassroots' organizing, participation in elections, and mass uprisings. Nothing worked. Yet the only lesson they seemed to draw was to shift tactics and try even harder along the same lines.

By contrast, there were few moderate leaders, and even those few were ultimately more respected in the West than by fellow Arabs. In the end, the greatest reputations belonged to the glamorous radicals who did so much to harm their countries. Egyptian President Anwar al-Sadat and Jordan's King Abdallah I were assassinated. And the environment corroded any moderate efforts to set a different course. To retain power against domestic and foreign foes, regimes used repression and had little interest in instituting real democracy, in part because this would have brought radicals to power. Sadat and Jordan's King Hussein, Abdallah's grandson, encouraged Islamic movements as a way to counter militant nationalists. Moderate Saudi Arabia and Kuwait paid off the radicals to leave them alone, only to find themselves threatened by those they had subsidized so generously, first by Saddam Hussein and the PLO, then by bin Ladin. King Hussein himself had to support Iraq during the Kuwait crisis of 1991 in order to propitiate his own people and his powerful neighbor, even though Saddam wanted to swallow up Jordan as well.

A key aspect that ensured this system's preservation was the ability of Arab nationalist and Islamist (but not liberal) leaders to use certain trump issues in silencing dissent, intimidating neighbors, and mobilizing their own people. By stoking and invoking such passionate issues as the Palestinian question, anti-Americanism, the defense of Arabism, and the protection of Islam, all other considerations could be overwhelmed and criticism made irrelevant. The centerpiece of this program was focusing attention on external enemies. After all, if foreigners were not to blame for the overwhelming problems facing the nation, the next likely culprit had to be the government itself. This is a common technique in politics, during all eras and everywhere in the world, but it has been used with particular effectiveness in the Middle East.

Syria's use of the Arab-Israeli dispute to justify and maintain its military presence and control of Lebanon as a satellite is a superb example of such an argument's indispensable usefulness. When Gibran Tueni, editor of the Lebanese newspaper *al-Nahar*, published an open letter to Syrian President Bashar al-Asad in 2000 asking him to withdraw Syria's army from Lebanon, Lebanon's President Emile Lahoud, always submissive to Syria, could squelch the rather mild request by responding, "This broken record is played with pro-Israeli motivations every time there are developments that may favor Lebanese and Syrian interests." Tueni answered sadly but uselessly, "It is a pity that someone who calls for the minimum standards of sovereignty and independence for his country is accused of treason."[11] Yet that complaint could be extended to the way any call for reform has been treated in the Arab world.

Saghia writes that the Arab regimes have the perfect responses for any criticism or questioning of their policies and behavior. They ask,

'Do you want democracy [so you can] become like Israel? Do you want [foreign] investment in order to join globalization?' . . . Because of such policies we have missed opportunities to take advantage of great world events. We gave priority to a policy of confrontation [with Israel] while postponing progress in the hope of completely achieving our rights. In order to justify this approach we said that progress is against us and is intended to plunder our treasures.[12]

11 *Al-Nahar*, March 27, 2000; and *Daily Star*, March 29, 2000.
12 Saghia in *al-Hayat*.

Any proposal for reform could be squelched by labeling it an alien Western notion, as if every import were a Trojan horse sent to weaken Arab resolve or Iranian morality and thereby make them easy prey to conquest.[13]

Since the Arabs were said to be imperiled by merciless and evil enemies – Western imperialism, Zionism, traitors at home – who were responsible for everything wrong, they must fight on and on, never losing but never winning. They could not devote more efforts to construction, for they must man the battlements. They cannot challenge their own governments, because the endless war requires national unity. And what could be better portrayed as an example of imperialist and racist thinking than the simple observation that Arab governments and societies might actually have some real responsibility for their own fate?

This has been a profoundly crippling tendency. If the proper question to be asked is, "Who did this to us?" the response must be to unravel a conspiracy, and the issue will be how to fight better. But if the question is, "What did we do wrong?" then the next step must be to figure out how to fix the problem by changing one's own thinking, methods, and institutions. Moreover, to argue that solutions were possible only when the "enemies" were defeated – which was never going to happen – meant the endless postponement of the steps needed to find real solutions. This was the catch-22 of Arab politics: Nothing can be done until Palestine is liberated or U.S. influence expelled, or until unity comes for all Arabs or Muslims, and since these things have not happened, then the desperately needed steps to solve the Arabs' problems must wait.

The emphasis on xenophobia and conspiracy theories builds a wall around the existing system that neither the arguments nor the actions of outsiders can penetrate. This approach fits perfectly, however, with the ideologies of Arab nationalism and Islamism. It is easier to make a bid to unite all of a country's citizens, or at least the Arabs and Muslims among them, if one can argue that they are all on the same side. Blaming problems on the regime or on any institution or sector within the state is more likely to provoke civil war than solidarity. When Islamists try to deny their opponents' Muslim credentials, they alienate large sectors of the population.

---

13 See Chapters 4 and 5 of this volume for examples.

By focusing on Israel or America as the real foe, radical regimes and groups also make it harder for their intended Arab victims to seek Western protection. The best way to discredit a government is to portray it as insufficiently nationalist or improperly Muslim. The best way to fight a regime is to claim that it is merely a front for the real enemy. As proof, it can be claimed that the regime does not struggle hard enough against foreign powers and influences, is too soft in fighting Israel or too friendly toward the United States. In order to protect themselves – and to use such accusations against their own enemies – politicians, parties, journalists, and governments compete in proving their militant credentials.

One by one, the forces that demanded democracy elsewhere in the world were subverted or co-opted in the Middle East. Since xenophobia displaced class there as the real grievance of choice, the political left was rendered irrelevant, merely another group clamoring to show its eagerness to defeat the common enemy. The statist economy weakened businesspeople and made them dependent on the regime. The intellectuals were intimidated by a political and intellectual atmosphere of perpetual McCarthyism; the greatest fear was to be labeled as anti-Islam or a Zionist agent or an American puppet, accusations that could destroy one's career and even jeopardize one's life. There could be no greater weapon to inspire conformity and self-censorship.

These myths of Arabism and Islamism have a tremendous life of their own that repels both facts and experiences. Arabs and Muslims have never united in practice, despite the broad commonality of rhetoric among them. They did not do so behind Nasser during the 1950s and 1960s, as both moderates and radicals refused to subordinate themselves to Egypt. Arab indifference was a major factor in defeating the Palestinians during the 1970s and 1980s; Arab opposition ensured Saddam's failure in 1990–91; and Muslim passivity ensured the failure of the Islamists and – along with the military prowess of pious Afghan Muslims fighting alongside the Americans – of bin Ladin and the Taliban in the 1990s and 2001.

After so much bloody Arab infighting – from the civil war in Yemen during the 1950s, to the Lebanese civil war of the 1970s and 1980s, to Saddam's brutal treatment of Kuwait – it is still generally accepted that Arabs shouldn't and don't fight each other. After a dozen inter-Muslim wars, ranging from Islamist–government battles to the eight-year Iran-Iraq war, Islamic clerics and many rank-and-file Muslims could still insist in 2001 that no one should help the American anti-terrorist war because that would mean the unprecedented act of fighting other Muslims. Several Arab countries did help the United States in its war against terror, but it was treated as a shameful thing that the regimes had to keep secret from their own citizens.

The myth of ultimate victory was as damaging as the illusion of achievable unity. Secular Arab nationalists as well as Islamists repeatedly claimed that the apparent balance of forces against them could be ignored because it was illusory. Thus, Ali Uqleh Ursan, head of the Syrian Arab Writers Union and a strong supporter of the regime, explained that the September 11, 2001, attacks proved "that the will of one man [bin Ladin], who chose to die to defend his honor, his rights, his people, his civilization, and his faith, is enough to realize his goal, even against a superpower and even on its own turf." If the people only woke up and showed the necessary willpower to resist "the tyranny, the despots, and the racism that exhale hatred, arrogance and imperialism," then everything could change. Indeed, he argued, "I maintain that this is the beginning of the collapse of the United States as the only dominant superpower in the world."[14]

This notion that, despite all measures of military and economic power, the Arabs or Muslims are about to defeat the United States is a constant theme used to justify the actions of radical states and movements. Bin Ladin himself recognized this natural tendency to go with a winner – and the consequent necessity of "proving" that the United States is weak and a loser. He told his colleagues as he exulted over his victory of September 11, "When people see a strong horse and a weak horse, naturally they will like the strong horse."[15]

In October 2001, as the United States was about to destroy the Taliban and chase al-Qa'ida's leadership deep into the Afghan caves, Ayman al-Zawahiri, a veteran Egyptian Islamist and close aide of bin Ladin, taunted, "Oh U.S. people, your government was defeated in Vietnam and fled scared from Lebanon. It fled from Somalia and received a slap in Aden [when the USS *Cole* was attacked]. Your government now leads you to a new losing war where you will lose

14 *Al-Usbu' Al-Adabi*, September 15, 2001. Translation in MEMRI No. 275, September 25, 2001.
15 Usama bin Ladin, videotape of a private meeting, November 9, 2001. Translation released by the U.S. Defense Department and broadcast December 13, 2001.

your sons and money."[16] Arab and especially Palestinian leaders frequently made similar remarks about the impending defeat of Israel in 1948, in 1967, and during two *intifadas*, each time just before Israel defeated them.

This certainty that victory will be theirs because they are valiant and the enemy cowardly, that God or historical inevitability is on their side, does not represent a realistic courage in the face of danger but rather a foolhardiness based on a misestimate of the odds. Faced with a choice between a compromise that they claim means surrender and continuing a losing struggle, the latter almost always wins out.

If the Arabs (or Islamists) can defeat America (or the West in general) by using special tactics that neutralize the enemy's great technological and military advantages, then any argument that good relations or concessions are needed is meaningless. The struggle can continue. As long as the struggle does not end, the Muslims and Arabs are not defeated. To accept defeat by changing words, policies, or ideas is to throw away everything. No matter how bad the material situation is at any given moment, the dream, hope, and belief that all will turn out differently is more important.

Bin Ladin's potential appeal was not that he introduced any new ideas but that he promised a new, supposedly better way to implement the old ones. His movement represented merely the latest version in a half-century-long series of attempts by Arabs to find some magic formula for achieving victory. Nasser, Ayatollah Ruhollah Khomeini, Saddam, the Asads, and many others had also seen the problems of Arabs and Muslims as stemming from the West, Israel, and local moderates who allegedly collaborated with them. After all, it was Khomeini's characterization of the United States as the "Great Satan" and Israel as the "Little Satan" that showed the irrational, demonic nature of this externalization of blame. All of these leaders had portrayed liberalism and democracy not as solutions but as alien tendrils from the most devious and devilish of enemies. And each of them and their ideologies, also like bin Ladin, argued that America and the West could be easily defeated if only Arabs or Muslims were willing to unite and fight.

---

16 Interview on al-Jazira television, October 7, 2001. Translation from U.S. Department of Commerce, Foreign Broadcast Information Service (FBIS).

The importance of bin Ladin's attacks and those of other suicide bombers was that they seemed to be the secret weapons to prove that the Arabs and Muslims would win. If Israel could be defeated by violence, there was no need to make a compromise negotiated peace. Neither concession nor acceptance was necessary. In the apparent triumph of today, all the defeats of yesterday are forgotten in the assumption that the same tactics will now work.

In its xenophobia and its definition of enemies, bin Ladin's ideas and those of his more established counterparts also paralleled earlier European totalitarian movements, even down to their common hatred of Jews and abhorrence of modern culture. In the broadest structural sense, these movements all represented – despite very different characteristics – a rejectionist response to progress at a critical stage of societal development. As communism had tried to seize control of liberalism and socialism, and as fascism had sought to appropriate conservatism and patriotism, so did radical Arabism seize control over nationalism, and Islamism try to hijack Islam.

Like communism, these Middle Eastern doctrines appealed to the downtrodden and asserted that their system was better than bourgeois democracy and greedy capitalism. Like fascism, they insisted that their system was superior to both corrupt capitalism and godless communism. And like those brands of European extremism that had triumphed in Russia and Germany, Arab nationalist and Islamist doctrines appealed to embittered nations that, having suffered defeat and humiliation, could not otherwise explain why they were weaker and less developed than others whom they considered inferior.

Even if bin Ladin and his closest supporters were to disappear, the choices already made by Arab regimes before September 11, 2001, would not easily be reversed. An entire generation's experience had been thrown away. The momentum built up by a half-century of failure and waste had not pushed the Middle East in a new direction. Those too young to remember those events directly had been taught that the radical interpretation had been right all along. Their leaders' big mistake had not been their preference for radicalism and rejection of moderation and reform, but their failure to fight firmly or fiercely enough for their cause. A foundation had been laid for decades more of misguided battle.

Instead of progress, Saghia concluded, "only dictatorship is spreading" in the Arab world, where one-party states continue to thrive although they have disappeared "not only in the Soviet Union but also in South Korea, Mexico and Taiwan. Nor has a leader emerged amongst us that would have the modesty of [Nicaraguan dictator] Daniel Ortega who accepted without bloodshed the results of the peaceful elections that demoted him."[17]

Comparative studies back up these assertions. Freedom House's *Freedom in the World 1999–2000* report classified fourteen of seventeen Arab countries as "not free" (the exceptions were Jordan, Kuwait, and Morocco, each of which had very limited liberty), far exceeding the proportion of such states in any other region. No Arab country was rated as having free media, and the manipulation of elections and suppression of nongovernment organizations were especially common.[18]

Ironically, "outsiders" are blamed for the Middle East's problems in an era when they clearly have limited influence there, and certainly less effective power than the West has in Asia, Africa, or Latin America. European influence in the area approaches zero, and the Soviet Union has ceased to exist. Perhaps the less the West needs to be feared in reality, the more convenient it is as a scapegoat, as that policy involves fewer risks. The United States could not change the regimes in Iran or Iraq, make peace in the Arab-Israeli conflict, or even persuade such long-time allies as Egypt and Saudi Arabia to support many of its policies.

And what is the nature of these all-important grievances? The dispute with Israel is very real, but when Israel is portrayed as a satanic, genocidal state whose crimes equal those of the Nazis and whose goals are regional domination, the destruction of the Arabs and Islam, and genocide against the Palestinians, it becomes impossible to envision a peaceful solution. Whatever the Arab complaints against Israel, the conflict could have ended years ago in compromise. There might have been an independent Palestinian state in the 1970s or 1980s, and certainly an equitable deal could have been reached in the year 2000. Syria might have taken back the Golan Heights in exchange for peace. Yet the very moment of a potential breakthrough became a prelude to the greatest explosion of violence, both actual and rhetorical, in decades.

17 Saghia in *al-Hayat*.
18 Adrian Karatnycky, *Freedom in the World: The Annual Survey of Political Rights and Civil Liberties 1999–2000* (Catay, NJ, 2000). For other Freedom House reports, see http://216.119.117.183/research/freeworld/2001/.

Beyond all the rationales, too, the issue of Israel has transcended geography. It seems that the Jews have come to play a role in the Middle East parallel to the one that had once been forced on them in Europe. They are most hated and slandered by the forces opposing modernization and democracy. They are the scapegoats who would subvert the nation, soil the true religion, act as agent of the foreigner, and seek political and economic domination. Their presence is the source of all difficulties, and their removal would solve all problems.

Similarly, hatred of America has gone beyond "rational" boundaries, not because Arabs or Iranians are "irrational," but because it is based not on analysis of facts but on the political function of sustaining local ideologies and political systems. The case against America is constantly recited in the Arab and Iranian media, in leaders' speeches, and in the writings of intellectuals. The overwhelming, countervailing case can almost literally never be found in Arabic or Persian. It seems that in the ledger book of the Middle East, there is only a debit and no credit column for entering the deeds of the United States. Whether the United States supported or opposed regimes, it was deemed equally reprehensible. Of course, the United States did back the shah of Iran, but President Jimmy Carter did not endorse violent repression of the Iranian revolution, and the United States later tried to make a genuine rapprochement with the new Islamist regime.

Indeed, the United States could not have acted less like an imperialist power. During the 1980s, it helped rescue Afghanistan from Soviet invasion and then provided large amounts of humanitarian aid without seeking any influence or domination there. For a quarter-century it provided Egypt with two billion dollars in aid every year, without which the regime might have crumbled. It helped the Arab side against Iran during the Iran-Iraq war. It saved Kuwait and Saudi Arabia from an Iraqi invasion but never tried to dictate their policies thereafter. American forces in the Persian Gulf were not used to take over the countries there. In Somalia, Bosnia, and Kosovo – where U.S. interests were not at stake – it engaged in humanitarian intervention on behalf of Muslims. Again, in each case the United States sought stability and good relations, not empire.

Finally, the United States worked hard to broker an equitable Arab-Israeli peace that both sides could accept. It was ready to be Palestinian leader Yasir Arafat's patron and organized massive aid for his Palestinian Authority (PA). Even when Arafat essentially destroyed the American-organized peace process, rejected President Clinton's own plan, and broke the cease-fires that he had promised to American leaders, the United States did not attack him or even take sides against him.

The United States, like every country, acted on the basis of its interests, including continued access to oil. But the point is that U.S. policy bene-fited many Arabs who had a vested interest in not admitting this fact. Oil and gas producers were well paid for their bounty, and the United States never sent gunboats to lower oil prices or to seize these resources for it-self. Thus, actual American policy behavior is insufficient to explain the high level of anti-Americanism, which really arose from the systematic excoriation of the United States by Arab governments and media.

In fact, the United States was a scapegoat for the failures of Arab politics and society. On a cultural and intellectual level, the export of American culture and ideas in the form of "globalization," "modern-ization," and "Westernization" were perceived as a threat by Arabs and Iranians jealous of U.S. success and frustrated by their inability to compete.[19] The real danger posed by America was that democracy, free enterprise, civil liberties, and an open culture could turn Arabs and Ira-nians against their own systems.

As for political and strategic matters, the United States had good ties with most Arab states over long periods precisely because those states wanted U.S. aid and protection. Generally, relations were bad only with the most radical states – Iraq, Syria, Libya, and Islamist Iran. The real problem was that these regimes, and also militant Islamist groups, saw the moderates' alliances with Washington as blocking their own efforts to conquer or control them. Ironically, having these Arab friends made the United States subject to more anti-Americanism; equally ironically, if American policy had not helped to stop the radicals, the Arab world would have suffered even more setbacks, repression, and bloodshed. If only America had not existed, ideologues argued, their revolutions would have succeeded.

The Arab world paid an extremely high price in blood and treasure for all these utopian notions and misperceptions. Nevertheless, despite this experience, Arab countries, movements, and intellectuals still overwhelmingly rejected a long-term, more pragmatic, free-enterprise strategy focused on the nation-state and requiring reform, moderation,

19 See Chapter 9 of this volume.

and democratization. In short, the idea was rejected that the Middle East had to become more like other regions in order to achieve the same relatively high level of political stability and socioeconomic progress.

Instead, as each highly touted solution failed, it became necessary to generate more anger and to direct it outward. The inability to transform the region, to improve internal conditions, or to make revolutions did not lead to the conclusion that these concepts were flawed, but only to a belief that success was being blocked by external factors. Islamist revolts could not seize power not because they lacked mass support or because rulers were so good at co-optation and repression, but because America kept them in power. The Arab world failed to unite not because their rulers wanted to keep power for themselves, but because of Israel's existence.

While dictatorships were fading away elsewhere in the world, unable to persuade intellectuals to cover up for them or the masses to follow them, those of the Arab world possessed the great secret eluding their counterparts elsewhere: how to bind the people to them by using trump issues and xenophobia to ensure their popularity. At a time when revolutionary movements were in abeyance in other parts of the world, having shed too much blood and left too many promises unfulfilled, they continued to flourish in the Middle East.

It is especially ironic that Middle Eastern governments were often mistakenly said to be too weak, lacking legitimacy and stability. In fact, though, they were so strong that they easily defeated reform movements, avoided the consequences of their own mistakes, and never had to make concessions in order to survive. Their poor economic management, foreign policy disasters, corruption, and incompetence were simply ignored as unimportant. No matter how naked the emperor was, he held the offensive, accusing everyone else of having no clothes.

There is simply no other way to explain the remarkable gap between performance and perception in the Arab world and Iran, the type of systematic failure that would have sent any Latin American or Asian regime crashing down in a few weeks. How else could the real and basic shortcomings of Middle Eastern systems be so easily brushed aside or completely ignored. As the Jordanian journalist Rami Khouri wrote in 1998:

The last decade's rates of economic performance and democratization remain among the lowest in the world. . . . The main problem . . . remains the exaggerated, unnatural, unchecked, and unaccountable power that has been accumulated in the hands of the central Arab state . . . . This has led to distortions and dependencies that are now visible, and increasingly corrosive and destructive but that had long been camouflaged by the decades of the Cold War, early state-building, the oil boom, and the Arab-Israeli conflict.[20]

But governments wanted to continue using "camouflage" to hide the real issues and their own poor performance. A "new Middle East" would rob them of these tools and perhaps bring about their own downfall. They understandably preferred to continue using trump issues in an effort to raise their level of legitimacy and disarm opposition. The less well they governed, the more successfully they seemed to hold onto power. They were not subject, collectively or individually, to accountability or replacement even after the worst mistakes or disasters.

In discussing the leadership of his own people, the Palestinian scholar Ziyad Abu Amr pointed out in 1996:

Yasir Arafat has been the leader of the Fatah movement since its establishment in 1965; George Habash has been the leader of the PFLP since its foundation in 1967; Nayif Hawatma has remained head of the DFLP since its formation in 1969; Bashir al-Barghuti has been secretary general of the Palestine Communist Party since its foundation in 1982; Shaykh Ahmad Yasin has been the leader of the Muslim Brotherhood Society in Gaza since the mid-1970s, and head of Hamas since it was formed in 1987 despite his imprisonment in Israeli jails since 1989; and Fathi al-Shiqaqi was the leader of the Islamic Jihad Movement in Palestine from its foundation in 1980 until his assassination in October 1995.[21]

The Arab world gained a reputation for instability because of the many coups that took place during the 1950s and 1960s. Yet after Hafiz al-Asad took power in Syria in January 1970, not a single Arab regime – outside of two marginal states, Yemen and Sudan – was overthrown during the following thirty years. Democratic reform movements remained minuscule, minor irritants for seemingly immortal dictatorships. Islamist revolutionary efforts were outmaneuvered and repressed in

20 Rami Khouri in the *Jordan Times*, June 30, 1998.
21 Ziyad Abu-Amr, "Pluralism and the Palestinians," *Journal of Democracy*, Vol. 7, No. 3 (1996), p. 88. The Popular Front for the Liberation of Palestine (PFLP) and the Democratic Front for the Liberation of Palestine (DFLP) were radical nationalist groups and members of the PLO.

state after state. Economic stagnation and military defeat – among other shortcomings – did nothing to displace governments, in sharp contrast to developments everywhere else in the world. Leaders who need not be concerned with being voted or thrown out of office, for whom performance was simply not a relevant consideration, were free to engage in any sort of repression at home or adventure abroad.

Indeed, governments did succeed in persuading the masses to ignore the issues most directly important in their lives, precisely the issues that usually shaped public opinion and political fortunes in other regions. Arab leaders could still govern by telling their people that they continued to carry on the good fight against Israel, reject American attempts to turn them into puppets, hold high the banner of Arab nationalism, and revere Islam. Yet in reality they did not fight Israel, turned to the United States whenever they needed its help, acted to suit their own self-interest, and interpreted Islam as they wished.

Leaders could even directly inflict suffering on their own people as part of their strategy without raising criticism or opposition. Thus, Saddam Hussein preferred to keep weapons of mass destruction rather than ending sanctions against Iraq. Instead, he used his people's suffering (magnified by Iraqi propaganda) as a lever to gain concessions. Arafat rejected realistic diplomatic solutions that would have included creation of a Palestinian state to which refugees would have been repatriated. Instead, in a misperceived bid to force an Israeli surrender or international intervention, he chose to launch still another war that cost his people many casualties, wrecked their infrastructure, and brought them no positive result.

Demagoguery acted as a viable substitute for governmental performance. Elsewhere in the world, rulers, systems, and ideologies were judged based on practical measures of performance: the ability to bring peace and personal security for their citizens, including material well-being, public services, and rising living standards. For the Middle East, the only important thing was having the right ideology and the proper enemies, rather than successful strategies and good policies.

The masses, of course, did not necessarily believe everything their regimes told them, any more than had citizens of communist states or other dictatorships. The Egyptian writer Hani Shukrallah scoffed,

We've become immune to nonsense – the manipulation of language into an instrument of equivocation, ambiguity, and sheer mumbo-jumbo. . . . And so well trained have we, as a people, become in this art that on occasion the hidden message is understood as the exact opposite of the outward meaning. Thus, for instance, when an official pronounces Egypt free of mad cow disease, Egyptians immediately start stocking their freezers with poultry.[22]

Nevertheless, governments continued to set the agenda of debate and the direction of popular thinking, keeping the terms of discussion and the limits on outside information and opinion quite restrictive. The kind of alternatives most important elsewhere were barely mentioned. A wall of language insulated them from the outside world, since only what was written or said in Arabic could have any effect.

Unlike other places, too, the opposition had nothing all that different to say, since it was overwhelmingly radical nationalist or Islamist. To put it simply but accurately, their critique of the government was that it wasn't doing enough, not that it should be doing something else entirely. Everywhere, the democratic, reform, and moderate oppositions were silent minorities, not even silent majorities. Even such vocal critics as Saghia and Shukrallah could only try to gain a hearing by insisting that reforms were needed to help the Arab world defeat Israel.

Yet was it so terribly difficult to understand the real disasters concealed by the claims of victimization and the demands for struggle? As Professor Fawaz Gerges wrote:

Economically and politically, the Arab Middle East is one of the regions left out in the world race to democratize and globalize. Authoritarianism and patriarchy are highly consolidated on every level of society, from the public sphere to the dinner table. These shortcomings, not U.S. foreign policies, are largely responsible for the lack of Arab development and progress. . . . It is high time for the Arabs to take charge of their political destiny and fully embrace modernity. This process requires structural reform from within and total engagement with the world, including the eradication of terrorism.[23]

What was unthinkable in the Arab world was quite possible in other Muslim countries. Turkey had embraced secularism, and Iran had accepted – though it had also subverted – electoral democracy. Even Pakistan's President Pervez Musharraf could lecture Islamic clerics

22 Hani Shukrallah in *al-Ahram Weekly*, March 8–14, 2001. http://www.ahram.org.eg/weekly/2001/524/op9.htm.
23 Fawaz A. Gerges, "The Tragedy of Arab-American Relations," *Christian Science Monitor*, September 18, 2001.

there, asking them why the Muslim world had 25 percent of the world's people and 70 percent of its energy resources, yet its combined economic output equaled just one-half that of one Western country, Germany. The reason, Musharraf answered, was that Muslim countries have allowed religious intolerance to stop them from educating their people, developing their economies, and establishing stable democratic governments.[24]

Arab intellectuals willing to complain about this dreadful situation were understandably few, especially among those still living in the Middle East, since they were routinely vilified and even threatened for trying to provide real help for their people, rather than just ideological opiates. Yet there was also a serious flaw in their trying to convince the masses and governments that following their advice would be a better way to achieve existing Arab aims. Governments and radical oppositions correctly worried that such steps would weaken them and alter Arab goals. After all, if the Arab world wanted the benefits of modernization and peace, it would have to accept a compromise negotiated agreement with Israel, discard anti-Americanism and anti-Westernism as a tool, adopt a nationalism based on specific states, privatize the economy and thereby take it out of the hands of government officials and their favored supporters, and modify its interpretations of Islam.

The reformers' presentations only highlighted the risks for the establishment implicit in such changes. Where the West and liberal Arabs saw opportunities, the rulers of the Arab world and Iran saw dangers. Discarding the trump issues that both preserved and paralyzed the regimes – Arab nationalism, the Palestinian issue, anti-Americanism and anti-Westernism, their claim to be defending a jeopardized Islam – would shatter their remarkable ability to survive as a ruling elite.

For the West, the fate of the USSR, the Soviet bloc, and communism suggested that free enterprise and democracy were superior systems. For Middle Eastern rulers, however, these cases suggested that they too might be shot or stripped of power if they tried to implement reforms. The West saw democracy as the basis for a stable state and society. But in Algeria, the military cracked down to ensure that Islamists did not

24 Quoted in the *Washington Post*, January 7, 2002.

win free elections, leading to a bloody civil war. In Iran, relatively free elections led to overwhelming support for a reform movement that also threatened to bring down the government.

Even Saddam Hussein well understood what kind of leadership was needed. "Do not give authority over public wealth," he told Iraq's people, "to him who builds his fame on wealth, nor over the media to him who builds it on ostentation, nor over the army to him who builds it on conquest . . . nor over national security systems to him who . . . acts treacherously in the dark and who is not afraid of God. Give each and all of these posts and titles to those who are strong, truthful and trustworthy." But even if the Iraqis knew they wanted such a virtuous, democratic-minded leader, they could never choose one. Saddam wouldn't let them.[25]

Indeed, in almost every respect the requirements for progress run sharply contrary to the interests of the regimes and their main supporters. In listing social and economic distortions that would have to be changed in order to ensure successful economic development in the Arab world, Khouri includes the "top-heavy maintenance of security" that has blocked "the rule of law."[26] But this simply means that the state has invested too much in the apparatus designed to preserve itself, a security and welfare system for the happiness and well-being of officers, whose support it needs to survive.[27]

Next, Khouri points out that the statist economy is discredited everywhere except in the Arab world. Yet this type of economy keeps wealth in the hands of the regime and its clients, denying economic assets to business groups that might demand further reform and even a share of power. Finally, he notes that "no Arab country has a democratically elected parliament [that has] had any significant impact on the policy-making direction of the state." Yet to share power with a legislature – which itself might be comprised largely of antidemocratic extremists – would not enhance the regimes' survival or even their stability under the existing system. If development requires "a more responsive and efficient state [that allows] public discussion and participation in decision-making; decentralization, . . . accountability

25 Speech of August 8, 2001. Text from the Iraq News Agency web site, http://www.uruklink.net/iraqnews/eindex.htm.
26 Khouri, in the *Jordan Times*.
27 See Chapter 7 of this volume.

and competition," all of these principles would require the existing regimes to give up their power.[28]

If this was the price of prosperity and peace, then the regimes, most of the intellectuals, the majority of opposition movements, and a large portion of the masses preferred something else. When the Syrian dictator Hafiz al-Asad died and his son, Bashar, stepped in to maintain the regime, reform-minded Arab writers were moved to despair. A Palestinian, Hani Habib, wrote, "The 'Syrian constitution' is in fact the constitution of all the Arabs from the [Atlantic] ocean to the [Persian] Gulf."[29]

Another Palestinian writer, Hasan Khadir, mourned, "After thirty years of autocratic and totalitarian rule" in Syria, Arab leaders still ruled "the same way he did. Do constitutions and democracies suit the Arabs, or is the Arab mind, perhaps, in a completely different place?" He concluded, "I admit that we are in a real mess. I also admit that the political culture of the Arabs is schizophrenic. . . . Will Arab intellectuals identify with their regimes from now on? The Arab intellectuals used to explain that they support the regime because it is progressive. How will they explain their support for a dynastic republic?"[30]

But there was a way for the regimes to continue cultivating popular support despite their failings. And it was this alternative, rather than the direction in which the previous half-century of Middle Eastern history seemed to be pushing them, that they chose at the onset of the twenty-first century.

---

28 Khouri, in the *Jordan Times*.
29 *Al-Ayyam*, June 14, 2000. Translation in MEMRI No. 102, June 16, 2000.
30 Hasan Khadhr, "And Now, a Dynastic Republic," *al-Ayyam*, June 13, 2000. Translation in MEMRI No. 102, June 16, 2000.

PARADIGM LOST

Cumulatively, the twentieth century's second half was a very bad era for Arab peoples and polities. Each year added to a seemingly endless list of problems and failures. Few if any of their basic foreign policy goals were achieved, and the gap between theory and reality opened up further during the post–Cold War era. At home, Arab countries lagged behind many others in the pace of their economic development and social progress; the Middle East remained less democratic and more repressive than any region on earth after the fall of communism.

Under normal circumstances, this situation should ultimately have led to a serious reevaluation – which indeed did happen during the 1990s – and change. Yet despite the demonstrated deficiencies of the radical expectations that almost always dominated Arab rhetoric and so often determined political behavior, these old ways were not rejected. Instead, they were merely revived, preserved, or just repackaged with new slogans and justifications. The region's dramatic daily events, colorful personalities, and frequent crises dazzle the eye and appear to involve continual transformation. Yet in the end, what is truly remarkable is how little Arab ideology and politics have changed despite the glaring inadequacies they have constantly showed.

But why has such an awesome gap opened up between ideology and goals, on the one hand, and events on the other? And why has the Arab world found it so hard to challenge and revise its own disproven assumptions and failed policies? The key to this apparent mystery is hidden in the issue of who is to be blamed for this unhappy history and pessimistic outlook. The overwhelmingly dominant answer in the Arab world and Iran has been to attribute responsibility to the United States, Israel, and traitorous – because they are insufficiently radical – rulers at home. The outpouring of anti-Americanism, both before and after the September 11, 2001, terror attacks on America, reflected this overall assessment that the United States was to blame for everything that had gone wrong in the Middle East.

But if America is responsible, of course, that means Pan-Arab nationalism, Islamist radicalism, dictatorship, badly run and rigidly statist economies, strategies rejoicing in violence and terror, and a media system dominated by propaganda have nothing to do with the Arab failure to prosper and progress. If these internal factors are irrelevant – or lacking only a more courageous and consistent application of the correct principles – then nothing needs to be altered. Yet if these things remain unchanged, the Arab world will continue to lurch from one embarrassment or defeat to another.

Those in the West who agree with the assessment that outside oppression is the true roadblock for Arabs and Muslims think that they are nobly helping the Middle East's people against their enemies. Echoing their views and explaining their grievances is expected to persuade the West to understand the Middle East and then to change its ways, thus solving the problem. Anyone who disagrees is said to be merely an apologist for imperialism and Zionism whose work does not deserve to be read and whose analysis need not be considered.[1]

In fact, though, these "pro-Arab" forces are reinforcing the Arabs' and Muslims' worst possible enemy: the unwillingness to confront the real issues and problems that have caused so many disasters and kept them from achieving more progress. At any rate, such arguments will never convince Western leaders or citizens, because they clearly do not conform to reality. The principal problem is not that the West misunderstands the Middle East, but rather that the Middle East misunderstands both the West and itself. As long as the real roots of the tragedy are ignored, there can be no major improvement in the region's sad fate.

In the 1990s, political, social, and economic systems were being challenged throughout the Arab world and in Iran as well, questioned by critics and even doubted by their masters. The failures of the past had exposed the existing order to severe criticism. It had become legitimate to cite the

---

1 See Martin Kramer, *Ivory Towers on Sand: The Failure of Middle Eastern Studies in America* (Washington, DC, 2001) for a discussion of these problems. Reactions to this monograph from Middle Eastern experts, many of them in private communications, fully demonstrated this point.

Western example, as well as those of other Third World countries, as something that might be imitated or adapted. Yet by the decade's end, a far more powerful reaction had set in against the reformers. Clearly, those benefiting from the status quo – those who controlled the states, the armies, the media, and much else – were not enthusiastic about alternatives and had the power to prevent change. Indeed, not only did they preserve the prevailing practices, the rulers effectively justified them and success-fully portrayed liberal critics as profoundly wrong and even traitorous.

What had so devastated the Arab world's predictions and expecta-tions? The answer is historical experience.

A series of events slowly and consistently chipped away at the Arab political and belief systems: military defeats by Israel in 1948, 1956, 1967, 1973, and 1982; civil wars in Lebanon, Iraq, and Yemen; the eight-year-long Iran-Iraq war; and Iraq's invasion of Kuwait. Islamist insur-gencies in Egypt, Syria, and Algeria were put down with heavy loss of life. There was no Arab unification, no Islamist revolution, no great eco-nomic progress, and no expulsion of U.S. influence. The Arab world did not go through a revolutionary social transformation. Instead, its dreams were shattered, and those it defined as enemies grew ever stronger.

The 1960s and 1970s had been terrible enough, but the 1980s brought even more bad news of Arab failures, defeats, and divisions. The year 1982 alone saw a triple disaster. First, the Syrian army massa-cred thousands of civilians in Hama, showing the hollowness of the radical regimes' populist, progressive rhetoric. Second, Iranian troops fought their way onto Iraqi territory, pointing out the genuine threat of Persian power and radical Islamism to Arab regimes. Third, Israel's army went into Lebanon and defeated the PLO and Syrian forces, thereby demonstrating Israel's continued military superiority, the Soviet and Arab states' unwillingness or inability to respond, and the readi-ness of some Arabs to ally themselves with Israel.

Israel not only remained stronger than the Arab states, but the balance of power seemed to tilt even further in its favor as huge numbers of im-migrants from the Soviet Union and expanding settlements on the West Bank suggested that time was not on their side. By contrast, Moscow's power continued to decline, and the USSR collapsed completely in 1991. Radical Arab regimes, even those possessing huge oil reserves, were un-able to show economic progress. The 1980–88 Iran-Iraq war further shocked the Arab world. The Gulf monarchies felt jeopardized by Iran and its potential for spreading Islamist radicalism. Their fear pushed these wealthy Arab states toward closer cooperation with the United States.

Nevertheless, so great was the old system's staying power that Saddam Hussein, champion of traditional Arab nationalist militancy and orthodoxy, was still the Arab summit's hero in 1990, insisting that Israel and the West could be defeated. But when he tried to bring unity through force by annexing Kuwait, the ensuing crisis demonstrated the dangers of Pan-Arab nationalism to Arab rulers. Saddam and his supporters used the Arab world's long-dominant ideology to legitimate Iraqi imperialism as well as Iraq's ultimate ambition to subordinate all other Arab states. If the unification of all Arabs was the ultimate goal, Iraq's action was a proper and patriotic (in Pan-Arab terms) step. But individual Arab regimes wanted to survive, and the fulfillment of their supposed dream was actually their worst nightmare. They would do anything to avoid being crushed by Saddam, even beg for American help or perhaps even consider making peace with Israel.

In failing to deliver on his promise of Arab victory and resurgence, however, Saddam graphically showed that the price of alleged glory would be more wars, defeats, and perhaps political suicide for other Arabs. For the Gulf monarchies, all the years of appeasing Iraq, billions of dollars in aid to Baghdad during the Iran-Iraq war, and mountains of Pan-Arab rhetoric had done nothing to protect them from Saddam. On the contrary, it had made them more vulnerable to this type of threat. His adventure showed them once more – and not for the last time – that the men most dangerous for the Arabs themselves were those leaders who actually believed and tried to implement their own slogans. Few governments were pleased at the prospect of becoming provinces or client states of Saddam's empire. The Gulf's residents, especially, did not like the prospect of being looted by him.

Most of the Arab world acted quite pragmatically in supporting the ensuing war to defeat Iraq. With their survival at stake, they chose to ignore the demonstrations and articles that cheered Saddam. No amount of talk about Arab solidarity, Islamic brotherhood, and the urgency of the Palestinian issue could mask the fact that Saudi and Kuwaiti interests profoundly conflicted with those of Iran and Iraq. In condemning Iraq, the Arab League even abandoned its rule that action could only be taken unanimously, and Arab states aligned with the United States to a degree hitherto considered impossible. Once Saddam was defeated on the battlefield, his attraction as the inevitable victor quickly dissipated for the Arab masses.

Other developments also showed the futility and danger of the old ways. The Cold War's end and the Soviet Union's collapse meant that there were no longer two superpowers for Arab states to play off against each other. The fact that the United States was now the world's sole superpower gave a far greater incentive to be on good terms with that country. And the fact that America was Israel's ally meant that maintaining, much less fighting, the Arab-Israeli conflict would be far more dangerous. The threat from Islamic radicals was another reason why Arab regimes could no longer play with the fire of conflict and crisis.

As a result of such trends, in the aftermath of the Gulf War and the 1993 Israel-PLO agreement it seemed that a major turning point was at hand in Middle Eastern history, the start of a new era of pragmatism and moderation. The decision of the PLO and several Arab states to make peace with Israel was the clearest sign that the most basic principles of Arab politics no longer applied. Perhaps an alternative mode of thought and policy was really possible. After all, even the Soviet bloc states, a model for the strongest Arab states, had come to terms with failure by transforming themselves.

Indeed, it was hard to believe that things could go on as they had for so long. How would the Kuwaitis and the Gulf Arabs generally maintain their support for an Arab nationalism that had almost destroyed their independence? Why would countries cling to systems that had so badly failed to redeem their promises? When much of the rest of the world was moving to democracy, would the Arab world remain bogged down in dictatorships that were repressive at home and that waged ruinous wars and provoked confrontations abroad? Would anti-Americanism remain so deep and bitter after the United States had saved the Arab world from Iraq? Could the Palestinians really choose to sustain a half-century-long struggle from which they had derived no material gain or real victory?

The moderate side in this battle of paradigms was aided by a variety of factors, including a declining Arab-Israeli conflict, a higher priority on economic development, the weakening of radical states, the readiness of Arab states to pursue their individual and disparate interests, and a new pattern of Gulf security arrangements ensured by U.S. protection. Kuwait, always the most anti-American of the Gulf monarchies, now cheered its U.S. liberators. American policy makers believed that Saddam would soon fall.

Without Soviet backing, the radical forces were severely handicapped. The Madrid conference of 1991, itself a product of the Kuwait crisis, was the start of the most promising Arab-Israeli peace process in a half-century.

In the aftermath of the 1991 war, it seemed that the old ways could no longer continue for the Arab system amid a growing sense of their futility and wastefulness. A writer for the newspaper *al-Sharq al-Awsat* called the Arab and Islamic world's situation "either a race to suicide or a deliberate plan to exhaust and disarm our nation."[2] There were civil wars in Yemen, Algeria, Iraq (with the autonomy of a UN-protected Kurdish region in the north and rebellion in the Shi'ite south), and in non-Arab Afghanistan. International sanctions restricted both Libya and Iraq, while U.S. sanctions also targeted Sudan and Iran. Riyad Najib al-Rayyes wrote in *al-Nahar* that after "two destructive wars . . . a strong united Iraq became a humiliated, besieged and divided Iraq."[3]

Consequently, it appeared that these views were being challenged and replaced by ideas and practices more in line with those of other regions. Understandably, many in the West thought that a big change was inevitable and that a new, better Middle East must emerge. Based on their own philosophy and experience, they could not envision the possibility that pragmatism could lose or that ideology could retain any importance compared to the possibility of material betterment.

In the most significant U.S. policy statement explaining such optimism, President Clinton's National Security Advisor Tony Lake said he thought there would be a new era, one in which moderate Middle Eastern states blocked the influence of radical countries and groups. "The extremists will be denied the claim that they are the wave of the future. They will have to confront the reality of their failure [while moderate] governments find the strength to counter extremism at home as well as abroad."[4]

In contrast to Western confidence, Arab weakness and disunity were visible everywhere. With Iraq's defeat, still another idol had been toppled with remarkable speed and ease. Egypt's leading newspaper, *al-Ahram*, called Pan-Arab nationalists an "extinct Arab tribe."[5] Declarations of

---

2 Cited in *Middle East Mirror*, May 27, 1994. The reader will hopefully forgive the second use of this remarkably apt image.
3 *Al-Nahar*, cited in *Mideast Mirror*, May 10, 1994.
4 Tony Lake, transcript of a lecture at the Washington Institute for Near East Policy, May 17, 1994.
5 *Al-Ahram*, May 17, 1994.

dedication to Pan-Arabism, the Palestinian cause, and fighting Israel or America seemed to fall out of fashion. There was talk of such exotic new concepts as "Mideasternism," the idea that all of the region's peoples – Arabs, Israelis, Turks, and Iranians – should cooperate across national lines, just as other areas of the world had done successfully.[6]

A long list of factors seemed to have changed decisively:

- Radical regimes were weaker and more divided than at any time in decades, forcing them to be cautious about bullying their neighbors or attacking Western interests.
- Moderate states no longer wanted to accept the radical regimes' ideology or leadership. Peace, stability, and economic development seemed to be more desirable ends than an endless struggle posing such risks to their prosperity, interests, even to their survival. They were reluctant to be dragged into Arab-Israeli confrontations and worried more about radical regimes and internal threats than about Israel.
- Arab governments seemed to act more individualistically – forming alliances with the United States, moving toward peace with Israel, and pursuing other policies as it suited their interests. While Iraq claimed that its takeover of Kuwait was a victory for Pan-Arabism, most Arab regimes thought its motives to be greed and imperialism. The Kuwaitis discovered that all of their devotion and donations to Arab causes had not shielded them from Iraq's invasion, and that their aid to the Palestinians had not stopped Arafat from helping Saddam. In opposing Iraq's aggression, the Arab League decided to act in future on the basis of consensus rather than unanimity. Similarly, when Egypt, Morocco, Jordan, some Gulf states, or the PLO decided that their own interests might dictate peace with Israel, they were undeterred by criticism that this defied Pan-Arab or Pan-Islamic ideology.
- Regimes and secularists felt menaced by radical Islamist movements and feared that new crises might be exploited to overthrow them.
- There were hopes that Syria, after having participated in the anti-Iraqi coalition and showed an interest in peacemaking with Israel, would join the moderate camp.
- There were expectations that Iraq's regime would remain isolated and weak, perhaps even falling from power.

6 For an interesting example of this discussion, see *Mideast Mirror*, June 17, 1994.

- It was thought that the reform movement in Iran, supported by an overwhelming majority of the people, might triumph and abandon the revolution's militant policies.
- Moderate Arab and especially Gulf Arab states were ready to work closely with Washington in order to survive Iraqi, Iranian, and domestic revolutionary threats.
- Some discernible progress was apparently being made in several countries – including, for example, Egypt, Jordan, and Syria – toward more open societies, stronger civil societies, and democratization.

In contrast to that apparent alternative future, the actual modern history of the Middle East had been largely a story of Arab defeat and failure on seven fronts. Yet by the same token, the attempt to change that basic paradigm in the 1990s also met with defeat and failure on these same issues.

First, during the twentieth century's second half, there was the breakdown of the Arab state system in the context of counterproductive efforts to bring Pan-Arab unity. For a very long time, Arab nationalism had been the Arab world's hegemonic ideology. No Arab state could easily take any major foreign or domestic action without justifying it within this framework. Yet this very structure of Arab politics inspired constant battles and betrayals among states as they sought to dominate or escape domination by other countries.

Shaped by the belief that one state, leader, or idea could dominate the region, the Arab world plunged itself into repeated crises that caused misery, defeat, and stunted development.[7] Despite an expectation that charisma and revolution could transform the region and bring the quick achievement of all the Arab nationalist goals, the region saw the failure of Egypt's President Gamal Abdel Nasser to bring about unity through subversive persuasion during the 1950s and 1960s, and the

---

7 Contrary to Arab perceptions, Israel and Turkey were the only countries among the area's stronger states that were uninterested in regional power, in part precisely because each saw itself as the nation-state of a limited ethnic group on a very specific territory. Of course, the whole structure of regional rivalry feeds Arab suspicions that the region's non-Arab states are engaged in the same great game. Turkish and Israeli nationalisms do not have this goal. Kemal Ataturk's insistence that Turkey's existing borders be retained is one of that country's most basic principles. Some Israelis did favor a claim to just one area – the West Bank and Gaza Strip – as part of what they saw as the historic land of Israel. This goal was abandoned in the 1990s when peace seemed possible. The objective of Israeli strategic doctrine had been to maintain sufficient defensive strength to deter any number of states from attacking it.

nightmare of Iraqi President Saddam Hussein's attempt to bring unity through force during the 1980s and 1990s. Yet in all the years up to the 1990s, proper ideology – not material success – was seen as the measure of both doctrines and leaders. For example, though Nasser's ambitions and errors cost his country huge casualties and financial losses, he remained a hero to many throughout the Arab world.

During all these years, the Arab candidates for regional power or subregional domination and their smaller neighbors waged a costly, sometimes catastrophic, struggle in which tens of thousands of people died, huge amounts of resources were wasted, economic development was slowed, and living standards were held back. Progress toward democracy stagnated, and Arab intellectual life was crippled by these obsessions. The Palestinian cause, supposedly the focus and beneficiary of Arab cooperation, became a playground for this competition, which delayed a solution, thus continuing the Palestinians' suffering from violence, occupation, and life in refugee camps. In the end, the West was not expelled; Israel was not destroyed. Literally nothing good for the Arab cause came out of all these decades of suffering, turmoil, crisis, and catastrophe.

Instead, the drive to impose Arab brotherhood and homogeneity brought constant quarrels and splits, intensifying interstate conflict. For the idea that there should be one leader of the Arabs or of the region as a whole inevitably ignited rivalries, including those between Iraq and Iran, Syria and Iraq, Egypt and Saudi Arabia, Syria and Jordan. Arab states took different sides – or at least espoused conflicting strategies – on every issue. Even when they reached joint decisions, they were notoriously unable to implement them. During the Cold War, they called in competing patrons, the United States and the USSR, to fight their local battles.

What Pan-Arab nationalism really did was to furnish a popular ideological cover for nation-state imperialism. By accepting and promoting such concepts, Arab states and leaders were undermining their own freedom of action and even their own sovereignty, as various Arab regimes (and Iran also) interfered in each other's internal affairs, sponsoring political factions and terrorist groups. There were civil wars in Yemen, Sudan, Algeria, Lebanon, and Iraq (where the Shi'ite south rebelled and the Kurdish north became autonomous). Syria and Libya supported non-Arab Iran in its war against Iraq. Even the Iraqi and Syrian branches of the Ba'th Party bickered over which was the proper leader. Libya's

ruler, Muammar Qadhafi, whose claim to leadership sometimes quali-
fied as comic relief, stirred up deadly mischief everywhere.

Ironically, the very obsession with unity resulted in a level of regional
cooperation far lower than that found in Europe, Asia, Africa, and
Latin America, where countries were usually able to work together to
preserve existing borders, avoid wars, and reduce conflict among themselves. In short, the emphasis on Arab solidarity was the very factor
that created high levels of inter-Arab conflict. The limits on the expression of individual states' interests and differences held back development and undermined stability. Yet instead of recognizing these facts,
the debate of the 1990s ended with a reaffirmation of the view that the
real Arab problem was an insufficiently high level of unity.

Second, the prophesied ideal revolutions either did not take place at
all or produced terrible governments. Arab nationalist republics never
came to power in Morocco, Jordan, Saudi Arabia, and other countries.
Nevertheless, these "reactionary" monarchies showed considerable
staying power. But where such coups did take place – as in Egypt, Syria,
and Iraq – the resulting regimes were also far from satisfactory and certainly failed to keep their promises of rapid development, inter-Arab
cooperation, and military triumphs. They were considerably more repressive than the kingdoms they replaced and did not necessarily do a
better job of governing. While on the positive side they carried out land
reform programs and empowered some new social groups, they also
came to embody the problems of incompetence and corruption that
they were supposed to solve. A highly symbolic last straw was when
Syrian President Hafiz al-Asad died and, in monarchical style, was succeeded by his son.

By the 1990s, too, the moderates were less intimidated by the radicals than ever before. The Gulf monarchies were wealthy and could depend on U.S. protection. The radical regimes were on the defensive. The
loss of the USSR denied them both diplomatic support and low-cost,
high-quality weapons. Iran, Iraq, Libya, and Syria were divided by their
own diverse ideologies, ambitions, and interests. Iraq and Libya faced
international sanctions, while Iran was damaged by U.S. sanctions.

Yet the 1990s did not ultimately bring a moderate victory. Timidity,
doubts about U.S. reliability, fear of domestic reaction, their own mistrust of reform, and other factors made the regimes return to old habits.
Once again, the Arab consensus accepted the idea that militant Arab

nationalism was still the ideal, that its lack of success was not due to internal shortcomings but rather to the machinations of the United States and Israel. Advocates of real democracy remained a small minority in every country. As in the past, the extremists were allowed to set the region's rhetorical tone, permissible limits, and agenda.

Third, the Arab states and the Palestinian movement were unable to destroy or even to defeat Israel. Instead, Israel became stronger and could not even be dislodged from the territories captured in 1967 except through negotiation and compromise. Many different strategies were tried, yet all failed to eliminate that country. Rather, the costs of continuing the conflict steadily damaged Arab interests and weakened Arab states.

For many decades, regional strife in the Middle East seemed to revolve around the Arab-Israeli conflict, though observers often exaggerated this factor's centrality. This issue engaged far more Arab rhetoric than action, partly because it was easier to rail at Israel than to address difficult, divisive problems at home or the real conflicts among Arab states.

But in reality, each Arab regime and movement manipulated the issue to promote its interests, mobilize domestic support, and gain an edge over rivals. Syria defined Israel and the West Bank as its property, "southern Syria." Jordan asserted its own claim to the West Bank. In Lebanon, factions alternately courted and attacked the Palestinians during the civil war. Despite mountains of anti-American rhetoric over the issue, the Arab-Israeli conflict rarely affected any state's relations with the United States.

Calculated self-interest also determined how Arab rulers acted toward the PLO. They promoted their own puppet Palestinian factions in an effort to seize control of the organization. Jordan fought and expelled the PLO by force in 1970 when it threatened the country's internal stability. Egypt made a unilateral peace with Israel in 1979 in order to regain the Sinai and its oil fields, which Israel had captured in the 1967 war. In 1983, Syria's alleged devotion to the Palestinian cause did not stop it from splitting the PLO in a takeover attempt. The Syrian army chased pro-Arafat forces from Lebanon; Syria's Lebanese clients attacked refugee camps in Lebanon, killing hundreds of Palestinians.

In addition, Arab states, rulers, and factions accused each other of being too cowardly or corrupt to deal with the issue properly. Regimes usually did not want to fight Israel, because they thought they would lose or would pay a high price with little gain. Their rivals and radicals who did not hold power themselves argued that the war could be won, despite past experience and the balance of power. If only all Arabs or Muslims united; if only they used conventional, guerrilla, or terror tactics; if only they devoted all of their resources to the conflict; if only they were willing to take more risks; if only they were able to frighten the Americans from the region or to free themselves of U.S. influence, then they could defeat and destroy Israel. With the alternative of making a compromise peace unthinkable – or extremely dangerous for anyone who advocated it – the Arab world remained a prisoner of this fantasy for many decades.

And this dream constantly boomeranged on the Arab states and societies themselves. It led to military defeats in the 1956, 1967, 1973, and 1982 wars, with accompanying losses of territory, money, prestige, and stability. Other results included Jordan's short and Lebanon's long civil war, the boycott of Egypt after the Camp David peace agreement, violent attempts by Arab states to take over the PLO, and the assassinations of Jordan's King Abdallah I and Sadat, along with many others. Using this issue demagogically, every Arab ruler could justify any policy. Democracy, economic reform, and any other change could be declared impossible to consider under the endless conditions of war. The Israel issue was the opiate of the Arab world, an addiction that could not be broken but that provided false satisfaction and distraction to the masses.

Yet over time, these realities did have an effect. The Arab-Israeli conflict seemed to subvert the Arab states' own stability and well-being, creating a dangerous permanent atmosphere of crisis that drew Arab countries into losing wars, provided a rationale for dictatorship, justified counterproductive economic and social policies, and inhibited necessary cooperation with the United States. It fostered revolutionary Islamic movements, expensive arms races, catastrophic civil wars, and the possibility of invasion by an Iraqi dictator.

In short, actually engaging in the conflict no longer served the interests of Arab regimes. Oppositionists still advocated battle, but their words did not set state policy. Diplomatic advances and negotiations further reduced the conflict's importance. The radical states were militant in rhetoric but did little in practice. Moreover, they were badly divided among themselves. Arab ardor was further dampened as Israel proved that it could defend itself. Threats, terror, war, and mass uprisings were all unable to drive Israel out of the West Bank and Gaza.

Thus, the conflict's high costs and defeats gradually pushed most Arab states to reduce their involvement with the Arab-Israeli issue, which increasingly appeared to be anachronistic, since there was no rational reason to believe that the situation would change in the Arabs' favor. Gulf Arab states were preoccupied by the Iran-Iraq war and Iraq's seizure of Kuwait. As time went on, Arab states became even less involved with the issue, being as unwilling to wage war as they were unready to make peace. They did little to combat the Israeli invasion and military victory in Lebanon in 1982, to help the *intifadas* that began in 1987 and 2000, or even to aid the Palestinian Authority. With Iraq (as well as radical Islamist movements and Iran) a clear and present danger to the survival of Arab regimes, it was harder to act consistently as if Israel was the principal threat.

In 1991, the Palestinians too were at the low point of their fortunes. Their *intifada* had petered out, and their latest hero, Saddam Hussein, had been defeated. Their ally, the USSR, and its Soviet bloc had collapsed. Arab states were less willing to help them, and the cut-off of Kuwaiti and Saudi aid had produced a financial crisis in the PLO. Around 350,000 Palestinian refugees had fled Iraq or been forced out of Kuwait. The United States, which the PLO had viewed as its archenemy, was the world's sole superpower. Israel appeared to be stronger than ever. If ever there was a time for the Palestinians to make a compromise peace, recognizing that they could not achieve all of their goals, the 1990s offered that opportunity.

During the 1990s, then, there was a serious reconsideration of Arab strategy on this issue. The conclusion of an Israel-PLO peace agreement in 1993 and its implementation, face-to-face bilateral and multilateral negotiations, a treaty between Israel and Jordan, and Israeli willingness to make dramatic concessions made peace seem possible.

But was the Arab-Israeli conflict really no longer a useful political tool? If peace were to be made, this precious instrument would be lost to Arab politicians. And if they reached a negotiated settlement, the benefits were not precisely overwhelming. Such a step might well make them more insecure. Demands for democracy, economic reform, and political change would multiply. At the same time, there would be many who might succeed in persuading the masses that this peace was "treason." The rulers took this issue seriously, even when they did not yield to such threats to unleash domestic revolutionary upheavals.

The history of the ensuing Syria-Israel, and Palestinian-Israel peace processes is very complex. Jordan did make full peace with Israel, and several other Arab states took steps in that direction. But the two main Arab protagonists were unable to reach an agreement with Israel, even after Israel offered to meet virtually all of their demands. Arguably, this failure on the Arab side could be attributed to a weak leadership, afraid to make tough decisions and incapable of altering public opinion; an inability to break with the past, including an overwhelming suspicion of Israel; or to a range of other factors. In some ways, though, the truth was that the Arab regimes were strong – and that refusing to end the conflict was a major source of their strength, like Samson's hair or Popeye's spinach.

The bottom line was that the Palestinians and Syrians proved unable to meet the challenge of achieving a compromise peace with Israel – even one that met most of their demands – and that other Arab states would not shake loose from their veto power in order to end the conflict. The conclusion the Arab world seemed to draw from this experience was not a need for greater compromise and conciliation, but instead a duty to strive for more effective violence, mobilization, and steadfastness in pressing old demands. By the end of the year 2000, Arab attitudes had reverted to those of twenty years earlier. Israel was demonized to astounding levels, and the old belief in the possibility of total victory returned in the minds of a new generation that had not experienced the frustrations and defeats of the past. It was easy for the Arab masses to believe – as their leaders and media told them daily – that only cowardice and treason could prevent Israel's elimination or encourage peaceful compromise with such a vile entity.

Fourth, the efforts to expel Western influence did not succeed. Indeed, given globalization, the Western cultural presence actually increased in the Arab world. Even Islamist Iran could not keep out American entertainment and fashions. On the political level, too, Arab countries brought in Western forces to help them. The radical states sought Soviet help in order to increase their regional leverage, fight Israel, and combat the moderates. The moderates turned to the United States to arm and save them. The Gulf monarchies asked the United States to convoy their oil tankers, sell them arms, and protect them from Iran during the 1980s. The Arab world turned to the United States to save

Kuwait and then to act as a broker in the Arab-Israeli peace process of the 1990s.

America's role and influence as the world's sole superpower was recognized and further consolidated during the Kuwait crisis. Thereafter, moderate Arab states continued efforts to maintain good relations with the United States and to use it as a protector, no matter how their public posture differed from that image. Even Syria tried to give the impression that it was cooperating with U.S. efforts to further the Arab-Israeli peace process. The Palestinian Authority became a virtual American client. And after a long struggle involving UN sanctions, Libya surrendered two intelligence agents to be tried in the bombing of a U.S. airliner over Lockerbie, Scotland, in 1988.

The most important aspect of the post–Cold War world for Arab states was the U.S. monopoly on superpower status, and it created a paradox. Radical and moderate Arab states resented America's status, both out of jealousy and for fear that it would be used against them. Even the moderates condemned the United States, while using it as a defender against the radicals, an arms supplier, and a source of aid. Expecting the United States to act as they would have done in its place, Arab leaders feared the United States might seek to control the Gulf, or the Middle East in general, subordinating them in an imperial manner.

In addition, while Arabs frequently complained that the United States was a bully, they also preferred to have such a powerful force on their side. Indeed, America's problems arose less when it was perceived as a bully than when it was viewed as being truly weak. Most noticeable and notable were the limits on U.S. power and influence, which could be attributed either to mistaken U.S. policies or to the Arab regimes' policies. The United States was unable to press the PA or Syria into signing peace agreements with Israel, despite that country's many offers of concessions on almost all the key points. Equally, it could not keep some countries from breaking the UN-mandated sanctions on Iraq or the U.S.-imposed sanctions on Iran. The United States had very little success in persuading other Arab states – especially Saudi Arabia and Kuwait, which it had saved during the 1991 crisis – to move closer to peace with Israel.

At any rate, why should Arab states show gratitude to the United States as their protector and liberator when they didn't need to do so in order to obtain the benefits? Indeed, there was an interesting counter-vailing factor on this point. To indicate dependency and appreciation for American help would justify U.S. demands for reciprocal behavior. By denying the United States had ever done anything to help them, the Arab states showed that they didn't owe America anything and could rightfully ignore its requests.

Far from legitimating better relations with the West, then, every American action was also counted as further proof of U.S. interference and perfidy. This was understandable on the part of the radical regimes, which wanted to isolate the moderates and deny them a protector. Yet the moderates also refused to say anything positive about the United States. When terrorists, most of them Saudis, killed more than 3,000 Americans on September 11, 2001, the state-controlled media in countries nominally allied with the United States – including Saudi Arabia and Egypt – were overwhelmingly hostile to the victim. They focused only on complaints about U.S. policy, while ignoring not only its efforts to mediate a mutually acceptable peace with Israel, but also all the aid and help the United States had provided to the Arabs directly. Years of experience of the high cost of combating U.S. influence and the benefits of working with America were not factored into Arab thinking and policies.

Fifth, the Arab states failed to maintain peace or security in the Persian Gulf. As a result, two bloody wars caused great loss of life and property, wasted tens of billions of dollars that could have been used for raising living standards, and endangered the very survival of the countries of that region. An arms race in the area also cost additional tens of billions of dollars that could have been better used. This problem was rooted in Iraqi aggression, fueled and legitimized by Pan-Arab ideology; Iranian ambitions, stimulated and magnified by Islamist doctrine; and the Gulf Arab monarchies' readiness to appease Iraq, combined with a reluctance to seek Western help sufficient to deter would-be attackers.

For a while after Iraq's defeat in 1991, it appeared that the Gulf Arab states had learned their lesson – that appeals to Arab brotherhood and Islamic solidarity too often provided cover to those who simply wanted to loot their wealth. Instead, the monarchies could work with the United States to deter both Iran and Iraq from disturbing their peace. Radical ideology and militant slogans had shown themselves to be like matches, far too dangerous to play with around so much flammable oil.

But while these regimes were indeed more wary than they had once been, old habits returned. Militancy was seen as providing insurance against the complaints of their own people and their neighbors. Payments from the Saudi government went to Usama bin Ladin to buy him off; Saudi private contributors gave to bin Ladin and other extremists out of a belief that they were the highest expression of Islam. Once again, there were moves toward appeasing Iraq, or toward viewing Tehran as the best protection against Baghdad. And the constant public disdain for America coming from the local elites and the state-controlled media undermined their real potential defender.

Sixth, Islamist ideologies failed as badly as their Arab nationalist predecessors. There were no successful Islamist revolts in Arab states, and even the one existing Islamist regime, in Iran, lost the support of the masses there.

Radical Islamism certainly did pose a threat to the existing order. Iran sponsored subversive and terrorist groups in the Gulf, in Lebanon, and among the Palestinians. In every country, too, Islamist groups arose and became the principal opposition movements, staging full-scale revolts in Egypt and Algeria. Often, though not by any means always, they contributed new problems of violence and instability to the already-existing heap of problems. Their cadre became strong voices opposing democracy and needed social reforms. In short, generally speaking, Islamist groups made things worse rather than better.

Yet the incumbent Arab regimes successfully adjusted their policies in order to defeat this challenge. Most Muslims saw these revolutionary groups as offering strange, even heretical, interpretations of Islam. In the 1990s, given the defeat of the radical Islamists, the way seemed open for the emergence of a true democratic alternative based on a vibrant civil society, which might eventually include moderate Islamist parties in some countries.[8]

Instead, however, the extremists got a second wind and again came to the fore. The apparent victory of Lebanese Hizballah over Israel in southern Lebanon was taken as proof of the idea that a guerrilla or terrorist

8 Actually, this transformation of Islamist parties and movements did happen to a large extent in Turkey. See Bulent Aras, "Fethullah Gulen and His Movement," in Barry Rubin, ed., *Revolutionaries and Reformers: Contemporary Islamist Movements in the Middle East* (Albany, NY, 2003); Birol A Yesilada, "The Virtue Party in Turkey," in Barry Rubin and Metin Heper, eds., *Political Parties in Turkey* (London, 2002).

force would inevitably triumph over a militarily stronger opponent. Arafat's turn toward violence in the year 2000 let Hamas and Islamic Jihad again argue persuasively that their path was the only proper one. The great "success" of Usama bin Ladin in striking at the United States in September 2001 seemed to show that his was an ideology that produced real fighters who would ultimately triumph, while the regimes stood by and did nothing. Thus, radical Islamist views remained equally or even more popular in the early twenty-first century than they had been a decade earlier.

Seventh, the Arab world had a relatively slow and often dismal pace of economic and social development. If it had not been for the existence of oil and gas – obviously a very considerable advantage, but one that has limits nonetheless – every Arab country would be an economic basket case. In many countries, radical regimes wasted huge resources engaging in war and imposing doctrinaire domestic policies. Dictatorship remained the principal type of government at a time when other Third World regions were overwhelmingly turning toward more democracy, civil liberties, and human rights, all of which can help to accelerate economic performance. This widening gap also had its costs, perhaps irreparable ones, as other countries filled economic niches and attracted investment that would be permanently lost to the Middle East.

During the 1990s, some awareness of these problems was a factor encouraging some reconsideration of the way Arab states were governed. The low oil prices prevailing in the 1990s made petroleum-producing states more nervous about their ability to continue providing domestic privileges and ensuring stability. To develop further, the wealthy states needed peace, stability, and good relations with the West. Poorer states could not depend on their rich "brothers" – who showed little interest in investing in the Arab world or in helping them – and thus hoped to obtain Western aid. Certainly, the economic situation and social trends were serious enough to set off alarm bells across the region, from Morocco all the way to Iran.

According to the World Bank, the Middle East – despite the opportunities offered by its immense oil and gas wealth – had the lowest overall and per capita economic growth in terms of gross domestic product (GDP) of any world region between 1965 and 1999, except for sub-Saharan Africa. The region had only a 3 percent annual growth rate, but even this figure is misleading because it was subverted by rapid population expansion. More revealing of the real lack of economic growth is per capita GDP growth, which was a mere 0.1 percent annually for this period. By comparison, South Korea's figures were 8.1 percent and 6.6 percent respectively, while Thailand's were 7.3 and 5.1 percent. Even India had 4.6 percent overall GDP growth and a 2.4 percent per capita growth rate. There was little or no real growth at all in Algeria, Jordan, Saudi Arabia, the United Arab Emirates, Iran, Kuwait, Libya, and Iraq.[9]

Looking at the most recent decades, the record is equally dismal. The Middle East had an average overall GDP growth rate of 2.0 percent between 1980 and 1990, compared to 8.0 percent for East Asia and 5.6 percent for South Asia.[10] The rate of growth in the Middle East rose to 3.0 percent for 1990–99, but even with the massive financial crises of 1997, East Asia still had an average growth rate of 7.5 percent for that period (until the crises, growth had been almost 10 percent), while South Asia stayed steady at 5.6 percent, and even Latin America faired better at 3.8 percent.[11]

Incomes did not grow very well either. Between 1986 and 2000, real per capita incomes fell by 2 percent a year – the largest decline in any developing region. For oil exporters, the fall in output per capita of 4 percent a year between 1980 and 1991 closely paralleled lower oil prices. But even the non–oil exporters in the region (such as Jordan, Morocco, and Tunisia) grew by less than 1 percent annually.[12] The average annual increase in per capita consumption was only 0.7 percent between 1980 and 1997, compared to 6.8 percent for East Asia. It stayed virtually the same, at 0.8 percent, for the Middle East for 1996–97, compared to 6.2 percent for East Asia, 3.9 percent for Latin America, and 3.4 percent for South Asia.[13] Given inflation, rising prices for other commodities, and population increases, per capita oil income in the Arab states did not increase appreciably between the 1970s and the end of the century.[14]

9 World Bank, *World Development Indicators, 2001*, (Washington, DC, 2001), pp. 24–6.
10 Anthony Cordesman, "Strategic Developments in the Maghreb: Economics, Structural Change, Productivity, Trade, and Per Capita Income," Center for Strategic and International Studies, 1998, p. 15; adapted from the World Bank, *Global Economic Prospects and the Developing World, 1996*, p. 6.
11 World Bank, *World Development Indicators, 2001* (Washington, DC, 2001), p. 196.
12 "Claiming the Future," World Bank, 1995, quoted from executive summary.
13 Ibid.
14 "World Bank MENA Regional Brief," World Bank, September 27, 2001. http://lnweb18.worldbank.org/mna/mena.nsf/attachments/MNABRIEF+English+2001/ $file/Mena+&+world+bank-01-+regional+brief.pdf.

One particularly Middle Eastern problem was the underutilization of female labor; another was the continued focus on agriculture.[15] Middle Eastern agricultural output improved only very slowly, with productivity gains averaging only 2.6 percent during most of the 1990s, versus 5.6 percent during the 1980s.[16] Yet while population grew quickly and agricultural productivity grew slowly, the amount of arable land per capita shrank steadily – by more than one-third during the last 15 years of the twentieth century. It was 0.29 hectares per person for 1979–81, and only 0.21 hectares for 1994–98. Meanwhile, only 11 percent of the labor force worked in manufacturing, compared to 30 percent in Europe, where productivity rates were much higher and large numbers of workers were involved in the higher-skill service areas and the professions.[17]

The Middle East lagged behind in the economic development needed to raise living standards and to provide housing, jobs, and education for its citizens. But it led the world in population growth, making it even harder to catch up. The fact that unusually high proportions of the citizens of these countries were young people also potentially contributed to social volatility. The region's population growth has been so rapid that something like 40 percent of the population is fourteen years of age or younger.[18] This figure is 50 percent in the Gaza Strip, 47 percent in Yemen, 45 percent in the West Bank, 42 percent in Iraq, 40 percent in Syria, 37 percent in Jordan, 35 percent in Libya, and 33 percent in Iran. Half of the Saudi population is under 15; 65 percent of Iranians are under 25; and in Algeria, 30 percent of the population is under 30 years old.[19]

In the early 1960s, the total population of the Middle East and North Africa was between 80 and 90 million people. By 1970, it was well in excess of 120 million. The World Bank estimated the total population at 174 million in 1980.[20] By 1999, it totaled 290.3 million. It is expected to reach 389.7 million in 2015, and 481 million in

---

15 World Bank, *World Development Indicators, 1997* (Washington, DC, 1997), pp. 14–17.

16 World Bank, *World Development Indicators, 2001*, pp. 194–6.

17 Anthony Cordesman, "Transitions in the Middle East." Address to the Eighth Mideast Policymakers Conference, September 9, 1999; World Bank, *World Development Indicators, 1997*, section 2.3.

18 Anthony H. Cordesman, "Stability and Instability in the Gulf," *Center for Strategic and International Studies*, April 1999, p. 13.

19 CIA, *World Fact Book, 2001*, http://www.cia.gov/cia/publications/factbook/index.html. (These statistics are updated from the Cordesman information.)

20 World Bank, *World Development Indicators, 1997*, p. 37.

2030.[21] The region had the highest annual population growth rate in the world and was tied for first with Latin America in terms of labor force expansion.

The population explosion was especially extraordinary in a number of places. The Gaza Strip and West Bank, Iraq, Libya, Oman, Qatar, Saudi Arabia, Syria, and Yemen had well over a 3 percent population growth rate.[22] The figures put a heavy weight on governments that can barely handle their current burdens:

- Egypt had a population of 41 million in 1980.[23] It was around 66 million in 2000. Although Egypt's population growth rate at the turn of the century was down to 1.9 percent, the World Bank projects a population of 93 million by 2030.[24] This demographic explosion has far outpaced the construction of schools and libraries.[25]
- Iran had a population of 39 million in 1980.[26] By 2000, it was over 69 million. The World Bank projects that it will be 96 million by 2030.[27]
- Iraq had a population of 13 million in 1980.[28] It had grown to 21.7 million by 2000, and Iraq's growth rate of 3.2 percent is one of the region's highest. The World Bank projects that it will have 39 million people by 2030.[29]
- Jordan had a population of 2.2 million in 1980.[30] It had reached 4.4 million by 2000, and the high growth rate of 2.6 percent is expected to produce a population of 8 million by 2030.[31]

21 World Bank, *World Development Indicators, 2001*, pp. 46–8; Anthony H. Cordesman, "Stability and Instability in the Middle East: Economics, Demography, Energy, and Security," Center for Strategic and International Studies, 1997. Adapted by Anthony H. Cordesman from World Bank database for world population projections, 1996, http://www.csis.org/mideast/stable/2e.html.
22 CIA, *World Fact Book, 1998*, in Anthony H. Cordesman, "Stability and Instability in the Gulf," p. 15. See also World Bank, *World Development Indicators, 2001*, pp. 24–6.
23 World Bank, *World Development Indicators, 2001*, pp. 46–8.
24 World Bank Group, World Bank Human Development Network, "Health, Nutrition and Population," world population projections, http://devdata.worldbank.org/hnpstats/files/EGY_pop.xls.
25 CIA, *World Fact Book, 2001*, http://www.cia.gov/cia/publications/factbook/index.html.
26 World Bank, *World Development Indicators, 2001*, pp. 46–8.
27 World Bank Group, world population projections, http://devdata.worldbank.org/hnpstats/files/IRN_pop.xls.
28 World Bank, *World Development Indicators, 2001*, pp. 46–8.
29 World Bank Group, world population projections, http://devdata.worldbank.org/hnpstats/files/IRQ_pop.xls.
30 World Bank, *World Development Indicators, 2001*, pp. 46–8.
31 World Bank Group, world population projections, http://devdata.worldbank.org/hnpstats/files/JOR_pop.xls.

• Syria had a population of 8.7 million in 1980.[32] With 17 million in 2000, and a high growth rate of 3.2 percent, a population of 28 million is projected by 2030.[33]

Growing urbanization is another factor with significant political implications. People in cities are more exposed to modern thinking, Islamist movements, and cultural contradictions. They seek and receive more education and require higher quality employment and housing. Consequently, they are more likely to have grievances and to express them. The region was only about 25 percent urbanized in 1960, 37 percent in 1970, 48 percent in 1990, and 58 percent in 2000. It is expected to be 70 percent urbanized by around 2015, with about 25 percent of the region's population living in cities of one million or more people.[34]

With slow growth, low investment, inadequate development of technology, and antiquated government and economic practices, how could there possibly be sufficient jobs, housing, and infrastructure for all of these people?

The Middle East has also done poorly regarding adult literacy. During the 1990s, male illiteracy (for those over age 15) declined from 33 to 25 percent, with female illiteracy going down from 59 to 47 percent. The combined total was about 38.7 percent in the year 2000, meaning that 68 million people in the Arab world could not read or write. This performance, however, was only slightly better than that of South Asia and sub-Saharan Africa. The Middle Eastern countries had triple the illiteracy of Latin America and East Asia. To make matters worse, the rapid increase in population meant that there were seven million more illiterate adults in the Arab world in 2000 than in 1990.[35] In Egypt, the average of all adult illiteracy in 1999 was a remarkable 55 percent, and in Iraq it stood at 45 percent. In Syria, while male illiteracy stood at only 12 percent, among females it was 41 percent. In comparison, the figure for adult illiteracy in South Korea was only 2.5 percent, in Thailand 5 percent, and in Peru just over 10 percent.[36]

32 World Bank, *World Development Indicators, 2001*, pp. 46–8.
33 World Bank Group, world population projections, http://devdata.worldbank.org/hnpstats/files/SYR_pop.xls.
34 World Bank, *World Development Indicators, 1997*, section 3.6; and Population Reference Bureau report on Arab world population, December 1996, in Anthony Cordesman, "Stability and Instability in the Middle East."
35 CIA, *World Fact Book, 2001*, http://www.cia.gov/cia/publications/factbook/index.html.
36 World Bank, *World Development Indicators, 2001*, pp. 94–6.

The number of personal computers (per 1,000 people) is another area – and an especially important one for education and future economic success – where the Arab world and Iran lagged far behind other countries at the turn of the century. While the figures for Kuwait (121.3) and the United Arab Emirates (102.1) are impressive, and for Saudi Arabia (57.4) respectable, these were exceptions. The overall average for the region was only 25.4, and in key countries with more political power, computers are rare – only 12 per 1,000 people in Egypt, 2.4 in Iran, 14 in Jordan, 10.8 in Morocco, and 14.3 in Syria. This compared to Peru at 35.7, South Korea at 181.8, and Israel at 245.7.[37]

Two positive developments that nevertheless contributed to growing population size and thus to a demographic imbalance and destabilizing social pressures were the decline in infant mortality and the increase in life expectancy. Infant mortality fell steeply, from 95 per 1,000 live births in 1980, to 60 in 1990, and to 44 in 1999. This was still higher than the rate in many countries – for 1999, the numbers were 39 for Peru, 20 for Romania, and 8 for South Korea – but it was a dramatic improvement, yet one that heightened social problems.[38] Life expectancy rose from 59 years in 1980 to 68 in 1999, tying the Middle East with South Asia as the world's most improved region.[39]

Morocco's situation is fairly typical in this respect. There, half of the rapidly increasing population is under the age of 25 and lives mostly in towns. Almost 65 percent live below the poverty line, and the situation is deteriorating. The head of a social welfare agency remarked, "Before independence people said the French sucked Morocco dry just for their own benefit. Nowadays the poor say the same about the middle classes and the rich." Similar concerns came from a young Moroccan teacher: "What counts most is loyalty and submission, not ability. That's why most young people have given up hope." All of these problems are integrally related to the nature of a system so self-confident that it need not make concessions to its own people. A businessperson complained, "If there wasn't so much corruption, the economy would be booming. But the civil service treats Moroccan and foreign investors like cash

37 Ibid., pp. 306–8.
38 Ibid., pp. 16–18, 114–16
39 Ibid., pp. 114–16.

cows and milks them dry." Many of the richest are army officers who have used their power to line their pockets.[40]

Given this whole range of problems, as one Arab assessment accurately concluded,

The Middle East is slipping behind in the . . . competition for markets and capital. States have interfered arbitrarily and ineffectively too often, created lopsided, uncompetitive state sectors, extended subsidies and entitlements which are difficult to withdraw or reduce, and depend too much on rising oil revenues. Economies are not diversified enough or integrated regionally. Population growth has raised a host of problems for states, from education and job creation to the need to trim subsidies and welfare systems. Most of the remedies for a more efficient private sector have important political implications, notably more transparency and greater rule of law.[41]

In the midst of this remarkable set of difficulties and failures, then, it is not surprising that many observers thought that the Middle East would find it imperative to make major shifts in its political and economic system during the 1990s. A break from the past seemed not only beneficial but inescapable if more decades of crisis, and possibly a collapse of several countries, was to be avoided. Even more important, however, was the conclusion of Middle Eastern rulers, intellectuals, and others that reform and democracy would not necessarily solve the problems of the regimes or the masses. Such changes could become major sources of instability, bringing suffering to everyone, as well as the loss of power and wealth by those who possessed it. Instead, populist regimes satisfied their people with the bread and circuses of

---

40 Ignacio Ramonet, "Morocco: The Point of Change," Le Monde Diplomatique, July 2000, http://www.monde-diplomatique.fr/en/2000/07/01ramonet.

41 "Entering the New Millennium, A Reformed Arab World," Jordan Star, December 30, 1999.

For more on these issues, see Bernard Hoekman and Peter D. Sutherland, "The Other Mideast Crisis: Economic Decline," International Herald Tribune, March 27, 2002; and a Council on Foreign Relations study, Bernard Hoekman and Patrick Messerlin, Harnessing Trade for Development and Growth in the Middle East (New York, 2002). Hoekman and Sutherland write that their research "reinforced what has long been known: privileged state enterprises, bureaucracy and red tape are significant obstacles to investment and growth. Of those surveyed, 20 percent said bribes averaged 2 percent to 9 percent of the value of consignments. The economic performance of many Middle Eastern and North African countries during the past quarter- or half-century has trailed most other regions, despite the advantage of great oil wealth. In the 1950s, per capita income in Egypt was similar to that in South Korea; today it is less than 20 percent [of that country]."

economic subsidies and ideological fulfillment. As Saddam Hussein assured his people, "If those who surpass you in material things and appearances outrun you, do not follow them. Choose your own honorable path. . . .Your clinging to these principles will be deeper in effect, firmer in stand and higher in position."[42]

And on some levels, the system was working. There had been no coup or revolution in a major Arab state (not including Sudan or Yemen) since the early 1970s. There is a big difference between the existence of internal conflict or violent opposition and such movements' ability to seize power. In general, rulers know their own societies well, can assess the relative threats, and are determined to stay in power by whatever means necessary at any cost required.

In this sense, the Middle East's decision not to switch to a new paradigm at the end of the 1990s was a rational choice. Yet when compared to other parts of the world, the tragedy of the area's situation becomes extraordinarily clear and increasingly depressing.

Each region has its own history, issues, power balance, political order, and structure that make its countries and peoples interact in specific ways. Still, there are some useful parallels. When these are examined, the Middle East can be seen as the exceptional region of the world. It is not that other areas don't have profound problems. They do. But in other regions, by the onset of the twenty-first century problems typically stemmed from innate difficulties of development and the ordinary clash of group or individual interests. There had already been a resolution – in theory if not always in practice – of the most basic issues. The Western model of development, democracy, and free enterprise was seen as preferable. Conflict among states had declined; national boundaries had stabilized; and both domestic and regional pluralism were accepted.

In the Middle East, though, difficulties arose from still-unresolved questions about purpose, direction, and identity. There was still a passionate argument over the desirable future, and strong resistance to even an adaptation of Western systems of thought and society. In other regions, disputes tend to be over details, methods, and variations on a theme, about how to best achieve an already agreed-upon end. In the

---

42 Speech of August 8, 2001. Text from Iraq News Agency website, http://www.uruklink.net/iraqnews/eindex.htm.

Middle East, totally different roads were still seen as preferable, and the restriction of free speech and open media made this debate more than a trifle one-sided.

During the last half-century, the Middle East was the part of the world where belief in the possibility of someone or something achieving regional hegemony played the greatest role both in public opinion and in the states' ambitions, actions, and relations. Equally, in a pattern recalling the historic international communist movement, revolutionary groups under Pan-Arab nationalist or revolutionary Islamic banners struggled to seize state power and to unite the region ostensibly from below, though often with an imperialist-minded regime's sponsorship.

Why was the Middle East different? The most honest answer is that no one actually knows. Many reasons can be put forward, but none of them can be proven or achieve a consensus accepting them as true. In a real sense, though, while this debate is tempting in intellectual terms, it is relatively unimportant in practical ones. What is truly significant is that these quite substantial differences can be readily observed and analyzed, providing some new perspectives on the problems of the Middle East.

One vital issue is the question of a region's definition and identity, both in international terms and in terms of specific countries. At some points in history – ancient, medieval, and modern alike – there have been leaders, governments, states, and ideologies that sought regionwide domination. An entire historical era, even centuries, have been required to prove that this kind of scheme would not work, or to stop some countries from trying to achieve this goal. Belief in the possibility of conquering, revolutionizing, or uniting a region has always been related to the idea that such an achievement would bring an overnight transformation to a higher social and economic level. Not only have such efforts been the result of ambitions from above, they have also attracted support from intellectuals and the masses as a panacea to solve all of their problems.

In Africa and South America, such efforts have had only a limited effect since the end of colonialism, with pan-nationalist movements quickly being replaced by individual nation-state nationalisms and a relatively low level of interstate conflict or subversion. The Organization of African Unity and the Organization of American States exist only to develop a minimal degree of cooperation among states. Even the controversial Cuban and South African issues have not upset these generally peaceful frameworks.

Arguably, Asia – both South and East Asia – has been more subject to drives for hegemony, especially from Japan in the 1930s and 1940s and to a lesser extent from China under communist rule in later decades. Yet even here, states have generally coexisted and accepted each other's sovereignty. In East Asia, the economic aspect of this regional cooperation has been especially fruitful, and the Association of East Asian Nations has few conflicts to resolve. While South Asia contains the serious India-Pakistan conflict, this is substantially a bilateral dispute over specific border regions.[43]

North America followed a different but quite successful route, as the United States and Canada became countries that grew to dominate the continent. During the last century there has been overwhelming cooperation, with hardly a crisis between the United States, Canada, and Mexico. The North American Free Trade Agreement symbolizes this productive interdependency.

Outside of the Middle East, the region most marked by perpetual battles for hegemony has been Europe. The main contestants have been Britain, France, Germany, and Russia. This international struggle was carried out under many banners: for king, czar, the emperor Napoleon, parliamentary democracy, fascism, and communism. In each case, though, the effort of a leader, state, or doctrine to gain regional hegemony – or to protect itself from those seeking it – was the motivating factor. After a century of peace, the twentieth century saw two world wars and a Cold War fought over this question. In the end, or at least one hopes it is the end, the inability of anyone to achieve the goal of hegemony through force or violence was clear. Europe was able to attain a high level of peace and regional integration by peaceful and cooperative means.

---

43 China had a brief war with Vietnam and had sought to spread communism to other countries. In the 1970s, Vietnam tried to develop a sphere of influence in Cambodia and Laos. India has never tried to gain dominance in the South Asian subcontinent, despite its involvements with Bangladesh's creation and with counterinsurgency in Sri Lanka. Arguably the three main cases of international conflict, however, could be seen as parallels to Arab nationalism's view that a single ethnic group should be united: China/Taiwan, North Vietnam/South Vietnam, and North Korea/South Korea. Yet these are very specific conflicts involving only two countries, Cold War ideological differences, and single states that have been partitioned in relatively recent times.

Simultaneously, within European countries, a parallel struggle took place over the social and political system to be adopted. Modernization had both advocates and passionate enemies. On one hand, reactionaries opposed change, viewing democracy as the rule of the mob, rejecting change as the enemy of nation, religion, and tradition. On the other hand, radical ideologies preached the need for an even more total transformation that would allegedly produce a utopian outcome. Civil wars, revolutions, violence, political struggle, and lively intellectual debate also characterized these battles.

The forces of extremism, intolerance, and stagnation repeatedly defeated in Europe (and in Asia, Africa, and Latin America to a lesser extent) had characteristics similar to those that dominated the Arab world: dictators seeking to destroy neighboring countries and conquer the whole region, governments imposing a single acceptable ideology, statist economies that did not work, cultural and theological systems that stifled creativity, systematic repression, lack of free speech, and so on. Europe had Napoleon, Hitler, and Stalin; the Middle East had Nasser, Khomeini, and Saddam Hussein.

But the history of Europe in the nineteenth and twentieth centuries – despite horrible wars, inequalities, and injustices – was also characterized by success. By the late twentieth century, a consensus had been reached that the best system comprised a certain type of representative democracy, regulated capitalism, and moderate nationalism. Another outcome was the construction of strong, stable, separate nation-states that respected each other's rights and existence; economic development; broadening democracy and social opportunity; rising living standards; and a flowering of civil society, cultural freedom, and intellectual achievement. In the end came peace, regional cooperation without domination, and the defeat of retrograde forces. Equivalent levels of turmoil in the Middle East have yet to produce even a realistic vision of such progress.

What makes the Middle East unique, then, is not the types of problems and processes it faces. Rather, the tragedy is that the Middle East is still in the midst of these struggles and that the wrong side is winning, the side that will ensure continuing turmoil. Without ignoring the tremendous difficulties faced by other parts of the Third World, relatively few international crises remain unresolved there. At the same time, the Middle East is still dealing with Islamist revolutionary movements, Iraq's dangerous ambitions, an Iran on the verge of civil strife, Gulf Arab monarchies where the world's fastest transformation meets the world's most intransigent traditions, a Pan-Arab nationalism subverting a stable regional order, the Arab-Israeli conflict, the unresolved Palestinian problem, Israel's control over the West Bank and Gaza, Syria's control over Lebanon, intense mutual suspicions among states, an arms race, the Kurdish question, civil wars in Sudan and Algeria, terrorism, ethnic strife, high population growth rates, potential water shortages, the general absence of democracy, violent anti-Americanism, and the increasing presence of weapons of mass destruction.

Equally, individuals, societies, countries, and the region as a whole still have not made the most basic decisions on identity, structure, and direction. Should the Middle East and the individual states be ruled by Arab nationalism or Islam? Will nation-states be sovereign, or should they be subsumed by some wider entity or cause? Is a patriotic dictatorship, paternalistic monarchy, parliamentary democracy, or Islamist *sharia* state the best form of government? Can Israel be accepted as an equal, legitimate country? Are economic development and civil liberties to be sacrificed in the name of political struggle? Would statism or some far more free enterprise–oriented system be better?

Indeed, it often seems as if this whole process of choice and implementation, which is far more advanced in other regions and countries, is still at an early stage of development – that decades, at least, must pass before a long-term evolution produces some generally accepted, stable, and workable order there. It might be said as well that the second half of the twentieth century showed remarkably little progress toward such an outcome. Even if this result is inevitable, it will not necessarily come soon.

The failure of paradigm change in the 1990s certainly postpones such progress toward what might be called "regional ripeness" even further, and there is no telling when the next crossroads of opportunity will come. After all, the 1990s debate and opportunities were products of a half-century of experience that will not necessarily carry over to the next generation. And in the Middle East, the next generation is a very large proportion of the population.

A second, related distinction concerns the model of civilization to adopt. The Middle East is the only region of the world where the modern type of society most influenced by the West has not been accepted, either in whole or as some type of clearly defined synthesis with the local one. This is not a value judgment but a factual observation. In Europe and North America, the places where Western civilization and ideas evolved, the Western model is accepted, albeit with many variations.

Yet Asia, Africa, and Latin America have also adapted this same basic pattern of behavior and worldview. While elements of the Western model are rejected and others are very much altered, this process has proceeded relatively smoothly and steadily during the second half of the twentieth century. Indeed, since the colonial period, Latin America has always accepted Western ideas, institutions, culture, religions, and languages (Spanish and Portuguese), giving them its own interpretations and variations. In Africa, too, despite many regional and local variations, these same basic structures – including Christianity and the English or French language – have been accepted and adjusted.

Certainly, this development has been more complex in Asia, where Western languages and religion have had far less influence. Still, many countries and cultures – notably Japan, South Korea, and India – have developed successful syntheses. Others have adapted a Western political ideology called Marxism to their traditional ways. Several countries have also showed a remarkable ability to employ Western technology and techniques in order to produce rapid economic development.

Only in the Middle East was there conscious, widespread, and systematic resistance to this type of change. Perhaps this was due to the lesser impact of forcible transformation from colonialism and to the power of a strong competing monotheistic religion. Again, though, understanding the precise reasons for this distinctiveness is less important than knowing that the difference exists.

Even in the Middle East, some groups made enthusiastic decisions to accept a Western orientation in the process of building their own nation-states or communities. These include Armenians, Jews, and Turks, as well as Lebanese Christian Arabs. Of course, in the Arab world and Iran the elites also adopted Western ways. Yet this approach did not permeate the societies or gain legitimacy. For example, the promotion of Westernization by Iran's shah became a factor in undermining his popular support and bringing about his overthrow.

Of course, the Arab world and Iran did import many things, both cultural and political, from the West and did adopt them. Nationalism itself was one such doctrine, as were the European socialism, Marxism, and fascism that became varieties of Middle Eastern radicalism. It could be argued that the Arab world did try liberal capitalism and multiparty parliamentary democracy in the 1930s and 1940s and discarded them because of their poor performance. But in the Arab world, the very fact that something was identifiably imported also made it suspect as such. There was a basic resentment that did not seem to exist elsewhere, even in Muslim societies outside the Middle East.

Nowhere else in the world are there explicit barriers to accepting large elements of Westernization, modernization, and globalization, at least in modified forms. Nowhere else in the world are there political movements and ideologies that reject the use of these elements as major ingredients in a new synthesis, whatever their commitment to protecting existing culture and religion. Nowhere else in the world are there states and regimes promoting systematic antagonism to these things.

Again, the basic issues faced by the Middle East are similar to those that confront other regions. Even the debate has many similarities. If Arab societies have had great difficulty in dealing with democratization, it can be said that, even in the twentieth century, some of the world's most terrible dictatorships have been found in Europe. Europe arguably took 150 years or more in managing the transition from autocracy to political democracy, and this history included many bloody episodes and setbacks. The same point applies to the development of civil liberties and rights. Equally, there is nothing surprising in the fact that the Middle East has lagged behind the West in economic development. The same is true for all areas of the world. Even the movement toward a strong element of secularism, about which Muslim societies have so many reservations, was difficult, prolonged, and remains incomplete in the West.

What is distinctive about the Middle East is that it seems to be having more trouble with these problems and to be taking considerably longer to handle them than its counterparts elsewhere in the Third World. Equally important, the side of the argument that has so far prevailed in the Arab world, and to a lesser extent in Iran, is the opposite one from that which had already triumphed elsewhere by the twentieth century's close. In contrast to other parts of the world, the outcome in that region is still very much in doubt.

A key element in this situation is how Arabs evaluate the basic problems that they face. Any discussion of how Africans, Asians, Europeans, and Latin Americans have debated their options would be a major undertaking in itself. On many occasions, the main responsibility was put on foreigners and outside forces. In Europe, the Jews were the most frequent scapegoat, said to be simultaneously the cause of current troubles and the subverters of nation, religion, and the traditional order. In Asia, Africa, and South America, lack of progress and other undesirable trends and events were attributed – sometimes correctly – to U.S. or European imperialism, and sometimes to regional communist states such as Cuba and China.

Yet rarely did this externalization of blame cripple the debate on the shortcomings of one's own state and society. The main emphasis of the debate was almost always on the internal factors causing problems and how to remedy them. Why didn't the economic system work better? Perhaps more capitalism, socialism, government regulation, labor unions, or other measures were needed. Why was there social injustice? Perhaps protection for the poor, civil society watchdog groups, social security systems, or racial fairness was needed. Why was there war and international instability? Perhaps there was a threat from dictatorships and imperialist ambitions; perhaps better understanding or improved commercial ties could help.

One irony is that the Middle East, where difficulties are obsessively attributed to foreign interference and exploitation, has a much weaker case in this regard than other regions. In Latin America, the United States could make or break governments. Africa suffered the depradations of the slave trade and rampant exploitation of raw materials, gaining little in return. Colonialism uprooted and remade the social order on both of these continents. China had the imposed opium trade; India was ruled by Great Britain for a century.

Why is it that these countries – victimized far more than the Arab world and Iran – were able, to use a psychological phrase, to "get beyond this," to get on with their developmental lives? Why is it that Kemal Ataturk, for example, founder of the Turkish republic at a time when his country was defeated and occupied by Western powers, stifled any anti-European resentment in order to follow the Western model?

Most Middle East complaints could have been made just as easily – often more easily – by those in other regions where such points never became critical issues. For example, a principal Middle Eastern grievance is to claim that the West drew artificial borders and thus prevented the unification of all Arabs or all Muslims in the region. But all the borders of Africa and Latin America, as well as those in North America and Asia, are also Western creations. It would be possible to charge that almost any country was an artificial Western-imposed entity, or that any country with an ethnic or religious majority or dominant group was illegitimate.

Consider, for example, what South America would look like if, adding to the already huge difficulties of economic development and state building, countries there were constantly maneuvering through war, subversion, propaganda, and terrorism for regional supremacy, or to try to impose a single concept of Spanish or indigenous culture or Catholicism on the continent. Imagine if Asia were full of competing nondemocratic rulers intervening constantly in each other's affairs, seeking to eliminate other states as not belonging to the region, and engaged in a constant vendetta against the West.

Or take the justifications used by dictatorships in order to win popular support and gain legitimacy. All such regimes, including those of the USSR and Nazi Germany, have employed the same basic arguments – that their rule and emergency measures are needed because of external threats, internal traitors, and the need to mobilize of all forces for development and survival. Yet in much of the Third World and even the Soviet bloc, unlike the Middle East, these rationales wore thin. Courageous activists and intellectuals campaigned against such claims and often won the masses' backing for their causes. Advocating democracy, human rights, and civil liberties, they frequently triumphed. Such a picture is simply absent from the Arab world, though it did happen among the people of Iran during the 1990s.

In accounting for all of these problems, distinctions, and preferred solutions, it should be clear – though one would never guess it from many Arab statements and the writings of many Western experts – that the sole or primary cause cannot be the Arab-Israeli conflict. This issue is simply not enough of a peg on which to hang all of the region's problems. Efforts to do so only succeed in obfuscating the range of issues that do exist. Indeed, such an approach is a leading cause of the aridity and weakness of so much of the debate within and about the Middle East. A country may be filled with impoverished people, plagued by corruption and government inefficiency, mired in undemocratic practices, and so on, but all of these issues can seemingly be made to disappear in an orchestrated passion on the Palestinian question.

This is not to deny the emotional intensity of this question. But it was no accident that this was the only issue on which governments "felt" themselves duty-bound to "yield" to public sentiment. And this very sentiment was continually fostered by the state-controlled media, educational system, official statements, and mosque sermons to a fever pitch. Indeed, it is no exaggeration to say that this is virtually the sole issue on which the public and the media have been permitted to vent their anger.

Yet there are scores of issues that merit and rarely receive such a critical examination. There are easily a dozen ways in which other regions differ from the Middle East to the latter's disadvantage:

1. Achieving economic and social development is considered a high priority, one that should not be blocked by ideology or international ambitions.
2. All ethnic and religious groups in the region are accepted and tolerated.
3. All states in the region are accepted and their sovereignty is respected, despite differences among them.
4. There is a very low level of conflict or subversion among states.
5. No country seeks to dominate or lead the region, because there is an acceptance of the fact that this is impossible.
6. Interstate war is deemed too unprofitable to risk.
7. Democracy is acknowledged as the best political system, even if it is not actually practiced.
8. There is a basic acceptance of Western ideas and institutions, along with ways of adjusting them to local culture and society.
9. Religion is not the main marker of identity or political loyalty.
10. "Quick fix" ideologies that promise to resolve social and economic problems through revolutionary transformation have declined or disappeared.
11. Political figures compete to convince the masses that they are moderate rather than militant.
12. There is an emphasis on finding solutions to domestic problems rather than attributing them to external factors.

None of these characteristics became dominant in the Middle East during the 1990s. Indeed, by the year 2000 it was hard to see any major change in how a single Arab state was being governed compared to the situation in 1990, or even in 1980, 1970, or 1960. There was no significant advance toward democracy anywhere, despite some small gains in the Gulf Arab states. Civil society remained extremely weak, with governments continuing to control or repress independent voices. Even the public debate over these issues was quite muted compared to the rest of the world.

This is a remarkable outcome, even though it is generally taken for granted. Political systems that don't work very well or that fail to achieve their goals are usually changed or at least seriously challenged. Policy premises that do not accord with external realities, thus producing real international failures, are supposed to be corrected or at least carefully reexamined.

Of course, the explanation is partly that the systems did function adequately in terms of keeping rulers in power and maintaining internal order. Not a single coup or real regime change took place in the Arab world between 1990 and 2000, or indeed between 1980 and 2000, with the exception of the peripheral states of Yemen and Sudan. Moreover, the basic political concepts shaping Arab politics remain fundamentally popular. It makes no difference that this is partly due to their reinforcement in state-controlled media and educational systems.

Externalizing the Arab world's problems – attributing them to American (or Western) imperialism, Zionism, and local traitors serving these enemies – has prevented the kind of reappraisal necessary to fix the internal factors at the root of the problems and catastrophes. Waiting for some charismatic hero to deliver them from evil – whether it be Nasser, Asad, Arafat, Khomeini, Saddam, or bin Ladin – has blocked the change from below needed to break down the barriers to progress. No matter how righteous or empowered or deprived of justice or sinned against Arabs feel themselves to be, this anger and resentment have advanced them not one step toward a better life.

In the end, though, while Arab ideology and foreign policies did not fit with the requirements of international affairs, economic development, or social progress, they did match the regimes' structural and domestic needs, and they well suited a public opinion shaped by a half-century of restricted debate and directed information. Regimes may sponsor suicide bombers, but they will not themselves commit suicide. Deciding that the proposed cure was worse than the defeat and stagnation it was supposed to cure, Arab societies rejected it. Nothing could be more richly ironic than Saddam Hussein's advice to the Iraqi people: "Do not select for posts of leadership those who claim higher roles for themselves in success or victory and disclaim their responsibility for failure or defeat."[44] But of course he and members of the elite throughout the Arab world preferred a situation that allowed them to shift the blame for their shortcomings onto others.

The Arab world was unable to escape its historical treadmill, returning largely to the patterns it had long followed. And so the hopes of the 1990s, the expectation that bad experiences would breed corrective changes, were disappointed. Instead, old patterns gained new life. The Middle East entered the twenty-first century with many attributes that it had hoped to leave behind:

- The Arab-Israeli conflict was not disappearing. Moderate states were not ready to pressure or help Syria and the Palestinians to make a compromise peace, even if almost all of their their demands were met. At best, there was a failure of nerve; at worst, governments and oppositions found inflaming and perpetuating the conflict to be too useful to give up.
- Prospects for serious economic or political reform faded in Syria, Iran, and elsewhere.
- Individual nation-states were still too restrained by the appeal of Pan-Arab nationalism to pursue their own interests. The tenacity of Arab nationalism and Islamist radicalism as transnational ideologies led regimes continue to meddle in other's internal affairs. Iran, Syria, Libya, Sudan, and Iraq sponsored armed groups seeking to take over in Algeria, Egypt, Israel, Lebanon, and other places.
- In the realm of public opinion, leaders took the safer, easier path of demagoguery, not only on the Arab-Israeli question but on many other issues. They made little attempt to educate the masses, who continued to worship the ideas that had held sway before 1990. On the contrary, government propaganda and rhetoric continued or even intensified radical, anti-American, Islamist, and other such sentiments. It should be noted that public opinion is not an unchangeable force of nature but something shaped over the years by the rulers themselves. With their sweeping control over public debate through the media, the educational system, the repression of dissent, and other means, Arab leaders have more control over this sector than do their counterparts elsewhere.

44 Speech of August 8, 2001. Text from Iraq News Agency web site, http://www.uruklink.net/iraqnews/eindex.htm.

- Progress toward democracy or the creation of a strong civil society remained extremely limited. Even Egypt cracked down on human rights groups and research centers making the mildest criticisms of government policy or even expressing independent positions on current issues.
- As sanctions weakened, Iraq reemerged on the Arab political scene and moved closer to relaunching its ambitions and seeking its revenge on those who had refused to be its victims.
- Within Iran, too, hopes for reform largely failed. President Muhammad Khatami, though elected by a wide margin and backed by a large parliamentary majority, proved unwilling or unable to produce actual change. And Iran's foreign policy remained as it had been before, supporting subversive and armed movements, as well as building long-range missiles and nuclear weapons.

Everywhere in the region, traditional models reasserted themselves. Moderate regimes did not become more moderate; radical regimes remained hard-line and grew in relative strength. Reform efforts failed, and the Arab-Israeli peace process fell apart. The United States was unable to use its sole superpower status to win any longer-term gains and dissipated the leverage it had enjoyed after the allied victory in Kuwait. Both Iran and Iraq, after being contained during the 1990s, were reemerging as regional powers in the twenty-first century's first decade. Lebanon was still a Syrian satellite. And the Arab states let themselves be wagged by Arafat's inability to make peace with Israel.

In an article for *Al-Ahram*, the liberal columnist Ridha Hilal provided the best obituary for the paradigm debate: "The calls for democracy and economic prosperity disappeared in favor of the slogan: 'No voice should rise above the voice of battle,' a slogan that returns to our life as if we are forever doomed to wallow in the mud of violence, dictatorship and poverty."[45]

45 Translation in MEMRI No. 198, March 27, 2001.

3

THE REGIME'S SUCCESS, THE NATION'S DISASTER

One of the main reasons for the failure of Middle Eastern political systems is that their disfunctionality is profoundly logical. In short, there are very sound reasons why they don't work very well. The regimes' strength has enabled them to twist societies, economies, and ideologies in order to ensure their own survival. Repression has always been an important tool toward this end, as in all dictatorships. But the Arab world has been distinctive in the fact that demagoguery has been the regimes' first line of defense, helping to ensure voluntary cooperation by business classes, religious authorities, intellectuals, and the masses themselves. As a result, these groups usually willingly pay the price of preserving the status quo. Even opposition forces have their assigned role to play in safeguarding the system.

All of the Arab world's leaders are essentially dictators, though of course the regimes and societies vary on many points. Some are nationalist/populist dictatorships (Algeria, Egypt, Iraq, the Palestinian Authority, Syria, Tunisia, and Yemen), while others are monarchical/traditional dictatorships (Morocco, Jordan, Saudi Arabia, Bahrain, Kuwait, Oman, Qatar, and the United Arab Emirates). Some are more repressive, and some allow considerable margins of freedom. Lebanon is the only country that can really claim to be democratic, albeit along strictly defined ethnic-communal lines. Yet it too is a dictatorship. The difference is that its particular dictator does not live in Beirut but rules from a neighboring country's capital, Damascus. Perhaps Kuwait and Bahrain have made the most progress, but in those places, as elsewhere, democratic developments are quickly reversible. The identical situation applies to Iran, where the same basic system – albeit in Islamist garb – has prevailed, though under challenge by an opposition demanding real change.

Even Egypt, a relatively mild dictatorship, has been ruled by the same self-perpetuating group since its 1952 military takeover. The president's powers are virtually unlimited. The police act under almost perpetual emergency law that allows them to hold people indefinitely, restrict meetings at will, and eavesdrop without a warrant. Egypt's economy is dominated by state-owned enterprises and strangling government regulation, with only very limited gestures toward liberalization and privatization. An independent civil society is impossible, since labor unions and other groups can be formed and operate only with government permission and high levels of intervention. The media are either directly or indirectly under close state supervision. Islamic law is supposed to be the basis of state law, and clerics and Islamists closely watch for any sign of deviation. Opposition parties face serious sanctions, and elections are always fixed to ensure victory for the governing National Democratic Party.

This system of populist dictatorship is rooted in some aspects of traditional society, but it developed to its highest form in Egypt, Iraq, and Syria beginning in the 1950s. Over time, rulers in these and other countries learned how to maintain and fine-tune it. The surviving monarchies kept their traditional links of solidarity but also adopted new elements. These same basic structures were built into the Palestinian movement and converted into a statelike system under the Palestinian Authority beginning in 1994.[1]

The principal elements of this system include the following:

State control of the economy. The directing goal and overriding purpose of economic life is not profit, productivity, or raising living standards but rather helping the government to stay in power. The economy provides money for the regime and its supporters and keeps funds out of the hands of their opponents. For the state, control is more important than prosperity. Individual businesspeople often succeed based far less on their merit or on filling some economic need than on the extent of their connections with the state apparatus. Privatization, free enterprise, and foreign investment challenge this control, and thus are generally unwelcome and always restricted. This is a very bad system for creating an efficient, internationally competitive, job-creating economy.

One of the wonderful features of oil wealth for the petroleum-exporting states is that it does not interfere with this system, since it can

---

1 This point is discussed in detail in Barry Rubin, *The Transformation of Palestinian Politics* (Cambridge, MA, 1999).

easily be isolated from the rest of the economy and kept under state control. Much of the massive influx of capital gained from the high oil prices of the 1970s and 1980s was squandered, used for consumption, put into safe investments in the West, or spent on war and weapons rather than being channeled into productive enterprises that might provide a basis for future development.

State control of the intellectual means of production. The goal and purpose of the media, schools, publishers, writers, and artists is to justify the regime and the dominant perspective, rather than to further a search for truth or the instrumental use of knowledge to bring progress. The state maintains a monopoly on defining who are friends and enemies, what is right and wrong, what is permissible and impermissible. All television, radio, and newspapers are either controlled directly by the state or subject to its tight regulation. Almost all Arabic-language newspapers published abroad and international television stations in Arabic are subsidized by particular states.

Such tight control of information creates a specific worldview for the citizenry. The direction of Arab public opinion is not some completely independent variable that drops out of the sky, but in large part is the product of a long-term indoctrination effort. The Arab masses are fed a steady diet of xenophobia, conspiracy theories, and negative news about the West and Israel that constantly reinforces existing attitudes. Public opinion can force a regime to make small adjustments, but there is virtually no case in modern Arab history where the masses' demands have gotten out of control and forced a government to change policy or to make a decision against its will.

Communal solidarity around the ruling group. In most Arab states, a specific minority subgroup of the population forms a special pillar for the regime's survival. This includes the Sunnis in Iraq, the Alawites in Syria, the Sunnis in Bahrain, and the East Bank (i.e., non-Palestinian, largely Bedouin) people in Jordan. For example, the dominant Sunni Muslim Arabs in Iraq are only 20 percent of the population, while Kurds make up 15 to 20 percent and Shi'ite Muslim Arabs from 55 to 60 percent. The Kuwaiti scholar Shafiq Ghabra has suggested, "The drive for unity with other Arabs, from Kuwait to Syria, is at its base a drive to keep Sunni Arab demographic strength in Iraq."[2]

2 Shafeeq Ghabra, "Iraq's Culture of Violence," *Middle East Quarterly*, Vol. 8, No. 3 (Summer 2001), pp. 2–12.

In societies where more traditional linkages still prevail, family and clan ties play a similar role as ways of constructing a solid and reliable base for government. The huge Saudi royal family, along with its allies through marriage and other means, forms a sizeable support group for the regime. In Lebanon, the whole country is organized along ethnic-communal lines defined by religious affiliation, each with its own parties and patronage systems, which form virtual states in themselves.

These privileged groups know that their individual prosperity, collective benefits, and at times even their physical survival depend on their ensuring that the regime stays in power. They are given special employment and material advantages in the bureaucracy, the military, and elsewhere that allow and encourage them to safeguard the existing order.

A well-organized benefits system for supporters. A large body of individuals has been created with a vested interest in the regime's approval. The state can directly determine who gets good jobs and promotions in every important sector, including the religious institutions, the huge state bureaucracy, the media, schools, and many economic enterprises. The masses benefit from subsidies ranging from basic commodities such as bread in the poorer states (e.g., Egypt) to a full range of luxury items in the high-income, low-population oil-exporting countries.

A well-organized punishment system for dissenters. The severity of the repressive apparatus varies widely, depending on the specific regime and its needs in different historical circumstances. Punishments range from warnings and beatings to loss of employment, torture, imprisonment, and even death. In some places, such as Kuwait, Jordan, and Morocco, the scope of what is permissible in terms of opposition and free speech is much wider than in other states, such as Iraq and Syria.

Redirecting the people's anger and frustration elsewhere. Regimes can allow some criticism as a safety valve. But it is always far preferable that the targets be foreigners (especially Israel, the West, or to a far lesser extent any Arab rivals of the moment). That is why Arab nationalist regimes can benefit from an Islamist opposition – even one voicing support for Usama bin Ladin – whose main fire is directed against outside enemies. Leaders and the media push public opinion in this direction, avoiding any praise for Western aid efforts, assistance to individual governments, or attempts to promote a diplomatic solution to the Arab-Israeli conflict.

The building of national solidarity around the regime. The regime is portrayed as the protector of the country, the Arab nation, and Islam against those who would allegedly destroy these cherished values. Since the regime claims to be under siege from enemies within and without, all citizens are called on to rally to its cause. No matter what criticism the regime's subjects may have of its specific policies, they can view it as a basically good and necessary ruler protecting them from the demonic forces of imperialism and Zionism. These countries are, as political science theory of the 1950s put it, mobilization states.

But rather than being mobilized by regimes for development purposes, as was originally predicted, the masses are being mobilized for a fruitless struggle designed to preserve the status quo. The success of this effort, however, depends on the more or less permanent existence of conflict and crisis. If issues like the Arab-Israeli conflict are resolved, alliances with the West openly defended, or a Western-style modernization explicitly embraced, this asset is lost. Thus, these enemies must be irreconcilably and enormously evil, worthy of neither empathy nor sympathy.

By engaging in systematic demagoguery, however, the government also brings problems for itself. Having created these bogeys, any regime that adopts a softer policy toward the West or Israel opens itself up to condemnation by neighbors and assault by internal opponents. Like a coachman who simultaneously whips the horses and keeps a tight hold on the reins, the rulers ensure a bumpy ride for themselves and their people. They don't want to go to war or to seek unprofitable confrontations, but they are periodically dragged into these situations – notably, for example, in the 1967 war with Israel – by their own behavior.

Sometimes, if the emergency is large enough – Egypt's difficult situation during the late 1970s, for example, when Sadat decided that peace with Israel was necessary, or the desperation of Saudi Arabia and Kuwait to save themselves from Iraq in 1990 – the usual pattern can be broken, and regimes will risk dispensing with their own version of political correctness. Still, there is always a price to pay for such actions, no matter how justifiable in terms of national interest. Sadat was assassinated within two years of the Camp David accords. The Saudi decision to admit Western forces onto its territory generated the angry renunciations of Usama bin Ladin, fueling his determination for revenge against either the regime itself or the Americans, who had "polluted" the Arabian peninsula by their presence.

74

The antidemocratic nature of the main opposition groups. The radical Islamist opposition does not criticize the system as such, but complains only that the regime is too timid and fights for the wrong cause, nationalism rather than Islam. Basically, it offers as a solution the imposition of the same structures, albeit in a "proper" form, in the service of the Islamist rather than the Arab nationalist cause. Caught between these twin authoritarian forces, the tiny democratic opposition is constantly faced with choosing the incumbent government as the lesser of two evils.

Much of the population is caught in somewhat the same situation. Understandably expecting a revolution to bring more chaos and violence, many people fear that things will be far worse during a change of regimes and somewhat worse under a new regime. In addition, a large portion of those who view themselves as being good Muslims regard the radical Islamists as having heretical ideas. As a result, rather than offering an alternative to the current rulers, the opposition becomes another reason for supporting the status quo.

The illegitimacy of the democratic alternative. Relatively small minorities – and by no means always the same people – advocate a range of changes, such as a more open economy, greater democracy, free speech, better relations with the United States, peace with Israel, and other ideas. They do this out of a genuine concern for their countries, their societies, and their people. Examining what is happening elsewhere in the world and looking at recent history with a critical eye, they have concluded that the terrible problems faced by the Arabs are caused by mistaken choices that can be corrected. While the number of such social critics and activists has been small, other such groups have succeeded in making dramatic changes in other parts of the world, including communist Eastern Europe.

In the Arab world, however, these liberals and reformists could be far more easily handled than had been the case for dictatorships in other regions. Their ideas were labeled as alien importations from the West, and they were accused of being imperialist and Zionist agents. It was also argued that the constant crisis of the Arab world made such reforms dangerous or an unaffordable luxury. The state-controlled media could exclude and attack the reformers and clerics denounce them as un-Islamic. Groups such as professionals, intellectuals, journalists, students, and teachers, who might be expected to embrace such ideas – as happened in other part of the world – were dominated by regime loyalists who shouted down the dissenters. In many places, professional associations were taken over by Islamists. In sharp contrast to experience in Africa, Asia, Europe, and Latin America, the liberals were hardly ever able to build a mass base of supporters. Thus, during the 1990s, the reformers lost the paradigm debate throughout the Arab world.

Only in Iran was the outcome somewhat different. Since Iran already had an Islamist regime – and, by definition, Arab nationalism had no appeal to Persians – there was space for a democratic opposition. And since it was an Islamist regime that was perceived as having failed, the reaction against that situation was more open to liberal ideas. Even there, though, the system held onto power with relative ease.[3]

The lack of class struggle. Since the working class remained small in the Arab world, and communism was shunned as too openly secular, Marxism mutated into regime-supporting nationalist doctrines rather than revolutionary movements. The working and middle classes remained relatively small and dependent on government patronage. The intellectuals were more often than not the standard bearers of authoritarian ideologies. The peasantry was generally quiescent, though it did benefit from land reform under the new regimes in Syria and Egypt. Also, communal identity remained more important than class identity. Thus the constituency for groups demanding greater democracy and civil liberties remained limited.

Lack of accountability. The fact that this feature of the dominant Arab systems is so taken for granted makes it all the more significant. Despite their responsibility for failure after failure, defeat after defeat, shortcoming after shortcoming, virtually all of the Arab states and the Palestinian movement were governed by the same type of regime for the last thirty or forty years of the twentieth century. Indeed, no matter what debacles they presided over, the same individuals remained in power until they died, usually of natural causes. Elsewhere in the Third World, governments that lost wars, presided over economic disasters, or became entangled in corruption scandals resigned. This did not happen in the Middle East. Even in the 1990s, the momentum was insufficient to

3 See Chapter 6 of this volume.

force significant changes in this pattern. Unlike their predecessors in the 1950s and 1960s, Arab ruling elites no longer paid for their mistakes.

Of course, there are many differences in how the various Arab countries are governed, especially regarding the margin of freedom allowed to citizens. In almost every instance, though, the state still has a virtual stranglehold over society, except in a few cases where it chooses otherwise. Freedom of speech is limited, and whatever opposition is allowed to operate (perhaps even allowed to hold a few seats in parliament) there is no question of the regime allowing a peaceful change of leadership. Except for a few cases – Cuba, North Korea, and perhaps China – the level of state control and dictatorship in the Middle East is higher than anywhere else in the world. And even China has managed to achieve prosperity through a major economic reform, a success that has eluded the Arab states.

As antimodern systems, barriers to future development, fomenters of war abroad and repression at home, radical Islamism and Arab nationalism manifest themselves in ruling and dominant opposition ideologies as the rough equivalent of communism and fascism in Western society. But the difference in the Middle East – in contrast to Europe – is that this basic structure dominated virtually every country in the region, arose from purely internal forces in each case, and lasted for a very long time.

In these regards, Iraq is an extreme yet highly illustrative case, showing how a regime can prosper while it brings catastrophe to its country. Iraq's rulers won one victory after another while Iraq and its people suffered devastating defeats. Enormous oil revenues earned during the 1970s and 1980s were thrown away on military spending and losing wars. Despite a costly war with Iran, a devastating military ejection from Kuwait, and massive revolts in the north and south of the country, the regime survived. It successfully lived through a decade of sanctions without making any major concession and then expelled the UN inspectors, while gradually but steadily reducing the international sanctions. During all this time, the country's elite continued to enjoy high living standards, even when forcing the country onto a rationing system.

When one considers what Iraq – with its huge oil and gas reserves alongside a relatively educated population – might have achieved during these years, the gap is awesome. Economic progress was sacrificed, hundreds of thousands of Iraqis were killed or wounded in the regime's aggressive wars, thousands of Kurds were systematically murdered by

77

security forces, the people's living standards were reduced, oil revenues were squandered, and the national infrastructure was wrecked.

Most remarkable of all was the fact that these problems were unnecessary and self-inflicted, arguably even from the standpoint of the rulers' own interests. Moreover, by the early twenty-first century, to judge by the Arab media, the blame for this situation and the Iraqi people's suffering belonged not to President Saddam Hussein but to an anti-Arab, anti-Muslim U.S. policy that insisted on maintaining sanctions. Indeed, this complaint was cited by Usama bin Ladin as one of the main reasons for his war on the United States, including the September 11, 2001, attacks on America.

Iraq's ambition to control the Gulf and rule the Arab world goes back to the 1930s, when its ideologists began portraying their country as the one fated to unite the Middle East under its rule. Saddam built on attitudes inculcated into Iraq's elite and people long before the regime came to power in 1968. He also promoted Iraqi nationalism in order to unite the country's disparate population of Sunni and Shi'ite Muslim Arabs and non-Arab Kurds. Both before and after Saddam rose to power, Iraq allied itself with the USSR, took a hard line on the Arab-Israeli conflict, sponsored terrorism, and tried to conquer the Gulf. While Iraq emphasized militant opposition to Israel, the lack of a common border usually limited Baghdad's direct role to extreme rhetoric, sponsoring anti-Israel terrorism, and opposing any diplomatic solution. After Egypt made peace with Israel, Baghdad led a rejection front in the 1980s, which included Syria, the PLO, and Libya, to isolate Cairo.

Yet despite its long history of militant posturing, Iraq could have become a peaceful, prosperous, and successful state in the last twenty years of the twentieth century. It faced no serious internal or external threats that could not have been handled far more easily. True, the United States had earlier supported the shah's Iran in order to contain Iraqi influence in the Gulf, and at one time Tehran sponsored a Kurdish revolt against Baghdad but stopped on the basis of an agreement with Iraq. Saddam was always in firm control of the country, and the shah fell to a domestic revolution. Israel was far away and posed no substantial threat to Iraq. Islamist Iran could not have successfully subverted the regime.

With oil reserves estimated at more than 112 billion barrels, second only to those of Saudi Arabia, and 118 trillion cubic feet of natural gas, Iraq would have had a bright future even with minimally competent government policies.[4] Instead, Saddam launched a war against Iran in 1980, sensing easy victory. Of course, he had his reasons. On the one hand, Iran seemed weak after its revolutionary turmoil, military purges, and loss of U.S. protection – a prize ripe for the taking. On the other hand, Saddam could worry that Iran's revolution would spread and might even appeal to Iraq's plurality of Shi'ite citizens.

Nevertheless, attacking Iran was a mistake that turned into an eight-year-long war. The war finally ended when it did largely because the presence of U.S. forces in the Gulf, convoying Arab tankers and sometimes attacking Iranian forces, persuaded Tehran that continued fighting might lead to U.S. intervention against Iran. Technically, Iraq could be described as the war's winner, but the conflict's high cost and the absence of any material gain made Iraq a very big loser indeed.

Once again, after the war, Saddam had another chance to take a highly profitable path by choosing either moderation or a strictly rhetorical radicalism. Gulf Arab monarchies had no intention to ask repayment of the huge loans they had given Iraq during the war. They were ready to use some of their oil wealth to pay Saddam for defending them in the past, and to ensure that he would not attack them in the future. The United States was on better terms with Iraq than it had been since its first revolution thirty years earlier, in 1958. Instead, Iraq's leadership launched a vigorous campaign to seize Arab leadership and mobilize the Arab world against the United States. Saddam thought – with hardly any evidence – that the United States would use its situation as the world's sole superpower to dominate the Arab world. He also argued that the United States was weak and cowardly, easily defeated by a show of Iraqi determination and Arab unity.[5]

The result was Iraq's August 1990 invasion of Kuwait. In January 1991, a U.S. coalition with overwhelming Arab support attacked the Iraqi forces and drove them out of Kuwait. By March, Iraq's army had been totally defeated. Both the north and south of Iraq were in revolt against the regime, led by Kurdish and Shi'ite dissidents respectively. If the United States had wanted to dominate the Arab world, it could easily have installed a new government in Baghdad and dictated its

---

4 Energy Information Administration (EIA), "Country Analysis Brief, Iraq" (Washington, DC, September 2001), http://www.eia.doe.gov/emeu/cabs/iraq.html.
5 For a fuller discussion of this issue, see Chapter 9 of this volume.

demands to the Gulf Arab states it had just saved. Instead, the United States decided not to intervene in Iraq, letting Saddam crush the revolts, and opted for a minimal presence in the Gulf.[6] As the scope of Saddam's repression became clear, U.S. policy backed the creation of a safe haven for Kurds in northern Iraq as an afterthought.

Nonetheless, Saddam continued his pattern of behavior. Holding onto his ambitions to lead the Arab world and to control the Gulf, he tried to outwit the rest of the world, keep or supplement his weapons of mass destruction, rebuild his armed forces, and reenter Arab ranks on his own terms. When his refusal to comply with the agreements ending the Kuwait war in order to retain his weapons of mass destruction led to long-term international sanctions, Saddam then tried to outmaneuver the sanctions as well by hiding arms, military equipment, deadly germs, and poisonous chemicals.

Sanctions, and the resulting suffering for Iraq's people, continued only as a result of a deliberate Iraqi strategy. Rather than end the sanctions by meeting his commitment to eliminate weapons of mass destruction, Saddam believed that he could wear down the rest of the world and mobilize international pressure to force an end to sanctions without having to make any concessions.

There were five main elements of this plan, which Iraq implemented throughout the 1990s and into the next century:

• To intimidate the UN by making threats and refusing to cooperate.
• To wear down adversaries by extending the need to maintain sanctions over many years, so that the West would tire of this struggle and make concessions or give up altogether.
• To fool the UN by a superficial pretense to cooperation and by supplying misinformation on the size of Iraq's manufacturing capacity and arsenal for weapons of mass destruction. In addition, Iraq circumvented sanctions by smuggling out oil and smuggling in forbidden goods through Iran, Turkey, and Jordan.[7]

---

6 The best account of the revolts and their suppression, detailing the regime's extraordinary brutality, is Kenan Makiya, *Cruelty and Silence* (London, 1976). An interesting feature of the book is a detailed demonstration of how Arab intellectuals downplayed and apologized for Saddam's misdeeds.

7 Youssef M. Ibrahim, "Iraq Said to Sell Oil in Secret Plan to Skirt U.N. Ban," *The New York Times*, February 16, 1995. For another example, see Carola Hoyos, "UN Releases Evidence of Iraqi Abuse of Sanctions," *Financial Times*, October 26, 2001.

- To undermine the coalition by offering some of its members – notably China, France, and Russia – lucrative oil, arms, and other contracts to be implemented when sanctions were removed.
- To gain support from international public opinion by depriving its own citizens of material goods, exaggerating the suffering, using most of its money to bolster the military and supporters of the regime, and blaming the problem on the United States. Portraying Iraq as a nation of hungry people and sick children was a superb propaganda tool.

Although he dug Iraq into an ever-deepening hole, neither Saddam's hold on the state nor his standing in the Arab world really diminished. Ironically, large elements of the West, which Saddam constantly claimed were eager to eliminate him, were far more eager to appease him. France and Russia as well as China campaigned for an end to sanctions, and most UN members were unwilling to confront Iraq in order to enforce them. The dangling of lucrative post-sanctions contracts won over greedy foreign powers and lobbies. As if that were not enough, Iraq had intimidated the world at a time when that country was weak and defeated.

In the Arab world and in much of the rest of the world, Saddam had won the propaganda battle. Iraq's people, of course, were not allowed to speak freely. As in other Arab states, public discussion was dominated by a regime that reported only support for itself. Although Saudi Arabia and Kuwait persevered in keeping Iraq from fully rejoining the Arab world, they were on the defensive. Saddam's intended victims were made to seem traitors to Islam and Arabism for seeking Western help in order to survive. Why should the Gulf Arab monarchies take risks if they knew the West would not get rid of Saddam and would probably leave them facing him alone some day?

Those against whom Saddam openly planned revenge competed to avoid his wrath. Other Arabs were ready to blame the crisis he had created and sustained on those seeking to protect them, the United States. They often spoke as if America were the threat and Saddam an innocent victim of unprovoked aggression. Usama bin Ladin, who supposedly should have hated Saddam for his secularism, his persecution of Muslims, and his efforts to gain power over Saudi Arabia, in effect sent suicide terrorists to fight on Baghdad's behalf.

A ruthless, aggressive, highly repressive dictatorship had succeeded in mobilizing tremendous sympathy among Western liberals as a victim and in gaining credibility for alleged moderation that it had done nothing to earn. The claim that Iraqis were suffering because of Western-imposed sanctions was sharply at odds with the facts.[8]

First, the nutritional and health crisis in Iraq was exaggerated by Baghdad's propaganda, which was accepted at face value by many who did not understand how a dictatorship – even one that had used poison gas against its own people – could manipulate good intentions. Data from the Food and Agriculture Organization (FAO) show that the average availability of foodstuffs in Iraq during the 1990s was consistently at or above 95 percent of the recommended optimal level, meaning it was always at or above 120 percent of the recommended minimum level. A UN report concluded,

Since the first food arrived in March 1997, foodstuffs worth almost $8 billion and health supplies worth about $1.5 billion have been delivered to Iraq. Although it is difficult to assess the impact of the program, the average daily food ration has gradually increased from around 1,275 kilocalories per person per day in 1996 [before the program] to about 2,229 kilocalories in October 2001.[9]

Second, to the extent it did exist, the cause of the problem was the policies of Iraq's government, which had refused to spend available funds or had diverted them to the leadership's benefit and to arms purchases. The West did not intend, nor did it benefit in any way from, the suffering of Iraq's people. It simply wanted an Iraq that was not an immediate threat to its neighbors. European powers wanted sanctions to be ended as quickly as possible. The United States was the main champion of sanctions, but it also preferred a quicker solution that would produce an Iraq without weapons of mass destruction, or even an Iraq without Saddam.

---

8 Michael Rubin, "Sanctions on Iraq: A Legitimate Anti-American Grievance?," *Middle East Review of International Affairs (MERIA) Journal*, Vol. 5, No. 4 (December 2001), pp. 110–15. Available at http://meria.idc.ac.il.

9 Food and Agriculture Organization of the United Nations Technical Cooperation Programme, "Assessment of the Food and Nutrition Situation, Iraq" (Rome, 2000), p. 8, http://www.fao.org/es/esn/Iraq.pdf. See also Hasmik Egian, "Oil-for-Food – the Basic Facts 1996–2001," office of the Iraq Program, December 2001, http://www.un.org/Depts/oip/latest/basfact_000610.html.

Even given the sanctions, the UN program to let Iraq sell oil in order to buy food and medicine was sabotaged by Saddam himself, who delayed the oil-for-food program for five years. His government kept more than half the imported medicines in warehouses and prevented food and medicine from reaching the groups and regions that most actively opposed him. Saddam's priorities are clearly revealed by his continuing disputes with the UN over the oil-for-food program. In December 1999, he insisted on underfunding food, medicine, and supplies for babies by $50 million in order to make room in the program for telecommunications and railroads, which he called humanitarian programs, but which actually had internal security and military purposes.[10]

Third, if the Iraqi government had not launched successive attacks on Iran and Kuwait, wreaking great devastation and wasting resources, Iraqi living standards would have risen far higher. Tens of billions of dollars were simply thrown away to serve the regime's ambitions instead of being used to develop the country. Huge military programs and two wars brought absolutely no benefit to Iraq's people.

Finally, if Iraq had complied with the 1991 agreements it would have lost only its weapons of mass destruction, leaving the regime in power and with large conventional forces. The sanctions would have ended years earlier.

"What we have seen," as the British Middle East expert Fred Halliday put it, "is the destruction of Iraq by its own leadership."[11] Yet from Saddam's point of view – reflecting a prevalent pattern for Arab regimes – there are real incentives for keeping disputes going. They are valuable domestically for mobilizing the masses behind the government, justifying hardships, delegitimizing opposition, and encouraging the funneling of resources to military rather than civilian needs. As the Kuwaiti scholar Shafeeq Ghabra explains, "From the regime's perspective, crises with neighbors such as conflict with Iran or Kuwait or a foreign power sensitize the Iraqi people to a common danger, which then justifies the imposition of even more control over the Iraqi people and bolsters the role of the military and security forces."[12]

10 For a comprehensive discussion of these issues, see U.S. Department of State, "Saddam Hussein's Iraq," September 13, 1999, and updated March 24, 2000. http://usinfo.state.gov/regional/nea/iraq/iraq99.htm.
11 Text of lecture given at the London School of Economics, January 23, 2001.
12 Ghabra, "Iraq's Culture of Violence."

Given this situation and the nature of the regimes, for Saddam – like his colleagues in other countries – making concessions is considered a sign of weakness that signals to both domestic rivals and foreign foes that the regime could be beaten. This explains why Saddam did not pull out of Kuwait even when warned that the U.S. military would attack him in January 1991, as well as his tough stands repudiating promises he made after the war. To this type of thinking, such flexibility could make conflict more, rather than less, intense. In addition, a readiness to compromise implies that the lost battle was wrong and unnecessary. These same criteria are used when judging Western behavior. If the dictator's enemies give ground, it proves that they were weak and their cause unjust. Restraint does not bring respect, much less gratitude.

Arab leaders often seem to believe that if they hold their own ground, the other side will yield. Even if the enemy is stronger, it is thought to lack the Arab party's – as Saddam put it – "courage, patience, and determination." In Saddam's own words, "You will never regret patience, no matter how long it lasts if it [lays a] foundation" for a later victory. Or, as he put it more graphically, "Do not provoke a snake before you make up your mind and muster up the ability to cut its head." [13]

In deciding to lead his nation into a decade of stagnation, however, Saddam ignored alternatives that would have served him just as well and Iraq far better. Saddam could have gained more, no matter how hypocritically, with a moderate strategy. Declaring himself the true friend and protector of the Gulf Arab monarchies, he could have reaped big donations from Saudi Arabia and Kuwait (partly because they would still fear him). He could also have built a working relationship with the United States, which would have supported him against Iran. When the Iran-Iraq war ended in 1988, Washington continued to provide Iraq with trade credits and other benefits.

A "moderate" Saddam could have kept tight control at home and never invaded Kuwait. Even after his defeat in Kuwait, he could have declared that he was a changed man and probably have reconciled with his Gulf Arab neighbors, who would have quickly reinitiated appeasement aid to Baghdad. He could have cooperated in giving up his

---

13 Speech of August 8, 2001. Text from Iraq News Agency web site, http://www.uruklink.net/iraqnews/eindex.htm.

weapons of mass destruction, which would have ended sanctions and let him quickly rebuild his conventional military capacity. Soon Iraq would have regained its place as an important Arab power, a contender for hegemony in the Gulf, and a militarily strong state.

Even at his most cynical, Saddam could have pretended to comply with his commitments. He could have cheated more carefully and selectively, limiting his concealment and obstruction of inspectors to a minimum in order to get away with it. Once sanctions were lifted, oil revenue would have poured into Iraq for the economic reconstruction effort, as well as to finance weapons purchases. In this context, Saddam could have launched a military build-up including weapons of mass destruction. He probably would have succeeded. Much of the West could have been bought off with lucrative contracts, most of the Gulf Arab states could have been intimidated by a mixture of threats and promises of friendship. No country – apart from the United States – would have protested his behavior, and even the United States probably would not have done anything.

Instead, Saddam cheated to such an extent that even his advocates were in a difficult position, and, as if that were not enough, he took adventurous actions and made extreme statements or demands just when his prospects looked better. The Iraqi leadership violated its commitments and tried to retain biological, chemical, and nuclear capabilities to a point where the inspectors could not be fooled. By constantly making threats and taking aggressive actions, Saddam made it hard for his friends in the Arab world and elsewhere – in countries such as China, France, and Russia – to champion his cause successfully. On this level, Saddam's behavior seems very foolish.

Nevertheless, this judgment must be tempered by the extent to which the Iraqi regime's strategy was effective. Saddam did stay in power without facing a serious challenge. His regime was able to preserve a fair amount of its unconventional capacity, never made real or major concessions, and at the same time managed to wear down the sanctions. Within a decade, Iraq was readmitted to full membership in the Arab world despite its intransigence, even maintaining its claim to Kuwait.

The Iraqi leadership could be reasonably satisfied with how it fared in the 1990s. In the terms that structure Arab regimes, then, Saddam's behavior was smart. But this type of politics had extraordinarily high costs: lost opportunities, wasted resources, lower living standards for the people, persecution of Kurds and Shi'ites, a dictatorial system engaged in ferocious repression, and many other negative features.

One reason for the regime's staying power was its long, careful preparation of a strong base of support. The courted forces included selected tribes, with key members being granted special privileges, subsidies, and high offices; the Ba'th party; the military and security apparatuses; and – at the broadest level – the Sunni minority as a whole. At the core was a highly committed sector comprising Saddam's family, clan, and others from his home region – people whose livelihoods, power, and even lives were dependent on Saddam's remaining in power.

Saddam was also not afraid to punish anyone for deviation. In 1995, he fired close relatives from the posts of minister of defense and chief of general security. Potentially most damaging of all was the defection to Jordan of his son-in-law Kamal Hessan and other relatives in August 1995. Hessan provided the UN inspectors with documents showing how the Iraqi regime had systematically hidden military equipment from them. But security forces murdered Hessan and his brother when they returned to Iraq in 1996, persuaded both by Saddam's promise of a pardon and by threats against their families.

In general, though, all of these groups remained loyal or servile. Because of this secure rear area, Saddam was able to act the role of victor rather than vanquished in the decade after the disastrous Kuwait war. In the agreement ending the fighting in April 1991, Iraq accepted UN Security Council Resolution 687 obliging it to cooperate in getting rid of nuclear, chemical, and biological weapons, missiles with a range exceeding 150 kilometers, and related research and manufacturing facilities. Thereafter, though, Iraq violated its agreements with little retribution.[14]

Iraq's obstructionism began almost immediately. It constantly blocked UN and International Atomic Energy Agency (IAEA) inspectors from looking at some places where weapons, documents, and equipment were hidden. The government misreported the quantity of arms it possessed and declared destroyed other things that it had actually concealed. There was "clear evidence that Iraq had taken advance

14 Center for Nonproliferation Studies, Monterey Institute of International Studies, "Chronology of UN Inspections Derived from an October 1998 UNSCOM document" (Monterey, CA, 1999).

actions at certain of the locations planned for inspection in order to defeat the purposes of inspection," wrote Richard Butler, who headed the UN inspection efforts. Other places were designated presidential palaces and thus closed to inspection.[15]

Nevertheless, based on the available evidence, the inspection teams concluded that Baghdad was concealing ongoing nuclear and biological weapons programs and hiding missile parts. The Security Council passed resolutions of complaint about Iraq's failure to disclose information about weapons facilities and demanded cooperation. Yet this did not stop Iraq from ignoring these demands and harassing the inspection teams.[16]

Despite continuing but conciliatory UN efforts, Iraq repeatedly sabotaged the investigations and dragged out the process. In February 1992, Iraq refused to comply with UN orders to destroy war materiel. In July, Iraq barred inspectors from its Ministry of Agriculture, where they sought documents. The Security Council once again, without avail, demanded that Iraq stop such behavior. By January 1993, Baghdad's behavior had led to U.S., British, and French air strikes. Iraq quickly promised to mend its ways. But this new era did not last very long.

In 1993, when former-president George Bush visited Kuwait, Iraq apparently sponsored a plot to assassinate him. In October 1994, Iraq said that sanctions must be lifted or it would stop cooperating with inspectors. It mobilized troops on the Kuwaiti border, hinting that it might again invade that country if sanctions continued. The Security Council adopted still another resolution stressing its determination, but without threatening retaliation against Iraq.[17]

Again the crisis dissipated for a few months. But the UN's experts became more and more convinced that Iraq maintained biological and chemical weapons programs and had hidden germs and equipment. In

---

15 Steven Lee Myers and Barbara Crossette, "Iraq Accused of Arms Violations that Could Result in Air Strikes," *New York Times*, December 16, 1998.
16 This chronology is drawn largely from the British Foreign Office Paper, FCO Daily Bulletin, February 4, 1998; and Greg Saiontz, "A Chronology of Diminishing Response: UN Reactions to Iraqi Provocations Since the Gulf War," Washington Institute for Near East Policy, Research Note 1, June 1997.
17 United Nations, Security Resolution 949, October 15, 1994. On the plot against Bush, see U.S. Department of Defense, Office of the Assistant Secretary of Defense (Public Affairs), news briefing, October 8, 1994, http://www.defenselink.mil/news/Oct1994/t101394_tbrfg100.html; and U.S. Department of State, *Patterns of Global Terrorism, 1993* (Washington, DC, 1994), http://www.fas.org/irp/threat/terror_93/statespon.html.

May 1995, Saddam again threatened to end cooperation if economic sanctions were not lifted by August. Kamal Hessan, however, had given inspectors more proof that Iraq had cheated and lied. Faced with this evidence, Baghdad finally admitted that it had manufactured biological weapons, had been trying to build nuclear weapons, and had made greater progress in producing nerve gas and missiles than it had previously divulged. Iraq then renewed its pledge to cooperate with the United Nations Special Commission on Monitoring (UNSCOM) and rescinded the deadline.[18]

After only a brief hiatus, Saddam provoked another crisis. Starting in March 1996, Iraq once again barred UN inspectors from certain sites until security forces had time to remove incriminating documents. In August 1996, Iraqi forces marched into the city of Irbil in the Kurdish safe haven of northern Iraq. The United States responded with cruise missile attacks on Iraqi targets and extended the no-fly zone in southern Iraq to the outskirts of Baghdad. The UN secretary-general held up a deal that would have let Iraq buy food in return for oil sales. Yet, year after year, Iraqi interference continued.

Throughout 1997, Iraq escalated its defiance. In June, it interfered with helicopter flights over some sites and barred ground inspections of others. Iraq's constantly shifting claims about its possession and destruction of weapons added to the skepticism. As one UN report put it, "Since the adoption of resolution 687 [in 1991], Iraq has presented not one but a series of different declarations on its proscribed missiles, related items and activities. At each stage, they reflected a different level of disclosure by Iraq, as well as omissions of proscribed weapons capabilities and activities that Iraq attempted to conceal."[19] By October 1998, Iraq had decided that it would no longer allow any inspection teams with American members, and these were ordered to leave the country.[20] The UN refused to accept that limitation, and this clash, coupled with Iraq's intransigence, led

18 For examples of Iraq's techniques, see Christopher S. Wren, "U.N. Weapons Inspection Chief Tells of Iraqi Tricks," *New York Times*, Jan. 27, 1998; and Richard Butler, *The Greatest Threat: Iraq, Weapons of Mass Destruction and the Crisis of Global Security* (New York, 2000).

19 Report of the executive chairman on the activities of UNSCOM, April 16, 1998. http://www.un.org/Depts/unscom/sres98-332.htm.

20 UN Security Council Resolution 1205, November 5, 1998. http://www.un.org/Depts/unscom/Keyresolutions/sres98-1205.htm.

to an end of the inspections altogether, which was of course what Baghdad wanted.

On October 31, 1998, the Iraqi government further restricted active monitoring activities.[21] Iraq also stopped supplying information on biological weapons, harassed chemical inspections, broke promises of access to buildings, and initiated new restrictions on the inspectors' work.[22] Butler reported, "Iraq's conduct ensured that no progress was able to be made in either the fields of disarmament or accounting for its prohibited weapons programs."[23] In December, Butler told the UN secretary-general, "In light of . . . the absence of full cooperation by Iraq," the inspectors could no longer conduct their work.[24] The inspections were ended, just as Iraq intended.

The story of Iraq's unconventional weapons, the inspection regime, the discoveries and concealments, and the UN responses is extremely complex. For the purposes of understanding how Middle Eastern political systems function and interact with the West, however, several general trends are most important.

First, Iraq had successfully defied the world and retained a considerable proportion of its weapons and facilities. The UN had destroyed many weapons, but the stockpile that remained was dangerous indeed. In his report to the UN Security Council of June 1998, UNSCOM head Richard Butler explained, "It is important to note the order of magnitude of the weapons retained by Iraq: two-thirds of the operational missile force; more than half of the chemical weapons and all of the biological weapons."

For example, despite Iraqi denials that it had any VX nerve gas, UNSCOM discovered that Iraq had a large production capacity and had made four tons of this highly toxic substance. The Iraqis had also continued work on such deadly poisons as sarin, tabun, and mustard gas. The huge al-Hakam factory had made huge amounts of anthrax and botulinum; Iraq claimed that it only produced animal feed. Iraq repeatedly furnished reports on its weapons research, production, and

21 Charles Duelfer, deputy executive chairman of UNSCOM, letter to the president of the UN Security Council, October 31, 1998. http://www.un.org/Depts/unscom/s98-1023.htm.
22 Richard Butler, letter to the UN secretary-general, December 15, 1998. http://www.un.org/Depts/unscom/s98-1172.htm.
23 Ibid.
24 Ibid.

arsenals that were shown to be false, after which Iraq simply revised the reports into new false versions.

What is especially ironic here is that some observers concluded that Iraq really did not have many workable weapons left, and thus could have cooperated more easily. If this is so, then what Baghdad was concealing was not actual arms but rather the capacity to make new ones quickly after sanctions ended. As one UN report pointed out, Iraq claimed

that it has unilaterally destroyed those of its prohibited weapons which were not destroyed under international supervision. While it is clear that in a number of weapons areas unilateral destruction did take place . . . Iraq's refusal to provide adequate and verifiable details of that destruction has meant that . . . the Commission has not been able to verify all of Iraq's claims with respect to such unilateral destruction.[25]

But whether he was hiding quantities of arms or merely information, equipment, and facilities, by being tough and devious Saddam Hussein had achieved his goal of keeping whatever he did possess.

Second, the international community basically accepted Iraq's unilateral rejection of the commitments it had made after being militarily defeated, on the verge of collapse, and accepting its terms of surrender. The United States did periodically bomb Iraq, helped maintain a Kurdish safe haven in the north, and gave some support to Iraqi opposition groups. Other countries, however, were eager to end the sanctions and even more eager – with a few exceptions – to avoid any retaliation against Iraq for its behavior. China, France, and Russia, wanting to collect old debts and win new contracts, constituted a virtual pro-Iraq lobby.

Saddam's delaying, harassment, and threatening tactics succeeded in wearing down most of the world. Brazil's UN ambassador and former foreign minister Celso Amorim complained, "Do we really need to have the Iraq problem on our table every six months? . . . We've all become very tired of the Iraq problem. Isn't there some way of getting rid of it, once and for all?" When it was suggested that disarming Saddam was a way to do this, he replied, "I'm afraid that's probably too much to ask." Amorim had just been appointed by the UN Security Council to head the next phase of the disarmament effort.[26]

25 Report of the executive chairman on the activities of UNSCOM, April 16, 1998. http://www.un.org/Depts/unscom/sres98-332.htm.
26 Butler, letter to the UN secretary-general, p. 216.

But Saddam did not become tired. Iraq was astute at manipulating foreign powers and buying influence among them, and so here too Iraqi conceptions worked. Like others in the Arab world, notably the Palestinian leadership, Iraq's rulers had developed a formula that seemed to produce good results with the West: sustain a crisis as long as possible, so that the other side will give up or make concessions; gain sympathy by trying to prove victimhood; and reject compromise, so that the enemy will be tempted to believe that only concessions will bring a solution. Intransigence becomes a very successful tool to outwit, outplay, and outlast all of an Arab regime's foes.

Third, the Middle Eastern response to Saddam's strategy was equally feeble and quick to erode. Saudi Arabia and Kuwait were reluctant to readmit Iraq into full participation in Arab circles. But all other Arab states were willing to forgive Iraq for its past trespasses and to ignore its ongoing ones. Iraqi officials professed themselves angry at continuing Gulf Arab cooperation with the United States, including letting Arab territory be used as bases for bombing raids. Still, Iraq made great progress in the Arab world while giving nothing on any issue and rejecting any apologies. Arab regimes and summits opposed any U.S. attempt to intimidate or overthrow Saddam.

Baghdad's Arab policy could have been more quickly successful if it had been more flexible, yet it also showed that an Arab regime could be forgiven by its peers for almost any misdeed. Such acts included using poison gas and mass murder against its own Muslim citizens (Kurds), attacking Muslim and Arab neighbors without provocation (Iran and Kuwait), firing missiles at Muslim and Arab population centers (Iran and Saudi Arabia), and using poison gas in attacking a Muslim neighbor (Iran). Allowing such regimes to enjoy good standing in the Arab world was not a formula that would persuade such governments to be more restrained and peaceful in dealings with their Arab neighbors.

The Iraqi regime's success included evoking tremendous sympathy among the Arab masses for the deprivations suffered by the Iraqis, often because of the regime's own policies. It was true that Arabs often claimed to distinguish between their attitude toward the Iraqi people and their feelings about the Iraqi regime. Nevertheless, the difference was usually meaningless in practice, and such sympathy objectively helped Saddam, since he benefited from any pressure against sanctions or retaliation. Moreover, while many blamed the United States for this situation – including bin

Ladin – very few publicly put the responsibility for the enduring sanctions and low living standards directly on the Iraqi government.

Fourth, despite Iraqi defiance, noncompliance, and threats, the sanctions gradually and steadily declined.[27] Over time, Iraq was given more and more loopholes and allowed to sell larger amounts of oil. The sanctions did not end entirely, and Iraq had to use some of its petroleum revenues to compensate its Kuwaiti victims and to pay the UN inspection program's bills. Still, Iraq's revenues went up steadily over time. Even after Iraq expelled the inspectors, the UN continued to make concessions to Baghdad. This was a clear victory for Iraq's intransigent strategy, both reflecting and encouraging a similar pattern in other Middle Eastern regimes.

Indeed, the feebleness of the commitment to combat Iraq's behavior and to maintain sanctions was a major factor in Saddam's own decision not to cooperate. As he affirmed on several occasions, "We have said with certainty that the embargo will not be lifted by a Security Council resolution but will erode by itself. . . . We do not expect or wait for a stage whereby the blockade will erode. Rather, this has started already."[28]

Fifth, the Iraqi domestic structure worked effectively to preserve the regime and its interests. Saddam stayed in power even as he inflicted suffering on his people. Massive repression played a large part in this outcome. Clearly, many Iraqis – especially Shi'ites and Kurds – hated the regime. Yet governments do not stay in power when they are backed by only a few dozen people. Nationalism was still a potent force, and the system's ability to survive under the most difficult possible circumstances was a testimony to its strength and durability.

Thus, on one level, Saddam was not "stupid," and his system had not "failed" in serving itself, even though it failed the Iraqi people by ensuring that sanctions lasted longer and that their damage would be deeper. It could even be argued that these results fell short of what a different Iraqi regime, with precisely the same goals but using a strategy that made a temporary pretense of moderation, might have achieved. For good reason, Saddam and his colleagues did not feel that they had failed, but rather that they had triumphed over devious, dedicated adversaries determined to eliminate them.

27 On the decline of sanctions, see, for example, Patrick Clawson, "Oil for Food or the End of Sanctions?," *Policywatch* No. 303, February 26, 1998; and Patrick Clawson, "Why a New Security Council Resolution about Iraq?," *Policywatch* No. 395, June 18, 1999.
28 Text of Army Day speech, January 6, 2000.

Saddam's international victories took place not because he was so strong but because the West and the Arab world would not counter or stop him. He put down Kurdish and Shi'ite revolts against him in 1991 with great loss of life just after being totally defeated in the Kuwait war. But the West stood by and watched the repression without doing anything. He threw the UN inspectors out of Iraq without any serious response. He survived because the West would not strive vigorously to overthrow him or give much help to opposition movements. He steadily weakened the international sanctions because the West made concessions in order to gain trade benefits or to reduce the suffering of Iraq's people, which was a result of the regime's deliberate policies. Even at a time when human rights were a powerful battle cry in other parts of the world, Iraq's repression was largely excused or ignored.

Yet ironically this reality ran directly contrary to a fundamental assumption of Arab nationalist and Islamist ideology used to justify such behavior in the first place: that the West was doggedly determined to weaken, defeat, and undermine them. While the anti-Iraq sanctions were often cited as proof for this claim, they also showed the opposite. The West invoked sanctions only to protect Arabs and Muslims from Saddam's aggression, and it was eager to end the sanctions if Baghdad gave it an alternative. If the West had really wanted to conquer the Gulf and dominate the Arabs, it could have brought down Saddam in 1991 and turned the Arab monarchies into protectorates using the military force and leverage it then possessed.

The Iraq case also does not illustrate the idea that the Middle East's difficulties stem from Western imperialist domination. Quite the contrary, it shows the primacy of indigenous problems and the West's reluctance to intervene or to impose its will or ways on the Middle East. The case of Iraq is simply a rather typical example of one regional power unilaterally deciding to initiate aggression against its neighbors. Equally, the Saudis and Kuwaitis were not betraying the Arab or Muslim cause but simply acting as victims of aggression who needed outside help in order to preserve their sovereignty. There have been dozens of such situations in Africa, Asia, Europe, and Latin America.

To maintain the distorted view that has dominated public Arab discussion of this issue often took tremendous acrobatics. For example, in one of his speeches Saddam said that Iraq had won a great victory over Iran thanks to help from God and despite "those who wished our people ill and our nation harm, backed by international Zionism, imperialism and the wicked Jews in the occupied land and in their accursed freak entity [Israel]."[29]

Yet the United States had actually supported Iraq in the war. At times, after the United States allowed Gulf Arab tankers to fly American flags as they violated neutrality and helped Iraq, U.S. forces became a virtual co-belligerent in the war against Iran. When a U.S. warship accidentally shot down an Iranian passenger flight in July 1988, this seems to have been the final blow persuading Khomeini to end the war, lest the Americans join the conflict on Iraq's side. Even Israel, while glad to see two of its enemies fighting each other, preferred an Iraqi victory to an Iranian one. Indeed, Iraqi propaganda had deliberately sought to win support from American Jews by portraying an Iranian victory as more threatening to Israel.[30]

Nevertheless, if Saddam could get political mileage out of anti-Americanism after the United States had helped him "win" the war against Iran, it was simply one more example of having one's cake and eating it too, seemingly a viable strategy in the Arab world. This conclusion, however, is not altogether true. As noted earlier, there was a high price to be paid for such behavior and thinking, seen most graphically when Saddam's calculation that America would not fight him over Kuwait proved mistaken.

The Iraqi government's view that it had enemies everywhere was largely a self-fulfilling prophecy. Its own actions were the source of its troubles. Thanks to Saddam, even the Saudis and Kuwaitis turned against Iraq. They may never have truly loved that country, but they had been quite willing to talk and act as if they did. The practical effect of Iraq's actions was to increase the country's isolation, sustain sanctions, and postpone the day when it could rebuild its military. This crisis, which was allowed to continue long after the Kuwait war ended, might have been dispensed with after a few years.

To a large extent, the victories of the dominant Arab system were paper victories, triumphs that filled the mind and preserved the status quo. Despite such tactics, Palestine did not become independent; Iran did not become an Islamic utopia; Syria remained economically backward;

---

29 Iraq News Agency, August 8, 2000, http://www.uruklink.net/iraqnews/eindex.htm.
30 Barry Rubin, *Cauldron of Turmoil* (New York, 1992), pp. 135–8.

Saudi Arabia only postponed its crisis of modernization; and Iraq did not shake off the sanctions or destroy its enemies.

Nevertheless, Iraq's leaders will never admit that their difficulties arise from following an unworkable ideology and policy. Rather, they insist that the other Arabs are just not trying hard enough to let them succeed. In this respect, Saddam's words are fairly typical of his counterparts elsewhere and of their Islamist opponents:

The youth want to rebel and unleash the Arab nation's potency [against both Israel and the Gulf Arab monarchies, but they are held back because] of weakness in the minds of those who have become accustomed to abasement to the degree of addiction, from among rulers and kings who have no concern but to appear on their chairs and thrones as if they really rule. . . . [They] have sold out their souls and have appointed [the occupying foreigner] to rule. . . . Whatever they find saleable they have sold to the United States and Zionism, thus becoming mere agents getting commissions deducted from the wealth of their own people and getting ignoble authority chairs to sit on. . . .[31]

On one level, this is just the kind of vicious polemic that characterizes much of the Middle Eastern political debate. At the same time, though, such arguments set the boundaries of permissible thought for everyone else. The defeat of the radical cause, the failure to achieve total justice and all of the Arab nationalist or Islamist demands, is said to be caused not by material conditions, the international or regional balance of power, or to wrong tactics or goals, but merely to cowardice and the betrayal of those who wish to fight. Egyptian journalists, Lebanese politicians, and Usama bin Ladin all claim to adhere to this same basic set of ideas. Regimes that do not want to pursue such dangerous and counterproductive policies are denied legitimacy. In response, they feel compelled to mimic the rhetoric and some of the policies of their persecutors.

This worldview is dressed up as a championing of proud principle over tarnished pragmatism. Saddam told his people, "Let not easy paths lure you when you find that the paths that cause your feet to bleed lead to the summit."[32] Iraqis and the Arab people in general should be willing to suffer and bleed for their principles and, if they did so, victory would be

31 Speech of August 8, 2001. Text from Iraq News Agency web site, http://www.uruklink.net/iraqnews/eindex.htm.
32 Ibid.

theirs. This idea has governed the Arab rulers' ultimate refusal to grant comprehensive reforms and the Arab people's refusal to demand them.

It could be argued, though, that Saddam paid less attention to another of his aphorisms: "Benefit from your own lessons lest you should be burdened with the accumulated price you pay for them and then you will get drowned."[33] But perhaps he was not so heedless. After all, Saddam did not drown. It was his own people, victims, and enemies who might suffer that fate.

33 Ibid.

4

SYRIA

The Test Case for Reform

Syria is the most revealing test case for the failure of change in Middle Eastern politics. Had Damascus moved from the radical to the moderate camp, it would have decisively shifted the overall balance, making a breakthrough toward a new and different Middle East. Syria's participation in the Gulf War coalition of 1991, its readiness to negotiate with Israel, its severe economic and social stagnation and strategic vulnerability – all topped off by the coming to power of a new generation of leadership – provoked expectations that it would undergo dramatic change.

Like so many of the Arab regimes' policies during the twentieth century's second half, Syria's strategy was both brilliant and useless. The regime survived, its foreign maneuvers worked well much of the time, and Syrian control over Lebanon was a moneymaker. But what did all of this avail Syria compared to what an emphasis on peace and development might have achieved?

It was a Western idea that desperation at their country's difficult strategic and economic plight would make Hafiz al-Asad – and Saddam, Arafat, and other Arab or Iranian leaders as well – move toward concessions and moderation. But the rulers themselves reasoned in exactly the opposite way: Faced with pressure to change, they usually became more demanding and intransigent.

Often, at least up to a point, this strategy worked, as the West offered more concessions in an attempt to encourage the expected reforms. Yet to the regimes this behavior seemed the result not of generosity or proffered friendship but of Western fear, greed, or their own superior strength and tactics. This perception encouraged continued intransigence in hope of reaping still more benefits. Eventually, this process destroyed any possibility of moderation, though not always Western illusions.

Syria's militant style of politics and policy arose from the country's history, the regime's ideology, and the ruling Alawite minority's need to prove its nationalist and Islamic credentials to a skeptical Sunni Muslim majority. By declaring itself guardian of Arabism and the Palestinian cause, Syria rationalized its own national interests in order to gain influence over or weaken its neighbors and to make itself a viable candidate for leadership in the region. "Syria's main asset, in contrast to Egypt's preeminence and Saudi wealth, is its capacity for mischief," explains Professor Fouad Ajami.[1]

Regarding its two weaker neighbors, Syria used these tools to gain hegemony over Lebanon and to intimidate Jordan. Doing its Arab "duty," Syria in effect took over Lebanon by sending in its army and creating Lebanese client organizations that would obey its orders. In Jordan, Syria fomented subversion through proxy groups in an attempt to obtain decisive influence over that country.

Syria struck at two stronger neighbors, Israel and Turkey, along similar lines, using revolutionary groups: Palestinian and Lebanese against Israel, Kurdish and Armenian against Turkey. These targets were non-Arab states, so Syria's constant emphasis on Arab nationalism denied them a normal regional role and the possibility of obtaining Arab allies against its ambitions. By maintaining the Arab-Israeli conflict, Damascus forced other Arab states to support Syria and blackmailed wealthy oil-producing countries into providing financial aid. Continuing the conflict while trying to subvert Arafat also allowed Syria to seek control over the Palestinian movement.

As for Egypt and Iraq, its main competitors for regional Arab leadership, Damascus sometimes cooperated, but each also tried to show that it was the best candidate for primacy. For a while, Syria knocked both countries out of the running by organizing an anti-Egypt boycott after Egypt made peace with Israel in the late 1970s, and by siding with the U.S.-led coalition to isolate Iraq after its invasion of Kuwait. While Syria never had the financial resources or strategic weight to consolidate these advantages, Damascus was always able to ensure that the Arab system protected its interests and supported its positions.

1 Fouad Ajami, "Arab Road," *Foreign Policy*, No. 47 (Summer 1982), p. 16.

Finally, the Syrian regime was always hostile toward the United States for very good reasons of its own that never changed over time. Syrian goals favored instability; U.S. interests preferred stability. The main friends of the United States – Egypt after the late 1970s, Israel, Jordan, Turkey, and an independent Lebanon – were Syria's enemies, rivals, and targets for intimidation. Syria's allies – the USSR, revolutionary groups, Egypt under Nasser, Islamist Iran, and at times Iraq – were opposed to the U.S. goals and role in the region.

Yet despite all of these enmities and rivalries, Syria was successful in winning Western and Arab acceptance of its control over Lebanon. Similarly, Syria was able to get through the weakest period in its history by using the 1990–91 Kuwait crisis to overcome many of its international problems. Before that event, as Moscow's best regional ally, Syria was the state hardest hit by the decline of Soviet power. It was on bad terms with all of its neighbors, threatened by Saddam's drive for leadership, undermined by the end of Saudi subsidies, and short of money for buying weapons.

Syria managed, however, to escape its dilemmas without having to make many concessions or any internal changes. At a time when there were international or U.S. sanctions on Libya, Iran, and Iraq, Syria was the only radical regime to escape this fate. By joining the anti-Iraq coalition in 1991, the Asad dictatorship, despite its human rights violations and support for terrorism, was joining the "free world" side. The U.S. defeat of Saddam weakened Syria's most determined foe. The coalition, which had gone to war to save Kuwait from Iraq, turned a blind eye to Syrian control over Lebanon. Lebanon was too valuable for Damascus to give up, since it brought benefits both to Syria's poor – up to a million of whom had found better-paying jobs in Lebanon – and to its ruling elite, which profited from smuggling, monopolies, drug trafficking, and other enterprises. Asad had also escaped his isolation from the Arab world. As a reward for his stance against Iraq in the Kuwait crisis, Saudi Arabia gave Asad's economically prostrate government two billion dollars, which was spent on buying arms from Moscow.

The same pattern of using minimum change and hints of moderation to win much larger gains can be seen in Syria's policy on the Arab-Israeli conflict. Even in exchange for all the Golan Heights, any peace settlement would be costly for Syrian interests. If Israel were ever accepted in .the region as a normal power, its new status would damage Syria more than ever because their interests would still conflict. Israel would try to block Syrian ambitions under far more favorable circumstances, and losing the Arab-Israeli crisis as an excuse would put Syria in a corner. Without being able to use Israel as a threat, how would the Syrian regime persuade Gulf Arabs to give it money, Lebanon to accept permanent satellite status, and its own people to tolerate such poor living conditions and absence of freedom? A Palestinian state would not welcome Syrian influence. And an increase in U.S. prestige and power in the region would be the last thing Damascus wanted.

At the same time, the benefits of peace – for the regime, at least – were minimal. The return of the Golan Heights would not solve any of Syria's foreign or domestic problems. Even with a peace agreement, Syria would still need to maximize military spending while still lacking either a reliable source of arms or enough money to keep the generals satisfied.

There would be no real economic bonus, as any additional U.S. or European aid and investment would be minimal. The Syrian regime also did not want to accept the alleged benefits of opening up the economy, as this step would weaken the rulers and deprive them of the profits they reaped from controlling the statist economy. At any rate, the biggest beneficiaries from peace and far-reaching economic reform would be Sunni Muslim businessmen – some of whom supported the Islamist democratic opposition – who did not love the regime and would then be in a better position to challenge and eventually overthrow it.

Superficially, it had seemed that Syria would desperately want to make peace with Israel and to regain the Golan Heights as soon as possible. Using the logic of their own politics, most Western observers thought that this was the most obvious thing in the world. But in reality, such an outcome would be that regime's worst nightmare. Without this advantage, Syria would be reduced to a third-rate power with far less influence in the Arab world. The ideal policy was one by which Syria's rulers could appear to negotiate seriously, preserving a good relationship with the West, while avoiding any actual agreement in order to protect their domestic and inter-Arab fronts.

One way to do this was to demand so much that Israel would never be able to agree. This approach was a win/win situation, since Syria could simultaneously appear to be moderate in the West and steadfast in the Arab world. The repeated diplomatic failure to broker a Syria-Israel agreement did not derive merely from a refusal to move the border a few meters in one direction or the other. Much deeper forces were at work, and the outcome was a basic consequence of Syrian national interest, perceptions, and geopolitics as interpreted by the country's leadership.

Israel's government was ready to return the entire Golan Heights to Syria up to the international border as part of an agreement that would bring full bilateral peace. Not only was this endorsed by Prime Minister Ehud Barak, it had also been secretly accepted by his predecessor, Benjamin Netanyahu. Clearly, Syria knew that it could get back its national territory at any time.

The ostensible sticking point was Syria's demand to annex about 20 square kilometers of territory on Israel's side of the international border that Syria had seized in the 1950s. This demand contradicted Syria's own position that obtaining territory by force was unacceptable, as well as the principle of returning to the international border that had prevailed in the Egypt-Israel and Jordan-Israel agreements. While the area involved was small, it was of vital strategic importance to Israel, but not to Syria. Syria did not need this flat piece of land for defense, since it held the commanding heights above. By contrast, however, holding this territory would let Syria instantaneously destroy Israel's access to its main water supply – the Sea of Galilee – and even claim much of that lake. There was no chance that any Israeli government would ever agree to such terms. Syria's procedural demand that Israel must concede all of this land, plus the entire Golan, before any other issues were even discussed obviously doomed the negotiations to failure.[2]

Thus, contrary to the Western expectation that Syria badly wanted and needed peace, Damascus was in no hurry to change anything. Nearly a quarter-century after Sadat had made peace with Israel, Syrian Foreign Minister Faruq al-Sharaa was still arguing that he should not have done so: "Egypt was the biggest Arab country, Arab solidarity then was in good shape, and the international balance of power was better. But Sadat was defeated from within [himself]. . . . The brave

---

2 For the text of the U.S.-proposed Israel-Syria agreement, see *Ha'aretz*, January 17, 2000.

Egyptian Army was not defeated, and the Egyptian people . . . were not defeated either."[3]

Syria's rulers, like their counterparts in Iraq and other Arab states, seemed to consider the vital secret of proper policy to be showing intransigence in difficult times precisely in order to deny your adversary any concessions. This was a key argument of the regimes against those among their own people who urged reform in order to deal with their rulers' multiple shortcomings. In Sharaa's words, "Despite the successive retreats and setbacks on the Arab and international levels, including the catastrophe of the [Kuwait war of 1991,] which opened the region to the United States, the West, and Israel, Syria did not submit to others or to their double standards."[4] One would never guess, incidentally, that Saddam had claimed during the Kuwait crisis that those "double standards" included Syria's occupation of Lebanon.

It may have seemed unlikely that Syria would be able to deal with this difficult dilemma on its own terms, yet that is largely what happened. Sharaa noted that Syria's plan had worked. Damascus had stuck to its maximal demands, a strategy that would ultimately sabotage the negotiations. But by appearing cooperative, Syria had escaped from isolation and the possibility of U.S. pressure. Sharaa explained, "For almost half a century Israel has been claiming that it wants peace with the Arabs, but it cannot get it. It has also been claiming that the Arabs are warmongers. Israel has succeeded in deceiving the world public, especially the Americans." But now Syria would prove that Israel was the true warmonger.[5]

Even in the unlikely event that Israel would meet Damascus's demands, Syria could continue the struggle by other means. Israel was much too strong for the Arabs to fight, Sharaa continued, and he deprecated the military option by saying that Israel, not the Arabs, would gain more in any war. "At any rate, we have tried 50 years of armed struggle and we are now alone," without allies for waging war on Israel. Perhaps it would be better to put the emphasis instead on "political, economic, commercial, and cultural competition."[6]

3 Speech to the Arab Writers Union Conference, January 27, 2000. Text is from *al-Usbu' al-Adabi*, February 12, 2000. See http://www.awu-dam.com. Translation from FBIS.
4 Ibid.
5 Ibid.
6 Ibid.

And even if, as happened in the year 2000, Israel was ready to make enormous concessions in exchange for peace without agreeing to such a complete surrender, the Arab side could simply demand even more. In Syria's case, this meant an insistence on annexing Israeli territory and that Israel make all concessions before Syria began discussing what it would give in exchange. In Lebanon's case, it meant redefining the country's borders in order to insist that Hizballah could keep fighting because Israel still held a tiny piece of land (the so-called Shaba farms sector) that hitherto no one had considered part of Lebanon. In the Palestinian case, it meant destroying negotiations on relatively minor issues along with the Palestinian demand that Israel let all Palestinian refugees live there, and thus be in a far better position to destroy it.

The Israelis would lose if they did not accept Arab demands, Sharaa explained, "because we would have won the Arab and international public. The Arabs will stand by us whether they like it or not because we will tell them: We have made every effort." If the Israelis were to concede on every point, such a peace would not be permanent either. The goal of any negotiation would be to find a way to "disarm and neutralize" Israel. "This does not mean that we will lay down our arms in a state of peace." For 30 years the Arabs had already known, Sharaa suggested, "that the restoration of the whole of Palestine is a long-term strategy which cannot be achieved in one phase.... The first phase is regaining the occupied Arab territories and guaranteeing the Palestinian Arab people's inalienable national rights." He did not need to explain to his Syrian audience what the second phase and ultimate goal involved.

When Sharaa gave his comprehensive analysis in January 2000, it was hard to believe that this strategy would work as well as it did. A year later, though, it was already clear that the Syrian regime had weathered the crisis and avoided the danger of peace without making any basic change in its policy. It had broken certain taboos about direct negotiations with Israel; but, without paying any political cost, Syria had turned down Israel's offer to return all of the Golan Heights in exchange for peace. As Sharaa had predicted, the rest of the Arab world did unite to support Syria and to blame Israel for the breakdown of negotiations.

In addition, Damascus had rejected America's peacemaking effort and humiliated President Clinton, but the United States did nothing to pressure or criticize Syria for such behavior. Rather than changing a status quo that had repeatedly brought disaster and so hurt its own people's objective interests, the Syrian regime had won still another great victory in the service of the old order and its own preservation.

Important as it was, though, the Arab-Israeli conflict in itself was a secondary concern for Syria, as it was for the other Arab states. The real issue was whether enough momentum had accumulated as the result of past failures and current problems to alter any Arab country's political and social system.

What the peace process was supposed to do for Syria, like Iraq's very different sanctions compliance process, was to put an end to the old era of crisis and hostility and begin a new era of peaceful coexistence with neighbors and good relations with the West. Such a change would permit a flourishing of rapid economic development, free enterprise, democracy, human rights, and other good things. An end to these regional problems would let Syria focus on solving domestic problems. If this path were followed, the people would benefit, the countries would be strengthened, and past mistakes would be rectified. Such a formula, with all its imperfections, had generally worked elsewhere in the world. Why not in the Middle East as well?

Syria seemed ripe for this transition. Aside from more controversial political questions, its economy was in shambles.[7] Once one of the region's more industrialized countries, Syria, shackled by a Soviet-style economic structure, had fallen steadily behind even compared to its Arab counterparts. "A restructuring effort at all levels is needed," said Nabil Sukkar, an economist who headed a Damascus consulting firm. Rateb Shallah, president of the Federation of Syrian Chambers of Commerce and Industry, warned, "It is not feasible to postpone decision-making, because we will lose the chance for reform."[8]

Having some oil resources, but far less than the rich Gulf states, Syria was hard hit by low petroleum prices during the 1980s, and its economy slumped badly as a result. The situation was not helped by President Hafiz al-Asad's costly and futile drive to gain military parity with Israel. The USSR's collapse meant the end of Soviet bloc aid

---

7 Eyal Zisser, "Syria's Assad, the Approach of a Fifth Term of Office," *Policywatch* No. 366, February 5, 1999.

8 *New York Times*, January 27, 2000. See also Roula Khalaf, "Syria's Golden Opportunity," *Financial Times*, October 13, 1999.

and cheap weapons. The Gulf Arab monarchies' reduced oil incomes and new priorities made them uninterested in giving money to Syria. At a time of rapid population growth, Syria's society was put under further strain. The combination of stifling bureaucracy, price controls, low interest rates, an overpriced currency, overregulation of the private sector, suspicion of high technology, low pay, high prices, the absence of a private banking system, and rampant corruption did not help matters.

It seemed that the country faced a stark choice. On the one hand, Syria could embark on a program of massive reform in order to reduce government controls; it could foster trade, unleash the country's able commercial sector, and attract investment by opting for peace and stability. On the other hand, it could continue to decline and perhaps head straight for a huge crisis that could bring the regime's collapse.

But the former alternative was not as obvious or attractive as it seemed, at least from the standpoint of the nation's rulers. Their perspective on the economy was very different from that of foreign observers and local businessmen. For them, the goal was not to provide higher living standards or more successful development but rather to enrich the elite and to ensure that the maximum possible resources flowed into their own control and were kept out of the hands of potential rivals.

Regarding economic liberalization, Syria also had a unique problem. The Alawites, the government's main supporters, greatly benefited from regime patronage in business as well as jobs in the bureaucracy and military. But the real private businesses and real entrepreneurial skills overwhelmingly belonged to the Sunni Muslim majority, which generally disliked the regime. Thus, privatization and deregulation would weaken Asad's base of support, while giving more power and assets to those who would like to see him fall.

If prosperity required opening up the society to foreign influences and to domestic freedom, this road – and not the route of continued militancy and dictatorship – seemed the real highway to disaster. A Syrian merchant, expressing the frustration of his fellows, complained, "The only logic I can see in this system is that someone wants the industry in this country to be killed."[9] But this evaluation was not quite right. The government did not want to kill the goose that laid the

9 *New York Times*, January 27, 2000.

golden eggs, but simply was determined to keep most of the eggs for itself, even if that reduced overall egg production.

Consequently, the government's alternative was quite different from the one recommended by the West and by its domestic critics. Perhaps in reference to this choice, President Bashar al-Asad remarked, "Often, some people astonish me when they refrain from conducting an analysis and tend to improvise positions that are, usually, verbal and sentimental, are not based on the developments, and do not solve the problems."[10] On both the economic and political fronts, the regime had its own plan that was less conducive to economic well-being but perhaps more effective for purposes of holding power than were the suggestions for reform.

This economic strategy used a combination of factors. Keeping a hold on Lebanon would provide jobs for Syrian workers, who went there to earn double the pay they received at home, and would enrich the Syrian elite through a range of activities that included smuggling and drug production. Lebanon provided another benefit, since Iran subsidized Syria in exchange for Damascus' giving Iran's client Hizballah a free hand there. Helping Iraq avoid sanctions, through smuggling and an oil pipeline, could also help. Finally, a rise in international oil prices, which zoomed upward in 2000, would provide the necessary cash to survive.

As for political reform, the regime would continue the policy it had always used, perhaps the only one it was capable of implementing. Continuing tight control would show that the regime was in charge and discourage dissent. Very small reforms would provide a safety valve, maintain hope, and fool foreigners. The largest possible military budget would keep the generals happy and loyal. Inflaming the Arab-Israeli conflict would, as it had always done, mobilize the masses' support, silence dissent, and provide an ideal excuse for keeping everything the same.

This is not to say that these definitions or choices were so clear-cut or conscious. Sometimes it seemed that there was a genuine puzzlement or ignorance about any alternative system. "I am amazed," explained Bashar, "by the insistence of those who are influenced by what is going on in the Western society, and especially American society, that the press is 'the fourth governing authority' [estate]. How can the press be

---

10 *Al-Safir*, July 16, 2001. Translation in MEMRI No. 244, July 20, 2001.

a fourth governing branch in our backward Third World, where the leader does not share the rule with others?"[11] In addition, there may have been differences of opinion within the Syrian elite, about which outsiders know little; but the harder-line logic always prevailed.

Bashar al-Asad, however, was the man who was supposed to break this cycle. When his father, Hafiz, died in June 2000, the thirty-four-year-old Bashar was quickly elevated to the office. The Syrian constitution, which required that the president be at least forty years old, was quickly amended. Bashar was then elected with 97.2 percent of the vote in an uncontested election.[12] It was a very strange situation: A radical regime that had always rejected hereditary monarchy as disgusting now behaved as if Syria were a family fiefdom.

The idea that Bashar was a Western-educated reformer rested on very thin ice. He had spent only two years in Britain, studying medicine, when he was called home after his older brother Basil, the family's crown prince, fatally drove into a bridge abutment in 1994. As on-the-job training, his father put him in charge of Lebanon and made him a colonel in the elite Republican Guard. It was said that Bashar was fond of the internet because he was chairman of the Syrian Computer Society. Actually, though, like the presidency itself, he had only inherited that job when Basil died.

Ridiculing the idea that Bashar might bring reform, Muhammad al-Hasnawi, a Syrian dissident writer living in London, remembered the mother of a political prisoner jailed in Syria, who had wept when she heard about Bashar's succession: "Her natural intuition," he wrote, "taught her that the tragedy will continue. . . . Has this fact, which is understood by an illiterate woman, escaped the attention of people like us, who want to lead the public opinion and the modernization?"[13]

In his inauguration speech, Bashar suggested, "We are in dire need of constructive criticism and in order for the criticism to be constructive, we must think objectively and examine each issue from different points of view."[14] But there are limits to that reconsideration, and any

---

11 Ibid.
12 Michael Eisenstadt, "Who Rules Syria: Bashar al-Asad and the 'Alawi Barons'." Washington Institute for Near East Policy, June 21, 2000.
13 *Al-Quds al-Arabi*, February 20, 2001. Translation in MEMRI Inquiry and Analysis No. 49, February 16, 2001.
14 Syrian Press Agency, July 17, 2000. Translation in MEMRI No. 116, July 21, 2000.

solutions must be in the Syrian style: "We cannot apply the democracy of others to ourselves."

He did make some small changes. More than 600 political prisoners, mostly Islamists held for up to 20 years, were released. One prison notorious for ill-treatment and the military courts were closed. Bashar suggested that there be fewer pictures of himself and banners praising him displayed in public. A few newspapers ran articles supporting reform, albeit only under the government's leadership. Bashar met with several reformers and told them that they could criticize the state on economic matters, but only in the state-run Syrian press, which of course might not print their complaints. Small parties allied with the ruling Ba'th regime were offered the possibility of opening their own newspapers, and a satirical magazine was also permitted, but only with continuing censorship and on condition that they reflect the government line.[15] "When we discuss granting a permit to a newspaper," he explained, "the primary question is what is the goal of the paper [and] do the ideas of the newspaper serve the national and pan-Arab line."[16]

Those interested in change, however, wanted more. In September 2000, a manifesto was published abroad, signed by 99 Syrian cultural and intellectual figures. It urged the regime to end the state of emergency and martial law, in effect since 1963; to pardon all political detainees and exiled dissidents; to recognize freedom of assembly, speech, and the press; and to abrogate restrictive laws and stop spying on the public.[17] Their goal was to establish a multiparty democracy and strong civil society. Only political reform, they argued, could allow Syria to deal with its problems. The state-run media refused even to mention the declaration, and the regime briefly imposed a ban on foreign newspapers that printed the document. But no action was taken against the signatories themselves.

15 *Al-Hayat*, January 15, 2001. Cited in Eli Karmeli and Yotam Feldner, "The Battle for Reforms and Civil Society in Syria – Part I," MEMRI Inquiry and Analysis No. 47, February 9, 2001.
16 *Al-Sharq al-Awsat*, February 8, 2001. Cited in Yotam Feldner, "All Quiet on the Eastern Front, Almost, Bashar Assad's First Interview, " MEMRI Inquiry and Analysis No. 49, February 16, 2001.
17 The document was published in *al-Hayat*, September 27, 2000. Sections are cited in "Syrian Intellectuals Call for Political Reform," MEMRI No. 131, September 29, 2000.

Encouraged by the apparent start of a new government-tolerated reform movement, more than 1,000 Syrians, within the country and abroad, signed a second manifesto in January 2001 that went even further than the first one. It also directly urged the end of single-party rule and called for democratic elections under the supervision of an independent judiciary. Even the Muslim Brotherhood supported it.[18] Seventy Syrian lawyers signed another petition calling on the government to conduct political reforms, revoke emergency laws, and allow independent parties.[19]

Activists founded the National Dialogue Club, which held meetings at the home of Riyadh al-Seif, one of the few independent-minded members of parliament, to hear lectures on democracy and civil society. At a January 2001 gathering, Shibli al-Shami, the lecturer, spoke words that would have been – almost literally – unthinkable a few months earlier, "Since 1958," he said, "the Syrian regime has been a dictatorship. The main problem is oppression. The oppression is from the inside." Defending the Western model, al-Shami stated: "The West is not bad. The bad is you . . . who oppressed each other. The bad were those of us who used to write reports [to the secret police] against others. The British . . . taught me and gave me a doctorate in engineering. They have not benefited from me." He also stressed, however, that reformers should be patient, not ask for instant changes, and give the new leadership a chance to develop its programs.[20]

The planning minister couldn't even speak to the Syrian Society for Economic Science without Seif popping up from the audience, amid cheers from the crowd, to complain, "We have no transparency, no exact monetary figures, and no accountability. We don't have any development. We don't have dialogue. We don't have strong institutions. We have no anti-corruption campaign."[21]

Seif applied for permission to form a new party, to be called the Civil Peace Movement. At an organizational meeting of 350 people, he

18 *Al-Hayat*, January 16, 2001. Translation in MEMRI Inquiry and Analysis No. 47, February 9, 2001.
19 *Al-Quds Al-Arabi*, February 2, 2001. See also *al-Safir*, January 24, 2001. Translation in MEMRI No. 47, February 9, 2001.
20 *Al-Hayat*, January 13, 2001. Cited in Karmeli and Feldner, "The Battle for Reforms and Civil Society in Syria."
21 Ibid.

criticized "the Ba'th party's monopoly on power" and the fact that it "gives itself the right to govern the country and the society through Pan-Arab rhetoric that conceals leftist tendencies, while removing from the political arena any other ideas." Five professors who were members of the party stood up to accuse him of collaborating with foreign elements.[22]

Such charges were common in the regime's offensive against the reformers. Turki Saqr, editor of the ruling party's *al-Ba'th* newspaper, proclaimed, "Throughout its history, the Ba'th Party has had many battles against imported political ideas [that did not] comply with our national or pan-Arab situation." No one would be allowed "to import ideas from across the ocean and force them on our party and our people."[23]

The regime's accusations that reformers were agents of foreign powers and Shami's theme that oppression came from inside the country were especially significant. The battle between reform and the status quo revolved around the broader question of whether Syria's problems, like the rest of the Arab world's difficulties, were caused by internal or external factors.

If the Arabs' woes came overwhelmingly from imperialism and Zionism subverting and trying to destroy them, then only unity and solidarity could help them to survive. Internal debate and criticism, much less democracy, could not help the Arabs in their desperate struggle. To make matters worse, the reformers wanted to import the ideas and institutions of the enemy, the very forces of evil that sought to corrode Arab culture and independence. After a certain point, the conflict with Israel, hostility toward the United States, and the need to discredit Western ways were symptoms rather than causes of this situation, just as the Cold War was integrally related to the maintenance of communist rule in the Soviet bloc.

The alternative interpretation was potentially quite dangerous for the rulers. For if foreign powers were not the villains, then the domestic rulers – dictators and not patriotic champions in that event – would be responsible. If so, progress would require not the adversaries' defeat or diplomatic surrender but instead the replacement of Arab leaders and a

22 Ibid.
23 *Al-Ba'th*, February 1, 2001. Translation in MEMRI No. 48, February 12, 2001.

comprehensive shake-up of the entire system. The struggle was not so much a life-and-death issue for the Arab cause but a life-and-death battle for the ruling elites and their allies.

As a substitute for reform, Bashar's strategy was to prove himself tough by enhancing his credentials as a militant Arab nationalist, fighter against Israel, defender of revolutionary forces, and no friend of the United States. His stances strengthened the regime at the cost of the nation, yet they had the added benefit of being applauded by the nation. Like Saddam Hussein, Yasir Arafat, and other Middle Eastern leaders, Bashar made the "wrong" foreign policy decisions for the "right" domestic reasons. These leaders were not, however, following the demands of public opinion but rather were trying to control and shape public opinion, and world opinion, in a specific direction.

Bashar made all of his choices in this manner. He could have eased up on Syria's occupation of Lebanon, especially after Israel's unilateral withdrawal in 2000 had reduced any excuse for staying there. In response, though, Bashar only removed Syrian troops from Beirut itself to the surrounding areas. Syria's proconsuls continued to manipulate Lebanese politics, interfering with even the smallest decisions and lowest-level appointments. Such continued control aided the Syrian regime by bringing economic profit to all levels of Syrian society. Given the lack of international – much less Arab – pressure for a pullout, Syria could stay indefinitely at almost no political cost.

Bashar could have made gestures to improve relations with the United States at a time when the Clinton and Bush administrations were eager to reconcile and reward Syria. There were no efforts in that direction. After the September 11, 2001, terror attacks on America, the Syrian media adopted a very anti-American line, and the government would not join the antiterror coalition, except to give information on a few of bin Ladin's men who were not on the Syrian payroll.[24]

Bashar could have kept his distance from Iraq, viewed by the United States as the most hostile state in the region. Participation in the Gulf War coalition against Iraq in 1991 had been one of the few assets Syria possessed in its dealings with the West. Nevertheless, he moved steadily toward aligning with Baghdad. When Secretary of State Colin Powell

---

24 See, for example, Ali Uqleh Ursan, *al-Usbu' Al-Adabi*, September 15, 2001. Translation in MEMRI No. 275, September 25, 2001.

visited Damascus in 2001, Bashar promised him that he would not open an oil pipeline with Iraq, a move that would help Iraq to evade sanctions. A few days later, it was apparent that Bashar had lied to him and opened the pipeline.

Finally, Bashar could have taken a less extremist stance against Israel. Instead, he tried to prove that he was the most hard-line of Arab leaders. In his speech to the March 2001 Arab summit, for example, Bashar called for renewing the economic boycott, said no Israeli leader was interested in peace, and condemned all Israelis as war criminals more racist than the Nazis.[25] In front of the visiting Pope himself, Bashar made a remarkably anti-Semitic speech, claiming that the Jews "tried to kill the principles of all religions with the same mentality in which they betrayed Jesus Christ and . . . tried to betray and kill the Prophet Muhammad."[26]

It was on the home front, however, that Bashar faced his real test. Here, too, he had alternatives. In the London newspaper *al-Hayat*, the columnist Hazem Saghiya wrote an article entitled "The Speech that Bashar al-Asad Will Never Make," in which the president promises democracy and freedom in these words:[27]

The arduous times that Syria went through necessitated a regime that is no longer needed. The world has changed and so have we, or at least we should, so as to find the time to [deal with] our real problems and compensate for the long years we were busy handling problems that withheld our progress.

The Cold War has ended and sooner or later so will its Middle Eastern parallel. The [continuation of the conflict] is more harmful to us than it is to Israel, which is building a thriving technological economy while neutralizing its [internal] conflicts by the democratic means it has developed over decades.

Bashar goes on to tell his people that Syrians must "live as a normal state in a normal region." He then announces free elections, a multi-party system, the rule of law, release of political prisoners, the end of emergency laws, reduction of security controls, an anticorruption campaign, major economic reforms, and a reduced budget for the military, which has not performed well in wars. He pledges to withdraw from

25 *Tishrin*, March 28, 2001. Translation in MEMRI No. 202, April 2001.
26 *Al-Mustaqbal*, May 3, 2001; *al-Hayat*, May 4, 2001; and *al-Sharq al-Awsat*, May 6, 2001. Translation in MEMRI Inquiry and Analysis No. 56, May 24, 2001.
27 Hazem Saghiya, "The Speech that Bashar al-Asad Will Never Make," *al-Hayat*, June 25, 2000. Translation in MEMRI No. 112, July 6, 2000.

Lebanon. Once Syria took such stances, he explains, the world would support its position and Israel would be ready to make an acceptable deal.

This was, of course, not what happened. Instead, the regime proceeded to repress the opposition in a skillful way involving a minimum of violence. Much of the assault was verbal, simply letting people know that they must stop this nonsense about civil society or face serious consequences. The charge was led by those responsible for supervising the intellectuals. The Arab Writers' Association, a Stalinist-style government front group from which dissenters had resigned or been expelled, ran an article by Ahmad Ziyad Mahbak in its weekly claiming that Syria didn't need any more civil society:

> The correct meaning of the civil society must come from within our Arab culture whose roots are 4,000 [sic] years old and which will continue into the future by means of the will of the Arab people to realize its Arab identity. The meaning of a civil society cannot be imported from outside the homeland from powers that weave [plots] against this nation and have no interest in its revival or progress.[28]

From the regime's standpoint, the reform movement was not a group of people trying to make Syria better, stronger, and more prosperous but a malignant gang threatening the nation's survival. At a meeting of regime loyalists at Damascus University, Vice-President Abd al-Halim Khaddam insisted, "It is not the right of any citizen to destroy the foundations that the society is built on,"[29] warning that reforms would push Syria toward a breakdown like those in Algeria and Yugoslavia.[30] Mentioning these two specific countries was a good example of the regime's own fears, since the former had seen an explosive Islamist uprising, while the latter had been torn apart by ethnic strife.

The Islamist movement, crushed in 1982 by the army when it murdered thousands of people in the city of Hama, remained relatively quiet. But the communal issue, which was inescapably linked to the movement, still frightened the regime. The minority Alawites were the government's main beneficiaries and supporters, while the majority Sunni Muslims were

28 *Al-Usbu' al-Adabi*, December 16, 2000. Cited in Eli Carmeli and Yotam Feldner, "The Battle for Reforms and Civil Society in Syria-Part II," MEMRI Inquiry and Analysis No. 48, February 12, 2001.

29 *Al-Sharq al-Awsat*, February 18, 2001. Translated in Yotam Feldner, "The Syrian Regime vs. the Reformers Part II: The Battle of Ideas," MEMRI No. 51, February 28, 2001.

30 *Al-Hayat*, February 19, 2001. Translated in Yotam Feldner, "The Syrian Regime vs. the Reformers Part II: The Battle of Ideas," MEMRI No. 51, February 28, 2001.

not happy at losing their traditional power in Syria. Support for the Islamists – in religious terms, the Alawites' Muslim credentials were rather shaky – was one way in which the Sunnis had shown their displeasure. In addition, a large portion of private businesses were run by Sunnis (and Christians) who suffered under the regime's economic policies, which also impelled them toward a protest movement.

When Seif spoke of the need to have pluralist democracy in order to respect "the mosaic of religions and ethnic groups in Syria," he set off alarm bells in the bureaucracy. Leading government and Ba'th Party officials, such as Sulayman Kadda, warned, "Talking again about the national and religious mosaic in Syria will lead to the disintegration of the society and will harm [the state's] security and stability."[31]

According to Khaddam, himself a Sunni, this concept was a Western and U.S. plot to shatter countries by demanding self-determination for their ethnic groups. "There are no conflicts among Syria's people today but any opening of pluralism would increase that likelihood and endanger everyone." Khaddam stated that although the critics might not be conscious foreign agents, "even if their intentions are good the way to hell is still paved with good intentions."[32] Bashar didn't even leave that much of a loophole. "In criminal law," he explained, "the element of intent is significant in determining the punishment. On the level of the homeland, however, only the result determines guilt."[33]

As always, the Arab-Israeli conflict was one of the main weapons in the regime's arsenal for stifling dissent. Knowing this, the reformers carefully avoided mentioning that issue and put the focus on domestic affairs, precisely because they knew how vulnerable they would otherwise be. Still, this omission was used against them to hint that they were Zionist agents. Khaddam asked, "Was it mere coincidence that the reformers proposals did not include a single word about the Arab-Israeli conflict? Can any Syrian or Arab citizen's life be separated from what goes on in the conflict between the Arabs and Israel?"[34]

31 *Al-Sharq al-Awsat*, February 17, 2001. Translated in Yotam Feldner, "The Syrian Regime vs. the Reformers Part II: The Battle of Ideas," MEMRI No. 51, February 28, 2001.
32 *Al-Nahar*, February 19, 2001. Translation in MEMRI No. 51, February 28, 2001.
33 *Al-Sharq Al-Awsat*, February 8, 2001. Translation in MEMRI Inquiry and Analysis No. 49, February 16, 2001.
34 *Al-Sharq al-Awsat*, February 18, 2001. Translated in Yotam Feldner, "The Syrian Regime vs. the Reformers Part II: The Battle of Ideas," MEMRI No. 51, February 28, 2001.

Ali Diyab, head of the Ba'th Party's foreign affairs bureau, scolded, "The leadership and the state determine many issues in light of the conflict. Every economic, social or political measure must, at the end of the day, contribute to the solidity of Syria's position [in the conflict] and strengthen it; on the other hand, any initiative that weakens national unity and harms [these] efforts, serves the Zionist enemy."[35]

So when even Ba'th Party members asked Khaddam at a public meeting why the regime did not do more to solve the problems of corruption, incompetence, and the slow pace of reform, his answer was that the Arab-Israeli conflict permitted no changes at home. "This country is in a state of war as long as the occupation continues," agreed Information Minister Adnan Omran. "You have threats coming against Syria every day, and the capital is only 60 miles from the front line."[36]

The irony of this argument, however, was that the regime itself now had the power to end the conflict whenever it wanted to do so. In exchange for peace, Syria had been offered the return of every square inch of the Golan Heights. Was the real issue preventing a diplomatic resolution Syria's need for twelve square miles of land on Israel's side of the international border, or was the endless state of war really the government's insurance policy against domestic problems?

Instead of dealing with Syria's real issues, the rulers were given the opportunity to parade their own patriotic demagoguery and steadfastness at every opportunity. Bashar roared, "An inch of land is like a kilometer and that in turn is like a thousand kilometers. A country that concedes even a tiny part of its territory, is bound to concede a much bigger part in the future. . . . Land is an issue of honor not meters." And he added that this was his inheritance: "President Hafez al-Asad did not give in," boasted Bashar, "and neither shall we; neither today nor in the future."[37]

Nor would he give in to the demands for reform. In January 2001, Information Minister Adnan Omran proclaimed that, like ethnic pluralism, civil society was an "American term." Noting that the Egyptian scholar Saad Eddin Ibrahim was then on trial in Egypt for "receiving money from foreign countries" and the (false) charge of performing

---

35 *Al-Hayat*, January 21, 2001. Translated in Yotam Feldner, "The Syrian Regime vs. the Reformers Part II: The Battle of Ideas," MEMRI No. 51, February 28, 2001.

36 *New York Times*, March 12, 2001.

37 *Al-Sharq al-Awsat*, February 8, 2001 Translation in MEMRI Inquiry and Analysis No. 49, February 16, 2001.

"security missions at the behest of foreign sides," Omran declared that "neocolonialism no longer relies on armies." The implication was that the reformers were traitors and might soon find themselves in a court-room. The very next day, one of the main organizers of the civil society committees, the novelist Nabil Sulayman, was attacked by two assailants and badly beaten.[38]

The government reminded the public that martial law made it illegal for more than five people to gather for a political meeting without a permit. In order to obtain a permit, security agencies must be given two weeks' advance notice of any gathering, the speaker's name, a copy of the speech, and a complete list of attendees. Bashar explained that no timetable for the development process can be set because it depends on the "natural development of the society." And he admitted, "The development of civil society institutions is not one of my priorities."[39]

In March 2002, a Syrian court sentenced Maamoun al-Homsi, a leading opposition member of parliament, to five years in prison on charges of trying to change the constitution by illegal means. His only crime was to publish a manifesto asking the government to end high-level corruption and to restrain the security services. Riad Seif was also arrested in the autumn of 2001.[40]

The challenge was basically ended, and probably for many years to come. As'ad Naim, an exiled Syrian scholar, had predicted that the reformers, being insiders who had benefited from the regime in the past, were bound to return, "so that we can continue our lives as we lived them over the last thirty years, God forbid."[41] This was precisely what seemed to be happening. A critical opportunity for progress had been thrown away. Syria seemed to be set to continue following all of the ideas, policies, and leaders that had served it so badly for so long.

---

38 Gary Gambill, "Dark Days Ahead for Syria's Liberal Reformers," *Middle East Intelligence Bulletin*, Vol. 3, No. 2 (February 2001).
39 *Al-Sharq al-Awsat*, February 8, 2001. Translation in MEMRI Inquiry and Analysis No. 49, February 16, 2001.
40 BBC report, March 20, 2002. http://news.bbc.co.uk/hi/english/world/middle_east/newsid_1883000/1883891.stm.
41 *Al-Quds al-Arabi*, February 19, 2001. Translation in MEMRI Inquiry and Analysis No. 49, February 16, 2001.

5

IRAN

The People versus the Will of God?

Iran's Islamic revolution was an earthquake that shook the Middle East and seemed permanently to reshape Iran itself. Yet 20 years after its apparent total victory, the revolution's failures sparked a protest movement that captured some of the nation's institutions and won support from most of its people. Still, Iran did not become an example of a successful transition to democracy and moderation, but just another case of a dictatorial system, like those in the Arab world, that was very good at keeping power but not at much else. The most remarkable thing about postrevolutionary Iran was the dramatic rise of popular democratic expression coupled with its total ineffectiveness in altering the country's system and structure.

In many ways, Iran followed the pattern of the Arab world. The regime used the same basic techniques employed by its counterparts there. For Iran, as for the Arab states, the 1990s did not bring reform or a functioning democracy, even if, in contrast to Arab states, the masses were openly on the side of change. Modernization was blocked, radical foreign policies (though more cautious in deed than in rhetoric) prevailed, and dictatorship survived. Yet there were also significant differences. In Iran, the system faced far more serious challenges. Power was divided, and democratic forces were far stronger. Still, despite the partial change and hope visible in Iran, it too has been stuck in the process of shifting paradigms. The government accepted the result of relatively free elections, but then blocked them from having any real effect.

Why was Iran different from the Arab world? It is impossible to understand all of the historical, cultural, and other factors. What can be said is that the trump issues that worked so well in the Arab world – and that had also been effective in Iran at the time of the revolution – were now weaker there. An opposition that could be neither Islamist nor radical Arab nationalist almost inevitably had to become democratic. The regime still claimed that America and Israel were deadly enemies whose threat justified hard-line policies and whose evil nature disqualified the Western system as an option for Iran. Islam was said to be under assault by secularism and the West so that defending it required limits on freedom, rule by the radical faction, and suppression of domestic forces that demanded too much change.

But these arguments did not work so well in Iran. Islam was already in power, but by the same token it could not be idealized by the opposition as a system of government that would solve every problem. The Palestinian issue was promoted heavily, but it was also more distant and echoed less passionately with a non-Arab public.

Arab nationalism was not an option in Iran, of course. While benefiting to some extent from Iranian patriotic sentiments, the regime's Islamic orientation reduced its ability to use nationalism as a justification. "Race and nationalism," Khomeini had said, were themes promoted by foreigners and their allied local traitors in order to divide Muslims. "To love one's fatherland and its people and to protect its frontiers are both quite unobjectionable, but nationalism, involving hostility to other Muslim nations, is something quite different" and contrary to the Qur'an and Muhammad's teachings.[1]

Another reason for discontent was the fact that, as in the Arab states, Iran's regime had suffered a number of setbacks and failures, mostly of its own making. True, it was not directly responsible for the costly Iran-Iraq war, but its provocative revolutionary rhetoric, purges of the military, and break with Iran's U.S. protector had encouraged Iraq to attack. Even after the war ended, the regime's policies had contributed to high unemployment, resentment at its social restrictions, disillusionment with corruption, and demoralization at the failure of radical utopian expectations. Abroad, Iran had failed to spread its revolution.

The regime, however, was not without its assets. Even by the year 2000, about 25 percent of the population still felt the political enthusiasm of earlier times and liked the Islamist creed. Many individuals had benefited personally from the opportunities and upward mobility brought

---

1 Hamid Algar, ed., *Islam and Revolution: Writings and Declarations of Imam Khomeini* (Berkeley, CA, 1981). p. 302.

about by the revolution. Others knew that the government's patronage would help their careers or ensure their livelihoods. The dominant radical faction[2] still dominated the security forces, controlled the media, and managed the massive financial assets of semiofficial foundations. The moderates also understood that the radicals were willing to fight, while their own leadership feared a confrontation.

In this context, the reform movement had a leader who was effective at winning popular support but ineffective at winning the factional battle. President Muhammad Khatami emerged very much from within the Islamist ruling establishment. His father was a close friend of Ayatollah Khomeini, and Khatami himself is an Islamic cleric, albeit one who had studied Western philosophy in Germany and spoke both German and English. He had been cultural adviser to his predecessor, President Hashemi Rafsanjani, and head of Iran's National Library.

By training, personality, and worldview, he should have been the ideal leader to move Iran forward. He proposed a synthesis between Iran's society, including its brand of Islam, and the modern, heavily Western-influenced world. Khatami did not fear this challenge, nor did he view the West as necessarily inimical. Rather than seeing the borrowing of Western ideas and institutions as a zero-sum game, he thought that a "dialogue of civilizations" would be a two-way exchange of ideas through which Iran could also influence the West.[3]

According to Khatami's vision, Iran required a major transition. In the first stage, the revolution had overthrown a conservative monarchy that was seen as being too accommodating to the West and its political demands. The revolution had then ensured Iran's stability and identity. From this secure base, Iran could now afford to move into a second stage in which it might adapt appropriate Western ideas without being subverted by the West. Economic and political pluralism, the rule of law, and civil rights were absolutely essential for Iran's further development. If this did not happen, the revolution would have produced only a new

2 I prefer the label "radical" rather than "conservative" for the dominant Iranian faction. While it may be said to be "conservative" in maintaining the status quo that preserves its power and opposing major social changes, the faction's domestic and international goals remain radical in the tradition of Khomeini.

3 Interview with CNN, January 7, 1998. http://www.cnn.com/WORLD/9801/07/iran/interview.html.

oppressive dictatorship with its own corrupt elite governing on the basis of a rigid dogma.

Rather than being a threat to the revolution, Khatami thought, democracy would allow for its true fulfillment. Rather than ensuring the rejection of the West, the revolution would make it possible for Iran to stand up to the West as an equal, taking what it wanted without fear that borrowing requires submission and securing Iran's proper place in the world as an important power. These are concepts quite common among leaders everywhere in Africa, Asia, and Latin America, but not in the Middle East. The more one analyzes Khatami's approach, the more striking it is that there is no Arab Khatami.

At the same time, Khatami himself had very severe limits as a political leader ready to challenge the existing order. He was a mild-mannered intellectual, not a fighter. Khatami was also personally very much a part of the Islamist regime and wanted to reform rather than to destroy it. After all, he saw the reforms that he wanted to implement as being built on the Islamist revolution's achievements, not opposed to them. Nor did he want to be responsible for the massive bloodshed and destruction that a civil war would entail. Consequently, when the radicals gave him a choice between submitting to their sabotage or sanctioning rebellion, he always acquiesced. Within four years of his political career's start, he accepted his inability to use his movement's overwhelming electoral majorities to make actual reforms. Once Khatami himself gave up, the movement was at a dead end.

Things had begun very differently. In May 1997, Khatami was first elected with a landslide 74.5 percent of the votes, including strong backing from women and young people generally,[4] in a remarkable turnout including 91 percent of the eligible voters. Some of his supporters had such high expectations that they called that victory Iran's second revolution. He won so overwhelmingly despite the fact that his radical opponent had the regime's covert funding, backing from its media, and help from the security forces. Khatami also had strong support from like-minded reformers in parliament, many of whom wanted to go further and faster than he did. Yet

---

4 On the election results, see "Statistical Breakdown of Seventh Presidential Elections in May 23, 1997" (Khordad 2, 1376), *Salaam*, May 31, 1997, p. 7. http://persia.org/khatami/elections.html.

almost nothing happened, and the great expectations of change were disappointed.

The problem was not Khatami's lack of vision, nor was it any lack of readiness or support for him by the masses. Khatami's visit to a Tehran fair in May 1998 provided a typical example of his views and the popular response. As he arrived, the audience chanted, "Khatami is a hero – the hope of young people" and "Khatami, may God save you." He told the crowd the current task was "the consolidation of the system . . . when everything should be carried out in keeping with the law." Freedom was "the greatest element, which has always been sought by the human race." Yet freedom had to be kept in balance. Some of its enemies were "against freedom," seeking to limit it too much. Others wanted to abuse it by going too far. Khatami saw the middle ground as requiring moderation, avoiding either change that was too rapid or violent conflict. [5]

"We should all try to enhance our tolerance," Khatami explained. He wanted to create a free, law-abiding society. Perhaps, though, escalating the struggle too far could undermine that very objective. "We should try to pass through this critical juncture with tolerance and patience. And, God willing, establish a dynamic society, as our people and revolution deserve." [6]

The problem was, though, that the hard-line faction would offer tolerance and patience only if it could ensure that the revolution would not gain real power. His argument was that tolerance was the basis of stability, while his rivals had precisely the opposite viewpoint.

When we speak of a civil society it means that different institutions, representing different inclinations and thoughts, should exist and . . . have the opportunity to raise their voices and to express their views so that their words can be compared. What creates problems is not the diversity of inclinations and thoughts – the existence of diversity is a necessity of a dynamic society. . . . It is bad to hide one's inclination behind religion and sanctities, to present oneself as the embodiment of religion and sanctities, and to accuse others of being against religion, it is also bad to hide oneself behind freedom, to consider oneself the embodiment of freedom, and to accuse those who are against one of being the opponents of freedom and the supporters of suppression.[7]

5 Tehran, IRIB television, *First Program*, May 14, 1998. Translation in FBIS.
6 Ibid.
7 Ibid.

Whatever Khatami believed about the revolution, however, was totally antithetical to the views held by Khomeini and those who had led the revolt against the shah's regime. They had no interest in tolerating thoughts at variance with their own, ideas they considered to be opposed to God's will and representing the evil West. They had no interest in submitting their ideology to the test of free competition with others. When he accused the radicals of hiding behind religion and using it as a weapon against opponents, Khatami was challenging the regime's most basic trump idea, which it would never give up.

Khatami made similar points to the entire Islamic world at the December 1997 meeting of the Organization of Islamic Countries, held in Tehran. Since Islamic and Western societies were "not necessarily in conflict and contradiction," Muslims "should never be oblivious to judicious acquisition of the positive accomplishments of the Western civil society." He called for tolerance between Muslims and the West and also among countries with Muslim populations: "Living in peace and security can be realized only when one fully understands not only the culture and thinking but also the concerns as well as the ways and manners of others."[8]

Literally none of the other Middle Eastern leaders at the meeting thought in such terms. This kind of cultural synthesis, so accepted in other regions that one hardly needed to speak of it, was totally taboo in the Middle East. As in his advocacy of democracy, Khatami was asking them to give up a trump issue that was one of the main pillars of their rule.

To some extent, Khatami's views on the United States were more typical of his colleagues'. Iran, he stated, would never bow to the United States. "The fruit of our revolution is that we have freed ourselves from the yoke of our masters, and we will never submit to any new one. Today we are building our country ourselves, if we have shortcomings, they belong to United States and we can remove them."[9] But precisely because of this alleged victory, Iran no longer had to be afraid of America or to fight it. Again, Khatami was virtually alone. He might accept the consensus that America wanted to make everyone submit

---

8 "Mohammad Khatami, speech to Eighth Islamic Summit Conference, December 9, 1997, available on the website of the presidency of the Islamic Republic of Iran, http://www.president.ir/khatami/speeches/760918.htm.
9 Ibid.

and that the United States was responsible for everything bad in his country. But while Arab leaders frequently shouted defiance at America, the idea that friendship could be reached by treating it as an equal was totally alien to them.

Finally, and worst of all from the standpoint of his counterparts, Khatami also emphasized the need for tolerance and democracy within each country: "In the civil society that we espouse, although centered around the axis of Islamic thinking and culture . . . personal or group dictatorship or even the tyranny of the majority and the elimination of the minority has no place."[10] In effect, this was a call to overturn every regime in the Arab world.

The sharpest possible rejection of Khatami's ideas was given at the same meeting by his own colleague, Iran's spiritual guide and most powerful leader, Ali Khamenei. He responded that no rapprochement was possible with the West, whose "civilization is directing everyone towards materialism while money, gluttony and carnal desires are made the greatest aspirations."[11] Western influence had replaced sincerity, truthfulness, altruism, and self-sacrifice in many parts of the world, leaving in their place deception, conspiracy, avarice, jealousy, and other indecent features. And no dialogue was needed, because Iran and Islam had nothing to learn from the West. Any attempt at borrowing or synthesis would simply water down and poison their country's identity and independence.

Like his Arab counterparts, Khamenei viewed the West, not internal factors, as the cause of all the problems of his country and the region: "Most nations are deprived of scientific progress while a group [has] used their science and knowledge as a means to mete out oppression on others."[12] The implications here are typical of Middle Eastern doctrines, yet quite shocking nonetheless. Khamenei was charging that the West had not only plotted to dominate the Middle East and the world as a whole, but had also deliberately worked to hold back everyone else. By the end of the twentieth century, at a time when so many countries were advancing quickly by developing science and technology, such paranoid views were held only by marginal and crank elements

10 Ibid.
11 Speech at the opening ceremony of the eighth OIC summit meeting, Tehran, December 9, 1997. Translation in FBIS.
12 Ibid.

outside of the Middle East. Knowledge flowed freely throughout the world – except perhaps for the details of certain advanced weapons systems. Middle Eastern oil producers could buy anything they wanted; Middle Eastern students could study any subject throughout the West. Yet this had little effect on the official ideologies of the region's states.

"Western liberalism, communism, socialism and all other 'isms' have gone through their tests and proved their debility," Khamenei continued. "As in the past, so today, Islam is the only remedial, curative and savior angel." At a time when, whatever the shortcomings of the Western model, it was the ideal for imitation everywhere else in the Third World, only Middle Eastern ideologues and leaders viewed it as a failure. But, Khamenei concluded, why expect anything from the West or care what it thought, since "the notorious global Zionist media and . . . in particular the Americans" were trying to destroy the Iranian revolution.[13]

Thus, Khamenei and his allies sought to block Khatami's program both because of their own desire to hold onto power and because they viewed his ideas as extremely dangerous, even treasonous. Although Khatami could respond that his proposals were appropriate for the revolution's new stage, there is no question that Khomeini, the revolution's founder, would have rejected them with scorn and anger. For while Khatami was confident of Iran's ability to accept Western ideas, more cultural openness, and democracy, Khomeini had been dead set against any such notion. He wanted to build a wall around Iran, because without such a fortification he seemed to doubt whether Iran itself, the Islamic republic, or his version of Islam could survive at all.

Khomeini had explained his views on these matters in the clearest possible terms. For example, in 1980 – using words equally applicable 20 years later – he had claimed that Western propaganda against Islam and Iran was "intended to show that the revolution of Iran cannot administer our country or that the Iranian government is about to fall, since Iran supposedly lacks a healthy economy, proper educational system, disciplined army, and armed forces ready for combat." He had rejected this idea that "Islam in the present day is incapable of administering a country." In fact, he asserted that the revolution had inherited a "ruined and backward" state and then – despite many American

13 Ibid.

plots – had achieved great success in improving the situation. This should not be surprising, he concluded, since "Islam . . . for several centuries ruled over more than half the populated areas of the globe."[14]

Certainly, Khomeini was right that the system he had put in place could last, and that predictions of the Islamic republic's collapse were greatly exaggerated. But it was not some pure Islamic system, but rather one ruled by Islamists in which survival required many compromises, as had happened with other ideological revolutions. One important clue to this contradiction was Khomeini's claim that Islam had ruled for centuries. What might be called theocratic rule by Islam through its clerical experts – the system Khomeini favored for Iran and even for the whole world – had not lasted long at all. What did endure for centuries was the rule of political elites that used Islam as a support system and rationale to varying degrees. Indeed, this historic pattern was a structure that had a great deal more in common with contemporary Arab regimes than it did with the Islamic Republic of Iran.

At any rate, despite Khomeini's claims of both material and spiritual success, Iran's real problem was not that Western propaganda criticized the Islamic republic and found its government inadequate and incompetent, but the fact that its own citizens voiced these same complaints. The priorities, goals, and desires of the country's majority epitomized everything Khomeini detested. They demanded the freedom that he saw as corruption and immorality. Khatami and the reform movement were Khomeini's worst nightmare, a revival of the ideas and forces that he had hoped the Islamist revolution would stamp out forever. Intellectuals and professionals were now demanding the very freedoms that Khomeini had denounced as representing "infatuation with the West" and acting like those he had accused of being "in the pay of foreigners."[15]

Khatami, however, was certainly responding to dramatic social changes that were transforming Iran. By the year 2000, a majority of Iran's people were too young to remember the revolution, much less the rule of the shah. Their complaints were against the only government and system they had ever known – a revolutionary Islamist, not a monarchical one. Moreover, as elsewhere in the Middle East, massive

14 Ayatollah Ruhollah Khomeini, "Message to the Pilgrims," *Jumhuri-yi Islami*, September 13, 1980, in Algar, ed., *Islam and Revolution*, p. 303.
15 Ibid.

population growth and urbanization required more jobs, housing, and education. The radical regime has failed to meet these needs.

During the 1990s, when oil prices were low, Iran was in very bad economic shape, with high inflation, major unemployment, and a weak currency. Iran had not made full use of its potential assets as the world's third largest oil exporter, with 10 percent of the globe's proven reserves. Much of the problem had stemmed from government policies that discouraged economic growth. Khatami called Iran's highly centralized command-style economy "sick" and advocated diversification, privatization, and foreign investment.[16] The radicals defended the system as more conducive to social justice and national independence. They were suspicious of foreign investment as bringing political and cultural subversion, and when the government did negotiate with foreign companies, its demands were usually enough to discourage them from making deals. U.S. sanctions, a response to the regime's radical policies, and the subsequent reduced access to international capital markets made matters worse. While higher oil prices after 2000 helped Iran somewhat, Khatami was unable to make any economic reforms whatsoever.

The same situation prevailed in other aspects of Iranian life. Independent newspapers opened, criticized the radicals' policies and behavior, and were then shut down, with staff members sometimes imprisoned. They then reopened under other names, and the cycle repeated itself.[17] Tehran's popular mayor, a strong Khatami supporter, was arrested on trumped-up charges and sentenced to a prison term. Students now chanted, "Khatami, Khatami, where are you?" And Khatami accused his own supporters of, "attacking the foundations of the regime and . . . wanting to foment tensions and disorders." He warned, "Deviations will be repressed with force and determination."[18]

There were other signs that the hard-liners' stance was growing harder. During a meeting with his top officers, Yahya Rahim Safavi, the

16 Reuters, June 15, 1998.
17 Regarding the Iranian media, see A. W. Samii, "The Contemporary Iranian News Media, 1998–1999", *MERIA Journal*, Vol. 3, No. 4 (December 1999), pp. 1–10; and A. W. Samii, "Sisyphus' Newsstand: The Iranian Press under Khatami," *MERIA Journal*, Vol. 5, No. 3 (September 2001), pp. 1–11.
18 Azar Nafisi, "Voices of Iran," *Washington Post*, July 15, 1999.

commander of the Islamic Revolutionary Guards Corps (IRGC), attacked Khatami's government for letting newspapers criticize the radicals and for not crushing student unrest in Tehran or arresting critics of clerical rule. Safavi bitterly complained that "[l]iberals . . . have taken over our universities and our youth are now shouting slogans against despotism. We are seeking to root out counter-revolutionaries wherever they are. We have to behead some and cut off the tongues of others. Our language is our sword. We will expose these cowards."[19]

Safavi also condemned the government's foreign policy, brandishing some of the usual trump issues: "Can we withstand American threats and domineering attitude with a policy of detente? Can we foil dangers coming from America through dialogue between civilizations? Will we be able to protect the Islamic Republic from international Zionism by signing conventions to ban proliferation of chemical and nuclear weapons?"[20] As in the Arab states, the regime argued that reforms could not be made because they were a dangerous and unaffordable luxury during the permanent conflict.

The threat to the regime came, however, not from "international Zionism" but from its own people. On July 11, 1999, tens of thousands of students demonstrated to protest against the security forces' attacks and beatings on the campus of Tehran University. Khatami criticized the behavior of the regime's police and fired an officer involved, but then called for an end to demonstrations. As the number of protesters increased and demonstrations spread to other cities, so did their demands. With Khatami's support, the government banned demonstrations. Street battles broke out for several days. The regime organized a massive rally to support itself. Worried about the growing discontent, top IRGC commanders wrote a letter threatening Khatami. But their action was unnecessary. Quiet returned, and Khatami did not use his popularity or the anger of his large constituency to challenge the existing order.[21] Once again, the people had spoken, but the hard-liners had won. Khatami was a reformer, but he was certainly no revolutionary.

19 Michael Eisenstadt, "Revolutionary Guard Commander Sends a Warning," *Policy-watch* No. 314, May 7, 1998.
20 Ibid.
21 On the regime's threats and actions against the students, see "Iran Threatens Revolutionary Court Trials for 'Incitement,'" Human Rights Watch, New York, August 3, 1999. http://www.hrw.org/press/1999/aug/irano803.htm.

The reformers did very well in the March 1999 municipal elections, and after similar successes in the February 2000 parliamentary election, a close Khatami associate said, "The most important business of the [new parliament] will be to rewrite, amend and adopt certain judicial procedure laws and other laws."[22] But once again nothing happened, and for all practical purposes this victory was useless. The same thing occurred again after Khatami's overwhelming reelection triumph in June 2001, an election in which he received a remarkable 78.3 percent of the votes, though apparently disillusionment significantly lowered participation compared to 1997, as turnout was only about 67 percent.[23]

The hard-liners consistently outmaneuvered the reformists. Just before the previous parliament had ended, they had passed a law forcing journalists to reveal their sources or face arrest. Shortly after the 2000 parliamentary election, the Expediency Council, one of the many nonelected or semielected bodies that really ruled Iran, took away parliament's right to investigate institutions controlled by the radicals. These included the IRGC, the state-controlled broadcasting authority, and the fabulously financed foundations that controlled much of the nation's wealth. This action violated Article 76 of the Iranian Constitution, which said that parliament (the Islamic Consultative Assembly, the Majlis) had the right to investigate anything it wished.[24]

Thus, the reformists' election victories were negated, key institutions were kept under the hard-liners' unquestioned control, and large-scale corruption was protected from scrutiny. Khamenei repeatedly went on the offensive. For example, he addressed the regime's semi-vigilante Basij forces on April 14, 2000, at a Friday prayer meeting. He told them: "The country's constitution and main policies are insulted, small events are magnified. The atmosphere is filled with libel." Meanwhile, Khatami retreated. "Iran needs tranquility," he explained. "Debate and criticism do not mean pushing the country into

22 Cited in Gary Sick, "Iran's Elections: Out of Chaos, Change," *Middle East Economic Survey*, February 28, 2000. On the 1999 municipal elections, see "Iran Reformers Score Another Big Win, Sweep Tehran Elections," *The Iranian*, March 8, 1999, http://www.iranian.com/News/March99/sweep.html. For results of the February 2000 parliamentary elections, see A. W. Samii, "Iran's 2000 Elections," *MERIA Journal*, Vol. 4, No. 1 (March 2000).
23 For the 2001 election statistics, see http://www.iranmania.com/elections/.
24 Siamak Namazi, "The IRGC, Khamenei, and the Fate of Iran's Reform Movement," *Gulf* 2000, April 23, 2000.

chaos. Writers are responsible for guiding the country towards tranquility. . . . No action should be taken which may worry the leader [Khamenei], the nation, the faithful and the youth [about national security]."[25]

Indeed, after four remarkable victories at the polls – twice for president, and in parliamentary and municipal elections – Khatami and his allies failed to make a single major change in any Iranian law. If all of these successes did no good, it was clear that elections would never change anything in the future either. Whatever his good intentions, Khatami was powerless at best, and at worst had given up trying to institute reforms, much less a far-reaching restructuring of the government or society.

Thus, while he was the radical regime's greatest challenger, he was also in some ways its best asset. Unquestionably, there was more freedom of speech in Iran, but not much more ability to change anything. By providing anti-regime elements with such a good safety valve by letting them voice their complaints, he had in effect defused the internal conflict. His failure so discouraged the regime's opponents that many sank into passivity. Moreover, while it was quite understandable that Khatami and his followers did not want a civil war, bloodshed, and destruction, the hard-liners' monopoly on violence assured their continued rule.

Khamenei's personal and bureaucratic position was also unassailable. He had been a leading revolutionary imprisoned under the shah's regime, elevated by Khomeini to a leadership position in 1979, and wounded in an opposition bomb attack against the Islamic regime in 1981. After serving eight years as president, Khamenei was named to be Khomeini's successor as the revolution's spiritual guide in 1989. Khomeini himself had designed the system to assure the political primacy of the spiritual guide – as a man who knew God's intentions – over the president, who merely reflected the fallible will of the people.

Khamenei was not popular among the masses, but he didn't have to be. Khatami might be president, but Khamenei was the country's real leader. He remained commander of the armed forces, the state-controlled media, the court system, the intelligence apparatus (including foreign subversion), and the nuclear and missile programs. The IRGC and Basij forces were ready to back him up with their guns. The candidate

25 Ibid.

whom Khatami had defeated at the polls the first time, Khamenei's ally Ali Akbar Nateq Nouri, was speaker of parliament, and hard-liners could even depend on a comfortable legislative majority on most issues.

If any reform legislation did get through, it could be rejected by the radical Council of Guardians, appointed by Khamenei, which also supervised elections and had the power to veto prospective candidates. Khatami's own predecessor, Ali Akbar Hashemi Rafsanjani, headed the Expediency Council, which was more centrist but could also block or slow change. When in 1997 Khatami removed General Mohsen Rezai, the IRGC's head for sixteen years who was openly hostile to him, Khamenei appointed Rezai to a powerful post as the Expediency Council's deputy leader.[26]

Even Khatami's minister of defense for a while, Admiral Ali Shamkani, was a hard-liner. Khatami fired Minister of Intelligence and Security Ali Fallahian, who had been involved in terrorist activities abroad and violent repression of dissidents at home. But hard-liners forced the resignation of Abdallah Nuri, Khatami's popular interior minister, in 1998, and then jailed him for five years beginning in November 1999 on charges of spreading anti-Islamic propaganda in his newspaper.[27]

The cards were thus very much stacked against Khatami and his allies. In response to all the legal and extralegal measures taken against him and his followers, Khatami could only express his sorrow and call for patience.

Regarding Iran's foreign policy, Khatami did not even do that. Under the radicals' rule, Iran still tried to spread revolution and increase its regional influence. Like its Arab counterparts, however, the regime usually combined militant rhetoric with caution. Also like those other states, Iran's government spoke in the name of ideology – Islamism – while acting for its own benefit. As with the Soviet Union, doctrine was used as a cover in the pursuit of national and regime interests. Khatami was useful to the hard-liners, as he allowed the regime to portray Iran as a moderate and democratic state even as it

---

26 *Jane's Defense Weekly*, November 12, 1998, p. 30; Reuters, September 10, 1997; *Washington Times*, September 10, 1997.

27 "Khatami May Face Uphill Task for Musavi-Lari'a Approval," *Tehran Times*, July 16, 1998, http://www.salamiran.org/Media/TehranTimes/980716.html#HLN13;. "Jailed Leader Enters Iranian Poll Contest," *The Dawn*, December 14, 1999, http://www.dawn.com/1999/19991215/int1.htm.

continued to take extremist actions in subverting Middle Eastern governments, sabotaging the Arab-Israeli peace process, fomenting terrorism, assassinating dissidents abroad, and developing long-range missiles and nuclear weapons.

After an initial period of enthusiasm and expectation of imminent revolution everywhere, Tehran settled down to a more cautious strategy designed to avoid risking the regime's own survival by using violence in a covert and deniable manner. Radical movements were backed among the Lebanese and the Palestinians to strike against Israel, and elsewhere to try to seize leadership among their people and thereby make more Islamist revolutions. Khatami and other Iranian officials met frequently with leaders of Palestinian, Lebanese, and Egyptian terrorist groups. From time to time, Iran also held summit meetings to encourage and coordinate terrorist groups and give them aid.[28] A similar strategy, albeit on a smaller scale, was periodically used against the Gulf Arab monarchies and the American presence there. Iran also reportedly helped Islamist revolutionaries in Algeria and Egypt.[29]

Terrorism was also used by Iran's regime to eliminate dissidents abroad, as a way to "defend" the revolution; the number of those killed was estimated at 350 by a British parliamentary report.[30] These killings apparently included the murder of two former education ministers involved in dissident activities in France, in 1990 and 1996.[31] The semiofficial Fifteen Khordad Foundation put up a $2.5 million reward for the murder of Salman Rushdie, a British citizen who had written a novel ridiculing Khomeini, who, in turn, ordered his assassination, accusing him of insulting Islam's founder.[32]

28 Hillary Mann, "Iranian Links to International Terrorism: The Khatami Era," *Policywatch* No. 296, January 1998.
29 See Chapter 7 of this volume.
30 James Bruce, "New Strains in Iran's Links with Germany, France" Defenseweb, Pollux Publishing, 1996, http://www.pollux.com/defenseweb/1996/oct96/iran!.htm.
31 Foundation for Democracy in Iran (FDI), "FDI Condemns EU Laxism for Mazlouman Assassination," Action Memorandum 014, May 28, 1996. http://www.iran.org/humanrights/960528.html; and Thomas Sanction, "Iran's State of Terror," *Time Europe*, November 11, 1996.
32 Barbara Crossette, "Iran Drops Rushdie Death Threat, and Britain Renews Teheran Ties," *New York Times*, September 25, 1998, http://www.ishipress.com/fatwa.htm; Benjamin Graves, "Vilifying Islam: The Rushdie Media-Spectacle," Victorian Web, Singapore, 1998, http://65.107.211.206/post/rushdie/satanic1.html.

In September 1992, four Iranian Kurdish nationalist leaders were shot dead at the Mykonos restaurant in Berlin. After investigation, a German court concluded that the attack had been ordered by "the highest levels in Tehran" and "Iran's political leadership." The court issued an arrest warrant in 1997 for Fallahian, whom it accused of being responsible for the plot. Germany's intelligence chief said that Fallahian had pressured him to influence the trial's outcome.[33] Shortly thereafter, Iranian secret police burst into the Tehran apartment of the German cultural attaché during a dinner party with Iranian writers, threatened him with violence, locked him in a room, and took away his guests for questioning about subversive activities.[34]

The European states largely ignored Iran's subversive and terrorist activities, partly because they believed that Khatami would change everything. These countries argued that a "critical dialogue" could persuade Iran's rulers to change their policies. But Iran reacted defiantly to any criticism, while profiting mightily from the absence of pressure. When European Union (EU) countries recalled their ambassadors from Tehran in response to the Mykonos case, Iran did the same in retaliation. When the EU wanted to return the ambassadors after only one month, Tehran refused to take back the German ambassador. German Foreign Minister Klaus Kinkel tried to appease Iran by professing that the Europeans were trying to reduce U.S. economic sanctions against Iran. Three months later, the EU accepted a humiliating compromise in which ambassadors would return to Tehran, but with the German envoy being "punished" by having to come back last. What had begun as an EU effort to punish Iran for fomenting terrorism ended with Iran punishing Germany for raising the issue.[35]

Commercial considerations were certainly an important factor in the Europeans taking a soft line toward Iran. In 1995, the EU had exported $11.5 billon worth of goods to Iran and bought almost $17.5 billion

---

33 Evangelos Antonaros, "Iran and the West," *Thesis*, Vol. 1, No. 2 (Summer 1997), pp. 26–33.

34 Kenneth R. Timmerman, "Writer's Fate Tests Iran and Europe," *Wall Street Journal Europe*, July 23, 1997. http://www.iran.org/news/WSJe_970723.htm.

35 "Iran Forbids German Ambassador's Return," *German News* (English edition), April 30, 1997, http://www.mathematik.uni-ulm.de/de-news/1997/04/301800.html; Hamid Reza Shokoohi, "A Glance at Four Years of Foreign Policy of Khatami Administration (Part I)" *Azma: Cultural, Social & Political (Weekly)*, June 2001, http://www.netiran.com/Htdocs/Clippings/FPolitics/010630XXFP01.html.

worth of Iranian oil and gas. After a meeting with high-level Iranian officials, French Foreign Minister Yves de Charet said that France was determined to become Iran's largest trading partner.[36]

Ironically, when in 1997 there was a scare that consuming Iranian pistachio nuts might cause cancer, the EU immediately banned their import.[37] By contrast, Iranian sponsorship of terrorism and human rights violations were not thought to require any strong action. Iran clearly believed it possible to intimidate Europe by responding to criticism with veiled threats of terrorism. This was the exact opposite of what critical dialogue was supposed to do. Instead of the Europeans charming and persuading Iran into changing its behavior, Iran was more successful in intimidating and pressuring Europe into acting differently. This European policy sent no message to the radicals that they needed to change policy in order to engage in commerce, nor did it help Khatami and the reform cause at all. Once it became clear that Khatami was unable to change anything, the Europeans did not reevaluate their theory that a soft line on Iran would help the moderates.

While belief in the erroneous notion that Iran was moderating its behavior reached its peak after Khatami's election in 1997, the two faces of Iranian policy were visible as early as the mid-1980s. In 1985, Rafsanjani had urged "prudence" and said that Iran would someday renew diplomatic relations with the United States, once it showed "repentance for the wrongs it has done in the past."[38] Yet soon thereafter, then Prime Minister Mir-Hussein Musavi told the Gulf monarchies, "You are facing a revolution that has roots in all countries and . . . the populations of your countries are less than that of Tehran alone."[39]

Despite the fact that the Gulf Arab states supported Iraq against Iran during the 1980–88 Iran-Iraq war, Saddam's invasion of Kuwait in 1990 gave Tehran a wonderful opportunity in the area. Tehran seized the chance to improve relations with Saudi Arabia and the other Gulf Arab states with a fair degree of success.[40] Meanwhile, the United States had

36 *Middle East Economic Digest*, August 12, 1995, and November 10, 1996; *Middle East Economic Survey*, February 11, 1997; *Middle East*, December 1996.
37 Associated Press, "Iran Claims U.S. Behind European Ban on Its Pistachios," October 19, 1997, http://www.farsinet.com/news/oct97.html; *The Economist*, September 20, 1997.
38 *Iran Times*, July 12, 1985.
39 *Iran Times*, March 14, 1986.
40 See Chapter 5 of this volume.

defeated Iran's enemy, Iraq, without Tehran having to do anything, a process that would be repeated a decade later when America overthrew another troublesome Iranian neighbor, Afghanistan's Taliban regime. In both cases, Iran benefited while continuing to attack American actions and presence.

As with other issues, Iranian restraint in practice did not mean moderation of its goals. Iran sought to use its enhanced relations with the Gulf Arab monarchies to press them for the removal of the U.S. forces protecting them from Iraq, and from Iran as well. At the 1997 conference of the Organization of Islamic Countries, Khatami urged the Gulf states to rid themselves of "foreign forces" and instead base their defense on a pact among local countries – presumably excluding Iraq – a situation that would leave Iran as arbiter of the area's future. Khamenei expressed a similar stance in harsher language, warning of America's "poisonous breath" and calling on the area's nations to "force the aliens to dispense with this intervention and . . . eliminate the pretexts for this improper presence."[41] The desire to drive America from the Gulf was apparently not limited to words, as U.S. officials became convinced of Iran's involvement in the attack on the Khobar Towers residential complex in Saudi Arabia in 1996 that killed nineteen American servicemen.[42]

Khatami would not challenge Iran's subversive and terror-sponsoring activities, which were the underlying cause of the U.S. sanctions, and was seriously constrained from any rapprochement with the United States, though he clearly favored such steps. Debates over foreign policy were more limited than those over domestic alternatives, though some even began to question the taboo against relations with the United States. Still, there were always limits. The official line was that, as Foreign Minister Kamal Kharrazi said in an April 22, 1998, speech, "America's policies prove that, as in the past, one cannot trust what American officials say."[43]

But even after the September 11, 2001, terror attacks on America, Khamenei rejected any direct talks with the United States and threatened to fire officials who spoke in favor of U.S. ties. Khamenei said that

41 Associated Press, December 9, 1997.
42 U.S. Department of Justice statement, June 21, 2001, http://usinfo.state.gov/topical/pol/terror/01062102.htm.
43 Cited in Cordesman, "Stability and Instability in the Gulf."

Iran had nothing to gain and everything to lose from official contact with the United States. "The Americans want to involve Iran in the Afghan conflict and make it a partner in the massacre of innocent people. They also want to show to the world that the Islamic republic has backtracked on its revolutionary ideals," he said.[44] This last point implied that Islamic Iran could never reestablish ties with the United States because this was contrary to its very identity.

As on other subjects, Khomeini had been unambiguous on this point: "America is the number-one enemy of the deprived and oppressed people of the world. There is no crime America will not commit in order to maintain its . . . domination. . . . Iran is a country effectively at war with America." Compromise with America would entail "humiliation" to which martyrdom would be preferable.[45] Khamenei and his regime were determined to maintain this tradition.

In order to do so, and to achieve Iran's continuing regional ambitions, the Iranian government embarked on a major program to build up its military. The lack of funds, however, required some creative methods. Iran tried to become self-sufficient, manufacturing many weapons or buying them from Russia, China, or North Korea. Yet it could not rebuild its ground, air, and naval forces without a massive expenditure of funds that the country didn't have. Iran's military expenditures, measured in constant 1995 dollars, peaked during the war with Iraq in 1986 at $14.8 billion. They dropped steadily down to only $5.4 billion after Iraq's defeat in the Kuwait war, and to $4.2 billion in 1995.[46] The volume of arms imported also declined.[47]

In this process, however, Iran turned to missiles and nuclear weapons as a relatively low-cost alternative that would increase its overall power. The longer-range missiles were capable of hitting targets as far away as Israel, Turkey, India, and Egypt, as well as all of the Gulf Arab states.[48] Admiral Muhammad Razi Hadayeq, the commander of

---

44 Reuters, October 30, 2001.

45 Algar, ed., *Islam and Revolution*, p. 305.

46 Arms Control and Disarmaments Agency, *World Military Expenditures and Arms Transfers*, 1996 (Washington, DC, 1997), Table 1.

47 Richard F. Grimmett, "Conventional Arms Transfers to the Third World, 1987–1995," Congressional Research Service, CRS 862F (Washington, DC, August 4, 1995), pp. 57–8, 67–9.

48 *Los Angeles Times*, October 15, 1997.

Iran's missile forces, claimed that Iran was the region's "strongest missile power."[49]

This does not mean that Iran was preparing aggression against any or all of these countries, but, given the radical faction's worldview, its peaceful intentions could not be taken for granted.[50] Even if they were never used, the possession of long-range missiles tipped with nuclear weapons would give Iran a tremendous ability to intimidate its neighbors into doing its bidding. Khatami never challenged the nuclear program, despite the fact that a big oil producer such as Iran had little need for such an alternative, and unreliable, source of power.

Ironically, the same regime that blocked the reform movement and in effect canceled the results of Iran's elections was then able to use the opposition's existence to portray itself as moderate without changing any of its policies. As a result, Iran was able to remain one of the world's most extremist governments – sponsoring terrorism, issuing militant threats against other countries, and developing weapons of mass destruction – while still getting the benefit of the doubt as a state moving toward moderation.

Despite its many differences, Iran's situation paralleled that of the Arab world. The struggle for reform had failed in both places, though in Iran it had opened a wider margin of freedom. Trump issues and radical, utopian rhetoric that justified the regime remained in command, though it was not always implemented in practice. Failed policies were not changed, and thus the problems they caused were likely to worsen.

Shahram Chubin, an Iranian political scientist living abroad, pointed out that the legitimacy of Iran's regime had become "bound up with what it can deliver, as opposed to what it can promise." Khomeini had sneered that "the revolution was not about the price of watermelons." Yet, Chubin noted, it was this material failure that had destroyed support for the government: "All the windy rhetoric about the revolution's virtuous aims bump up against the impoverishment of the nation."[51]

---

49 Associated Press, October 18, 1997.
50 Michael Eisenstadt and Azriel Lorber, "Iran's Recent Missile Test: Assessment and Implications," *Policywatch* No. 330, August 6, 1998.
51 Shahram Chubin, "Iran's Strategic Predicament," *Middle East Journal*, Vol. 54, No. 1 (Winter 2000), pp. 10–24.

Yet while these failures stirred open opposition, the regime was still easily able to hold onto power. In much of the Arab world, things had not even gone that far. "Windy rhetoric" was still sufficient to avoid the consequences of material failure. It was impossible to say, of course, whether people in Arab states felt the same way about their situations as did those in Iran. The stronger credibility of trump issues among Arabs may have reduced their discontent; and the presence of repression ensured that it would not be expressed, or at least that it would be channeled through Islamist movements proposing the same "solutions" that had failed in Iran.

Chubin's conclusion, though, applies perfectly to both Iran and the Arab states. When talking about the need for modernization and change along the lines accepted elsewhere in the world, "Opting out is a strategy for losers and fighting the inevitable is nonsense." The only rational policy toward globalization was "embracing it selectively and seeking to direct its course in the cultural domain," as had been done so successfully in Asia. By acting "as if others do not face comparable challenges . . . Iran typically casts itself into the role of victim, as the target of some conspiracy to undermine its independence, rather than as part of a world-wide phenomenon, a challenge which confronts everyone and calls for rational responses. Self-absorption limits Iran's capacity to understand its context, and react to it."[52]

Rather than deal with the actual challenges of development and globalization, Iran's rulers, like those in the Arab world, were able to transmute their country's problems into a plot by imperialism, Zionism, and local traitors to destroy Iran and Islam. In this context, of course, the proper solution was the hard-line faction's continued rule, international militancy, hostility to the United States, and developing weapons of mass destruction. The purported need to exclude Western influence justified the kind of statist economic policies rejected elsewhere, allowed corruption and incompetence to be covered up, and turned the rejection of democracy into a noble battle against spiritual corruption.

This very approach, however, also guaranteed that Iran would make little if any progress in solving its real problems. Under Iran's enduring system, the regime wins, the people lose, and God is supposedly pleased.

52 Ibid.

6

FORCE AND VIOLENCE
IN MIDDLE EASTERN
POLITICS

During the twentieth century's second half, the Middle East knew more international wars, repression, civil wars, terrorism, and revolutionary insurgencies than any other area in the world. Aside from its quantity and wide distribution, Middle Eastern violence was most distinguished by two factors. First, compared to that of other regions, far more of it was inspired and supported by cross-border rather than by purely domestic factors. This does not negate the importance of ethnic, ideological, and factional struggles for control of specific countries elsewhere, but cross-border sponsorship of subversion in the Middle East far exceeded that in any other region. Second, while violence elsewhere in the world tended to occur in specific countries at particular points in time, conflict – government, intergroup, and interstate – was a far more universal and long-term phenomenon in the Middle East.

Why is force and violence so pervasive in the region? There are, of course, a number of unresolved issues; but, after all, disputes can also be resolved by negotiations or compromise without resort to violence. The most important answer to this question is that the methods used in handling conflict depend on the attitudes and goals of the parties involved. In a situation where individual states, groups, or ideologies seek regional conquest or reject other countries' sovereignty, force will be an important aspect of interstate relations. Where revolutionary forces believe themselves to possess absolute truth and reject the existence of other communities, violence is a favored option. When peaceful reform is blocked and when political goals are absolutist, bloodshed is a likely outcome. If regimes think they can use violence at home and abroad to enhance their hold on power, with little risk to their own survival, they find it an attractive policy.

Still, one might expect that the failure of violence in internal and regional conflicts would discredit that tool. Indeed, the paradigm debate of the 1990s partly revolved around this question. Some argued that violence had cost the Arabs greatly without bringing any benefits. Iraq's defeated invasion of Kuwait, bloody abortive Islamist revolutions, and the inability of Palestinian or Arab state violence to eliminate Israel were cited as examples in support of this claim. Arab liberals insisted that the balance of forces would not allow this situation to change. The United States, Israel, and the Arab states themselves were too strong to be overturned by revolution, invasion, or guerrilla warfare. On the contrary, those deploying violence were the biggest losers.

Reformers suggested that negotiation and compromise, reduced military spending, democracy, and open debate leading to peaceful change were all superior to a test of arms in settling domestic and regional conflicts. By delegitimizing violence, moderate states would also make it harder for radical neighbors to attack them. In rejecting these alternatives, Arab rulers accepted the continued risk that their actions and rhetoric would bring massive violence even though they preferred to avoid outright war.

Yet violence was too useful to abandon as an instrument of statecraft, especially given the existence of so many rationales for refusing to do so. First, there was the belief, often vindicated in practice, that violence could be made safe for its practitioners. If they sponsored such measures in a covert way, responsibility could be avoided and retaliation evaded. Sponsoring terrorism was so attractive precisely because it bypassed the more dangerous and often losing proposition of using one's own military in conventional warfare. For example, Iran and Syria could back a whole range of groups in Lebanon, among the Palestinians, or in the Gulf at little cost, whereas the direct use of their armed forces would have led to serious and costly interstate conflict.

Second, there was a recurring ideological claim that the balance of forces was not as it seemed. Radical Islamist groups continued to argue that their very high motivation would allow them to overcome any military disadvantage and to overthrow regimes, destroy Israel, even to defeat the United States. A willingness to sacrifice oneself, combined with Allah's help, they insisted, would overcome enemies who were really cowards. Readiness to fight for a long time would wear out foes weak in morals and morale. Apparent triumphs – Israel's withdrawal from southern Lebanon and the September 11, 2001, attacks in the United States – stiffened this resolve. Huge numbers of people who would never have dreamed of joining such a campaign themselves cheered on these warriors and opposed any policy that would have "betrayed" them by compromise. Governments determined not to be dragged into conflict still sought to use such movements and the enthusiasm they inspired for their own purposes.

Arab regimes had mastered the difficult art of such brinksmanship during the golden age of coups during the 1950s, 1960s, and 1970s. In those years, military officers saw politicians – by no means inaccurately – as incompetent and corrupt, considered the military to be the only reliable institution in their countries, and believed that they could do a much better job of governing. But once a stable regime had come to power through a coup or had survived these threats, the rulers had learned a great deal about preventing their armies from intervening in politics.[1]

There has not been a coup or serious attempt to seize power by soldiers in Egypt since 1952, in Syria since 1970, or in Iraq since 1968. By contrast, Syria earlier had eight coups over twenty-two years (1949–71), while Iraq had three within ten years (1958–68). The last coups during which soldiers seized power for themselves in a major Arab state (outside of Yemen and Sudan) were those of Asad in 1970 and Muammar Qadhafi's coup in Libya in 1969. By the year 2002, only one of the fourteen main Arab countries – Libya – had a ruler who had originally seized power through a coup as a career military officer, and even he had become a full-time politician a quarter-century earlier.[2] In Algeria, the armed forces took control acting on behalf of the existing regime to prevent an Islamist electoral victory, but then held elections installing a civilian government.

Yet the civilian control over the military had a price, too. To keep armies harmless at home involved further reducing their already

---

1 For an analysis of the social and institutional management techniques of such regimes, see Barry Rubin, *Modern Dictators: Third World Coupmakers, Strongmen, and Populist Tyrants* (New York, 1987). The classic history of this period is Eliezer Be'eri, *Army Officers in Arab Politics and Society* (New York, 1969).

2 These countries are Morocco, Tunisia, Algeria, Libya, Egypt, Lebanon, Jordan, Saudi Arabia, Kuwait, the United Arab Emirates, Bahrain, Oman, Qatar, and Jordan. King Abdallah of Jordan was a career military officer but rules, of course, as heir of his father.

questionable ability to fight wars abroad.[3] Arab armies were too frequently defeated to encourage their use, especially against an Israel stronger than any probable Arab alliance. By the 1980s, the decline of the USSR, the traditional source of arms and external backing, and America's stature as sole remaining superpower had accelerated this trend. Consequently, employing proxies, subversion, and terrorism become more important means of power projection than the use of regular armed forces. Arab governments deployed a wide array of privileges and policies to ensure their generals' happiness, including high budgets to purchase arms and loyalty that drained money away from development and welfare spending. Such policies also meant allowing the military to engage in corruption and exempting the generals from criticism.

Year after year, decade after decade, the Middle East led the world in military spending, both in absolute terms and as a proportion of gross domestic product. The leading importer of weapons was Saudi Arabia, reaching a total of $11 billion in 1997 alone, an amount that leveled out in the following years only because of low oil prices. For the 1995–97 period, Middle Eastern countries imported $53.1 billion worth of arms (38 percent of the world total), compared to $35.5 billion for East Asia (25 percent), $25.8 billion for Western Europe (18 percent), and $4.2 billion for South America (3 percent).[4]

In 1992, Middle Eastern countries used a remarkable 48.2 percent of central government spending for military purposes. While this had fallen to 22.9 percent by 1997 – for a variety of reasons, including sanctions on arms sales to Iran and Iraq as well as lower oil prices – it still far exceeded the 16.6 percent expenditure by Eastern Europe and Central Asia, the number-two ranking region in this category. For specific countries, the proportions spent varied as follows: Algeria (5.9 percent in 1992, 12 percent in 1997), Egypt (8.5 percent, 11 percent), Iran (14.9 percent, 11.6 percent), Jordan (27.3 percent, 25 percent), Kuwait (96.3 percent, 26.8 percent), Lebanon (18.5 percent, 8.4 percent), Libya (16.4 percent, 19.7 percent), Morocco (14.3 percent, 12.9 percent),

3 For a discussion of the region's overall issues, conflicts, and balance of forces, see Barry Rubin, "The Geopolitics of Middle East Conflict and Crisis," *Middle East Review of International Affairs (MERIA) Journal*, Vol. 2, No. 3 (September 1998), pp. 39–45.

4 Bureau of Verification and Compliance, U.S. Department of State, "World Military Expenditures and Arms Transfers 1998," August 21, 2000. http://www.state.gov/www/global/arms/bureau_vc/wmeat98fs.html.

Oman (40.2 percent, 36.4 percent), Saudi Arabia (72.5 percent, 35.8 percent), Syria (39 percent, 26.2 percent), the UAE (40.5 percent, 46.5 percent), and Yemen (29.8 percent, 17.4 percent). The rates in Turkey (18.8 percent, 14.7 percent) and Israel (23.3 percent, 20.9 percent) were also high.[5]

Calculated in terms of gross domestic product (GDP), military expenditure in the Arab countries increased by 9.1 percent in 1998, to $44.4 billion from $40.7 billion in 1997. Total defense expenditure constituted 7.4 percent of GDP, more than triple the world average of 2.4 percent of GDP. The share of military spending in Egypt was 4 percent of GDP. Military expenditure in 1998 increased for the North African countries by 13 percent from the level in 1997 and amounted to $5.8 billion, with Algeria's share at about 40 percent. Such high levels of spending among Arab countries pulled resources away from health care and education, which for most countries of the region were well below world averages. UN statistics show that expenditures by Arab countries on basic services such as health care and education have been minimal. Jordan, the most generous in social expenditures, spent 3.7 percent of GDP on these sectors in 1998.[6]

In this context, governments have no incentive to end regional conflict in order to obtain some "peace dividend," since military budgets will stay high to ensure domestic stability. Equally, free speech and democracy are dangerous in this context, since people might start demanding less spending on the army. No "rational" appeal to put the priority on social and development spending in order to improve conditions for the country's poor will persuade leaders who know that they need a strong, contented military if they are to survive.[7] Yet government strategies have wasted even more money than this strategy required, buying the latest and most expensive weapons' systems either because the generals demanded them or because they raised the regime's prestige. There was no real oversight by civilian authorities, much less by such institutions as legislatures or the media, to criticize and curtail such behavior.

5 Eric Swanson et al., *World Development Indicators, 2001* (Washington, DC, 2001), pp. 294–6.
6 Ibid.
7 Gencer Ozcan, "The Turkish Foreign Policymaking Process and the Influence of the Military," in Barry Rubin and Kemal Kirisci, eds., *Turkey in World Politics: An Emerging Multi-Regional Power* (Boulder, CO, 2001), pp. 13–30.

Another mechanism created by governments for their own defense, not for national defense, was the creation of multiple military branches and intelligence services to spy on and compete with each other. This process meant not only wasted resources and poor coordination, but also unreliable intelligence gathering, since dictatorships put a premium on information that pleases rulers and discredits rivals rather than on accurate data.

For example, even before obtaining a state of his own, Arafat had created a dozen different intelligence units that feuded and fought among themselves while harassing and looting the citizenry. But Arafat wanted such inefficiency and conflict in order to ensure his own power. In one 1998 incident, the military intelligence service, led by Musa Arafat, a relative of the leader, raided an office of the Tanzim, Fatah's armed militia. The Tanzim then marched on the military intelligence headquarters in Ramallah, whose garrison opened fire and killed one youth, a nephew of a PA cabinet minister. The Tanzim issued a leaflet stating: "Musa Arafat and his dogs suck Palestinian blood by dealing with stolen cars, whorehouses, and selling weapons. They prefer to be Israeli prostitutes, working here as the Israeli intelligence arm to separate the Palestinian leadership and the Palestinian people."[8] Even when fighting against Israel, different forces refused to share ammunition and supplies. Arafat himself built up irregular forces, especially the Fatah militia (Tanzim), as rivals to his own security forces and also used them to stage terrorist attacks on Israel, for which he could then deny responsibility.[9]

Another aspect of this system was the creation of special elite units or completely parallel security forces with special links to the regime through communal, religious, and ethnic interests. The story of Lebanon was a cautionary tale on the dangers of ethnic pluralism. Its multicommunal system fell apart during that country's civil war, to be replaced by ethnic militias. By contrast, Iran had, aside from the regular military, the Islamic Revolutionary Guard Corps and the Basij militia, on whose backing the Islamic regime, or at least the hard-line faction, could count.[10]

8 *Palestine Report*, October 30, 1998; *Ha'aretz*, December 22, 1998.
9 Gal Luft, "Soldiers without Fortune: Palestinian Militarization in the Post Statehood Era," in Barry Rubin and Thomas Keaney, eds., *Armed Forces in the Middle East* (London, 2001), pp. 130–48.
10 Michael Eisenstadt, "The Armed Forces of the Islamic Republic of Iran: An Assessment," in ibid., pp. 231–57.

Saudi Arabia had both its regular forces and the tribal-based National Guard.[11] Jordan's forces were overwhelmingly comprised of "east bank Jordanians," mainly Bedouins, with only very limited numbers of Palestinians permitted to serve.[12]

In Syria, the same pattern was followed for Alawites from the community of the ruling Asad family, with special units based on family and ethnic loyalties employed to guard the leader and his capital. The Republican Guard, an armored division and the only military formation allowed in Damascus, was commanded for many years by a nephew of President Hafiz al-Asad. Two of Asad's sons, Bashar and Maher, were colonels and brigade commanders in this unit. After Bashar succeeded his father as president, his personal secretary commanded its security service. Unit 549, which provides defense for the capital, was headed by one of Bashar's cousins. Other special units guarding Damascus included the Special Forces and the Third and Fourth Armored Divisions, all commanded by Alawis. Defense Minister Mustafa Tlas, who took his post in 1972 and held it for the next thirty years, was an old comrade of Hafiz al-Asad from their student days.

In Iraq, this system has been developed to a peak of complexity and specialization. Kurds are not drafted into the regular army – though there are pro-regime Kurdish militias. In the regular armed forces, there is a large proportion of Shi'ite Muslims, who can even attain the rank of general. But the choicest positions are usually reserved for Sunni Muslims, especially those from tribes and areas close to President Saddam Hussein's home town; this is especially true in the complex hierarchy of elite units. As Amatzia Baram has written:

In the army, as opposed to the Republican Guard (RG), support for the president is far less staunch. Thus, the RG is placed between all army units and the capital city, and the Special Republican Guard (SRG) is stationed inside of Baghdad, and thus between the RG and the inner rings guarding the president. As long as the regime looks stable, the RG, the SRG, Special Security (SS), and the Palace Guard (or Presidential Guard, Himayat al-Ra'is) will remain essentially loyal to [President] Saddam Hussein. If he is removed they have too much to lose: power and prestige, higher salaries than those of their

11 Joshua Teitelbaum, *Holier Than Thou: Saudi Arabia's Islamic Opposition* (Washington, DC, 2000).
12 Alexander Bligh, "The Jordanian Army between Domestic and External Challenges," in Rubin and Keaney, eds., *Armed Forces in the Middle East*, pp. 149–61.

army counterparts, and other privileges that increase in relation to a soldier's proximity to the president."[13]

Another technique is to base promotions and assignments more on political loyalty than on ability, thus handicapping professionally able officers. The top command posts are often given to those with special connections to the regime through family – as happens with many Saudi princes and several Iraqi commanders – or through ethnic, geographical, or tribal connections. To put a premium on political loyalty makes eminent political sense, of course, since the regime's first priority is to stay in power, but it also lowers the military's quality. Less competent officers are eager to portray, or pretend, ideological zeal precisely in order to ensure their successful careers because they lack other assets for doing so.

There are many other characteristics that damage Middle Eastern militaries. Officers are frequently rotated to avoid letting them establish strong ties of loyalty with their subordinates. Initiative among individual officers is discouraged, a practice that has high costs during battles and military campaigns. As mistrust among officers is encouraged, they become reluctant to share information with each other. Coordination among units is inhibited, and combined operations can be made very difficult or even impossible. Officers suspected of other political loyalties or excessive ambition are periodically purged. The smaller Gulf Arab monarchies, with insufficient population but lots of money, ensure a depoliticized army by hiring non-Arab mercenaries.

All of the region's armies – except for Iran's, of course – try to keep radical Islamists out of the officer corps. Failure to do so can be costly for a ruler, as shown by the 1981 assassination of Egyptian President Anwar al-Sadat by a small group of soldiers at a military parade. In general, professional military formations – even in Iran – seem unsympathetic to radical Islamist views. Does this indicate some inevitable orientation? The armed forces typically have more contact with Western ideas and personnel than virtually any other Middle Eastern institutions. Perhaps the pragmatic and patriotic ethos of the professional militaries discourages traditional piety. Unquestionably, too, Islamists and strong religious believers are attracted to other professions, and frequent purges in many armies have kept their numbers limited.

13 Amatzia Baram, "Saddam Husayn, the Ba'th Regime and the Iraqi Officer Corps," in ibid., pp. 206–30.

Of course, a key element in successful coup avoidance is an Arab leader's personal connection to the armed forces. Egyptian President Mubarak and Syrian President Hafiz al-Asad were commanders of their countries' air forces. King Hussein of Jordan was a graduate of the British military academy and devoted great personal attention to the army. His son and heir, King Abdallah, was an officer who commanded important special units and would have stayed in the army had he not become king at such an early age. In Gulf Arab monarchies, some members of the ruling families pursue military careers and control key units.[14] Civilian leaders such as Saddam Hussein and Yasir Arafat frequently appear in uniform and claim military status. An exception proving the rule was the way in which Hafiz al-Asad prepared his son Bashar, an eye doctor with no military background, by quickly promoting him to high rank after it became clear that he would succeed his father.[15]

Finally, there are some important social and cultural factors that damage the capability of Arab armies. These are hard to measure and controversial to enumerate, but they surely include excessively rigid hierarchies and reluctance to take initiative. A retired American army officer with extensive experience as an advisor to Arab armies, Norvell de Atkine, has concluded:

Until Arab politics begin to change at fundamental levels, Arab armies, whatever the courage or proficiency of individual officers and men, are unlikely to acquire the range of qualities which modern fighting forces require for success on the battlefield. For these qualities depend on inculcating respect, trust, and openness among the members of the armed forces at all levels, and this is the marching music of modern warfare that Arab armies, no matter how much they emulate the corresponding steps, do not want to hear.[16]

Certain structural flaws in regional – especially Arab – military establishments are also important factors in limiting their political role and utility. The growing importance of high technology, rapid

---

14 Daniel L. Byman and Jerrold D. Green, "The Enigma of Political Stability in the Persian Gulf Monarchies," *MERIA Journal*, Vol. 3, No. 3 (September 1999), pp. 20–37; Sean Foley, "The UAE: Political Issues and Security Dilemmas," *MERIA Journal*, Vol. 3, No. 1 (February 1999), pp. 25–45.

15 Eyal Zisser, "The Syrian Army on the Domestic and External Fronts," in Rubin and Keaney, eds., *Armed Forces in the Middle East*, pp. 113–29.

16 Norvell de Atkine, "Why Arabs Lose Wars," in ibid., pp. 23–40.

communications, and flexibility in military strategy tend to play up the weaknesses of the Arab and Iranian armed forces. By contrast, security forces in Algeria, Egypt, and Syria have been more effective in defeating internal threats – usually from highly motivated but poorly equipped Islamic revolutionaries – where these qualities mattered less. But the armed forces of Lebanon and Iran collapsed when faced with major domestic conflicts.

Further, regarding the task of national defense and power projection abroad, the failure of Arab and Iranian armies has been an important factor in modern Middle Eastern history. Most obviously, Arab armies were unable to destroy Israel or even to defeat that country during the wars of 1948, 1956, 1967, 1969–70 (the "war of attrition"), 1973, and 1982 (Lebanon). There are few Arab victories that can be cited during the five decades of armed Arab-Israeli conflict. In power projection terms, the Arab states have failed to eliminate, dominate, defeat, or force significant concessions from Israel.

A second area of general failure in Arab power projection were the efforts to use military force to promote Pan-Arab nationalist objectives or, to put it another way, to ensure any Arab state's control over its neighbors or regional hegemony. Among these cases can be listed Egypt's failed intervention in Yemen's civil war and its unsuccessful effort to stop Syria from seceding from the United Arab Republic (1961), Syria's move (canceled because of Israeli threats) toward intervening in Jordan during the Jordan-PLO war of 1970, and Iraq's wars against Iran (1980–88) and Kuwait (1990–91). While Iraq can be said to have "won" the war with Iran, its victory consisted only in regaining the original border between the two countries, despite a high cost in destruction and casualties.[17]

There are only three cases in a half-century where such attempts to use regular military forces to expand an Arab country's authority can be said to have succeeded: Syria's domination of Lebanon from the mid-1970s on, using a 30,000-soldier expeditionary force; Morocco's successful expansion into the former Spanish Sahara, defeating a local insurgency; and Yemen's annexation of South Yemen. By contrast, as noted earlier, Iraq gained nothing from its military attack on Iran. Iranian

---

17 For an evaluation of the contemporary Iraqi armed forces, see Baram, "Saddam Hussein"; and Kenneth M. Pollack, "Current Iraqi Military Capabilities" *MERIA News*, Vol. 2, No. 4 (February 1998).

leaders never used conventional military means to extend the influence of their state and ideology, relying instead on more indirect methods, including propaganda, terrorism, and the use of surrogate clients. Such groups have included Hizballah, Hamas, Islamic Jihad, various organizations in the Persian Gulf, and also the direct covert operations of Iranian intelligence.

Israel can certainly be considered the most successful country in using power projection, though with the important reservation that Israeli objectives have always been limited – far more so than most Arabs have perceived – and defense oriented. These goals have included: preserving the state's existence, trying to prevent neighboring countries from letting their territory be used to launch third-party attacks on Israel, damaging the infrastructure of terrorist/guerrilla groups operating from other countries against Israel, and pressuring neighboring states to make peace, or at least deterring them from engaging in war. Another goal has been to stop or slow down the development of nuclear weapons by Iraq, achieved in the 1981 raid on the Osirak reactor.

Within this context, Israel's failures must be seen as more modest. The most prominent would be the inability to defeat Hizballah through Israeli operations and support for surrogate forces in south Lebanon. From the standpoint of deterring and reducing attacks on Israeli territory during the 1980s and 1990s, Israel's military was able to achieve a far better situation than had existed earlier. But it is important to note that Israel's decision to withdraw from southern Lebanon in 2000 was perceived in the Arab world as a tremendous defeat at the hands of Hizballah, a guerrilla force. It encouraged the Palestinians to wage a new insurgency and Arab states to proclaim that Israel could and would be defeated. Thus, the experience can be considered another example of the dangers of using regular military forces and an argument for projecting power in other ways.

Still another stimulus for Arab states to use alternative means of violence for power projection were limits on the support they received from outside powers. Since no Middle Eastern military can manufacture all of the arms and equipment it needs, finding a source for weapons and materiel is indispensable and of the highest political importance. When Nasser's Egypt turned to Soviet supplies in 1955, it was a major turning point in the region's history, as was Egypt's break with Moscow in the early 1970s and its move to the American camp in the late 1970s. The same can be said of Israel's loss of French supplies in 1967 and its switch to U.S. equipment during the 1970s, and of Iran's break with U.S. weapons necessitated by the 1979 Iranian revolution and the hostage crisis. Even during the period when the USSR was sponsoring radical Arab states, it discouraged them from going to war but supported the PLO and other guerrilla and terrorist groups, a situation further encouraging Arab states to use indirect types of force.

By the 1970s, the United States and the USSR were the only two powers able to supply all of a Middle Eastern military's import needs. By 1990, the Soviet Union had largely dropped out of the picture. The end of the Cold War with a U.S. victory penalized countries such as Iran, Iraq, Libya, and Syria that depended on Soviet weaponry.[18] The already wide technological gap between the two main suppliers would grow over time, with American equipment becoming increasingly superior to Russian armaments. Moreover, unlike the Soviet Union, Russia was not going to give cheap credit in exchange for political influence, and it demanded repayment of old debts as well.

The source of a country's weapons can have real influence on its politics and policies. For example, a U.S.-supplied Middle Eastern military is less likely to stage a coup against a pro-U.S. government. Such an army would also be less likely to attack Israel, since this would lead to the loss of U.S. spare parts. Lack of large-scale access to Soviet-style equipment given Russia's unwillingness to provide arms on credit has reduced the capacity of the Syrian, Libyan, and Iraqi militaries to stage offensive attacks. The exception to the U.S. monopoly is most glaring in the area of weapons of mass destruction, such as long-range missiles, nuclear arms, and chemical and biological weapons. Countries such as Iran, Iraq, Libya, and Syria can turn to alternative sources of arms and technology, notably China, North Korea, and Russia. This situation could make the Middle East an even riskier place, since these arms are both extremely destructive and available without political restraints.

18 For a discussion of U.S. military capabilities in the region, see Michael Eisenstadt, "U.S. Military Capabilities in the Post–Cold War Era: Implications for Middle East Allies," *MERIA Journal*, Vol. 2, No. 4 (December 1998), pp. 37–53; and Marvin Feuer, "U.S. Policy and Middle East Armed Forces," in Rubin and Keaney, eds., *Armed Forces in the Middle East*, pp. 41–67.

Iran or Iraq might use such arms to scare their neighbors into submission.[19] But since using these weapons is so incredibly dangerous, alternative types of violence would remain attractive even for those possessing them.

In short, then, since conventional war and direct engagement by national militaries seem to be unproductive or too costly, governments needed to use other means for projecting power. These instruments can include subversion, support for surrogate forces, terrorism, diplomatic solutions, and civil insurrections (notably the two Palestinian *intifadas*).

This analysis is not meant to imply that Middle Eastern armed forces are unimportant factors in the region's politics. On the contrary, in that part of the world, where war and conflict are most likely – and most often evidenced – military power is relatively more important than anywhere else. The conventional use of armed forces did not provide an adequate basis for waging the region's various conflicts, but their inability to resolve issues did not force a negotiated solution to those issues. Perhaps this is why Arab states have generally preferred an in-between state of affairs, a situation of no war, no peace.

Given this situation, the gap was filled by state-sponsored or state-assisted guerrilla and terrorist groups that were used to project influence and strike at enemies. In particular, four governments – Iran, Iraq, Libya, and Syria – were especially active in employing this strategy as a conscious and integral part of their foreign and security policies, developing a network of their own agents, as well as foreign clients and supporters, to carry out missions. For example, Iran backed Lebanese Hizballah and groups in the Gulf to spread Islamist revolutions; Libya used terrorists against Egypt and other neighbors; Syria stood behind Armenian and Kurdish groups against Turkey and supported a variety of Lebanese groups. All of these states assisted Palestinian terrorism against Israel. The efficacy of terrorism in fulfilling each regime's goals, however, varied widely.

19 See, for example, Bates Gill, "Chinese Arms Exports to Iran," *MERIA Journal*, Vol. 2, No. 2 (May 1998), pp. 55–70; Barry Rubin, *North Korea's Threat to the Middle East and the Middle East's Threat to Asia* (Tel Aviv, 1997); Barry Rubin, "China's Middle East Strategy," in Raman Kumarswamy, ed., *China and the Middle East: The Quest for Influence* (Thousand Oaks, CA, 1999); Robert O. Freedman, "Russia and the Middle East: The Primakov Era," *MERIA Journal*, Vol. 2, No. 2 (May 1998), pp. 1–8; Robert O. Freedman, "Russian-Iranian Relations in the 1990s," *MERIA Journal*, Vol. 4, No. 2 (June 2000), pp. 65–80.

State-sponsored terrorism's goal-oriented, "pragmatic" quality does make it vulnerable to the costs of punishment or failure. Countries and movements deploying terrorism have sometimes suffered international isolation, economic sanctions, and even military retaliation. The question is whether this punishment was sufficient to transform that policy from asset to liability. Moreover, using covert means reduced the chance of being held responsible, while the small forces employed limited the state's investment in the project.

It is crucial to understand that "terrorism" is not merely an epithet used to discredit movements but actually does describe a very specific and even logical political strategy to achieve certain strategic goals for states as well as for social revolutionary and nationalist movements. Terrorism is used to achieve the following objectives:

Demoralize, destroy, or gain concessions from another state or group. Those originating terrorism must believe that the targets would be weakened precisely because civilians and the entire society are being hit. The goal is to undermine the intended victims' morale and make adversaries appease or fear to oppose the sponsor. Such pressures, through direct attacks or intimidation, can also undercut international support for enemies or rivals by deterring their allies from helping them. In staging the September 11, 2001, attack on the United States, for example, Usama bin Ladin's forces believed that they would persuade America to retreat, constantly citing historical precedents – from Vietnam to Lebanon in the 1980s and Somalia in the 1990s – to prove this assertion. Those using terrorism against Israel believe that it is not a real, viable state and that its citizens are cowardly. Thus, sustained violence would make them flee or surrender.

Increase popular support and participation from the perpetrators' constituency. Groups often turn to terrorism when unable to develop other forms of revolutionary action due to a lack of popular support, their own incompetence, or effective government countermeasures. Terrorism's perpetrators must believe that those it would mobilize will consider its deeds acceptable and effective because of their tremendous hatred and dehumanization of the intended victims. Using terrorism – as in the case of bin Ladin's attack on America, or anti-Israel terrorism – is designed to prove that the target countries' military power can be circumvented and these states politically defeated by using such tactics. As a result, the groups involved will be seen as both heroic and successful, inspiring the masses to support them and their doctrines. If the terrorists' and sponsors' assessment is correct, the outcome will be a much larger terrorist movement. But if they are mistaken, the result will be to leave the group isolated as a marginal force, albeit one capable of disproportionate violence.

Advance a revolutionary or nationalist movement's efforts to overthrow a government or take over a given area. In the same way, the sponsoring regime hopes to advance its interests in reaching a well-defined, though not necessarily realistic, goal. Examples of sponsors' motives are Libya's efforts to overthrow moderate regimes and become the Arab world's leader; Syria's attempts to control Lebanon and the PLO, destroy or weaken Israel, lead the Arabs, and at times to block Arab peace with Israel; Iran's trying to spark Islamic fundamentalist revolutions and to gain hegemony over the Persian Gulf; and Iraq's drive to lead the Arabs, control the Gulf, and press other states into appeasing it financially. All of these forces also thought that this type of violence would help them to eliminate U.S. influence in the region and to destroy Israel.

It is important to note, though, that while revolutionary movements have found terrorism a useful way to mobilize support and to get revenge, such tactics have been extremely unsuccessful in making revolutions. As has also been shown in Europe and Latin America – though many Islamist groups did not understand this lesson – terrorism is not a strategy likely to trigger mass revolts.

Dictatorships have also found terrorism a way to strike against exiled opponents. Iraq's government, for example, ordered the murders of overseas critics during the 1970s and 1980s in Britain, South Yemen, Kuwait, and Sudan. During the 1980s, Iran's minions murdered oppositionists in the United States, France, Pakistan, West Germany, Britain, Turkey, and Switzerland. Syria and Libya have carried out similar activities.[20]

During the Cold War, support for terrorism could also be an important cooperative bond between the sponsoring states – especially Syria and Iraq – and the Soviet bloc. At times, assistance for such activities was part of Soviet aid to these countries. At the same time, alliance with the USSR protected sponsors from Western retaliation.

20 See Chapter 5 of this volume.

Sponsors' goals and effectiveness in using terrorism vary greatly. This strategy did offer Libya, Syria, Iraq, and Iran a low-cost, low-risk way of waging conflict, hiding behind shadowy connections and front groups that victims could not easily deter or punish. Beginning in 2000, the Palestinian Authority became a sponsor of terrorism for similar reasons and in similar ways. Consequently, these regimes consistently provided groups with money, safe havens, propaganda, logistical help, training, weapons, diplomatic support, and protection against retaliation. The ability to obtain genuine passports, send arms and explosives by diplomatic pouch, enjoy lavish financing, well-equipped training bases, and state-of-the-art explosives allowed Middle Eastern terrorists to operate more often and more efficiently than did potential terrorists in other parts of the world.

At times, terrorist groups took "credit" for their actions, but at other times – especially when states used their own agents in attacks, or when groups sought to maintain a separate, "legitimate" diplomatic option – cover names were used to reduce the likelihood of retaliation. The PLO[21] used Black September, while the Palestinian mercenary terrorist Abu Nidal employed such aliases as the Arab Revolutionary Cells (the April 1986 Syrian-backed bombing of a TWA airliner), the Revolutionary Organization of Socialist Moslems (attacks on British targets), and the Arab Revolutionary Organization (the June 1985 bombing at the Frankfurt airport). The Syrian-controlled Al-Saiqa group bombed Jewish community centers, stores, and restaurants in France as the Eagles of the Palestinian Revolution. Iran's minions were called Islamic Jihad, Guardians of the Islamic Revolution, and Organization of the Oppressed on Earth; Libyan surrogates employed Egypt's Revolution, among other names. But even when Arafat's bodyguards, security forces, and militia (the *tanzim*) staged terrorist attacks on Israeli civilians – in some cases openly taking responsibility – he was able to claim that he had no connections with these operations.

Events in Lebanon during the 1980s showed the incredible leverage that small groups of terrorists could have on public attention, national policies, and the international agenda. Terrorist attacks and kidnappings

---

21 On the PLO's uses and rejections of terrorism, and the employment of terrorism against it by sponsoring states, see Barry Rubin, *Revolution until Victory: The Politics and History of the PLO*, (Cambridge, MA, 1994) and "The Origins of PLO Terrorism," in Barry Rubin, ed., *Terrorism and Politics* (New York, 1991).

set off and extended the Lebanese civil war, led to the Syrian occupation and Israeli invasion, and drove out the Western forces trying to stabilize the country. Hostage-taking there almost wrecked the Reagan administration, which abandoned its most cherished principles in order to negotiate with Iran over freeing Americans being held in Lebanon by Iranian-sponsored groups. Backing similar groups helped to ensure Syrian control over the country and Iranian influence with the Shi'ite community there.

The level of potential Western opposition or retaliation was a key factor in assessing the relative value of a sponsorship policy. Radical states concluded that this strategy gave them more protection from Western opposition than if they pursued their ambitions without the ability to threaten potential opponents. In order to avoid being targeted themselves, European countries became less willing to act against the sponsors of terrorism. Western countries also worried that punishing terrorists or their sponsors could lead to the loss of lucrative commercial deals and access to oil. Even Britain, which took the hardest line among European states, was ready to abandon its old ally King Hussein of Jordan in 1970 in surrendering to hijackers who had seized British hostages.[22] Britain also reopened relations with Libya just a year after Libyan diplomats had murdered a British policewoman in London in 1974, and minimized retaliation against Iran for ordering the assassination of the writer Salman Rushdie.[23]

In 1986, for example, a Syrian agent who had entered England on a government employee's passport received an explosive device directly from the Syrian embassy in London for use against an El Al passenger plane. His confession implicated Syria's ambassador to Britain, two Syrian diplomats, and the deputy director of Syria's air force intelligence. The bomb was similar to those used in 1983 bombing attempts against El Al and in an explosion killing four Americans on a TWA plane over Greece. Yet this failure's cost for Syria was minimal: London only briefly suspended diplomatic ties.[24]

---

22 Douglas Davis, "Declassified Documents Show How UK Gave In to Terrorists." *Jerusalem Post*, January 2, 2001. http://www.csis.org/mideast/online.html#ME2000.
23 Mark E. Kosnik, *The Military Response to Terrorism* (Newport, R.I., 2000). http://www.nwc.navy.mil/press/Review/2000/spring/art1-spo.htm.
24 David Ottoway, "Syrian Connection to Terrorism Probed," *Washington Post*, June 1, 1986.

Other European states acted similarly. In 1977, France refused to hold or extradite Abu Daoud, a PLO terrorist leader. For years, it let terrorists operate in its territory as long as they did not commit violent acts there. Relatives of George Abdallah, a Lebanese terrorist imprisoned in France, planted bombs in Paris in a successful bid to force his release. In 1987, two West Germans were abducted in Beirut to prevent West Germany's extradition of Muhammad Ali Hamadi to the United States for air piracy and murder. Europe retaliated only in the most limited and temporary way – by withdrawing ambassadors from Tehran – after a German court ruled that high Iranian officials had participated in killing Kurdish leaders there, then surrendered to Iranian demands that they end this policy on Tehran's terms.

While the United States took a far stronger anti-terrorist line, it sometimes made concessions to sponsoring states and their agents, either because of terrorism or – given the strategic and economic considerations – in spite of it. Most notably, U.S. efforts to get Syria into the anti-Iraq coalition in 1990 and into the Arab-Israeli peace process in the 1990s prevented any action against Damascus's sponsorship activities. Nevertheless, the United States invoked sanctions against Iran and Libya because of their sponsorship of terrorism, which cost both countries billions of dollars.

The most sustained and ambitious wave of terrorism was that deployed as a substitute for ineffective Arab conventional military action in the struggle against Israel. This effort was pursued for many decades. During the 1990s, states and movements opposing a negotiated settlement focused on this strategy as a way to subvert any success in negotiations. This policy was not based on objections to the slow pace or details of the talks, but rather on fear that they might succeed. Peace would undermine the radical regimes and even further reduce the prospects for revolution. Those involved rejected Israel's existence not only on national interest and ideological grounds but also because the continuation of the conflict itself was so useful to them.[25]

A variety of groups participated in this battle and received help in doing so. Radical Islamist organizations – such as the Palestinian Hamas and Islamic Jihad, as well as the Lebanese Hizballah – and a

---

25 On Arab states' treatment of the Palestinian Authority, including their sponsorship of its terrorist rivals, see Barry Rubin, "Israel, the Palestinian Authority, and the Arab States," *MERIA Journal*, Vol. 1, No. 4 (December 1997).

number of non-Islamist Palestinian and PLO member groups all received backing from Iran, Iraq, Syria, and Libya. By attacking Israel, these groups helped to slow and damage the Israel-Palestinian peace process.[26] When Arafat himself became dissatisfied with the direction of the peace process – or decided that he did not want an agreement, based on what was achievable – he, too, turned to terrorist violence in 2000.[27] The ability to wage war and deny that one was doing so, despite the most vicious and deliberate strategy of murdering civilians, enables Arafat to maintain sympathy in the West and even gain support and protection from Western states. This episode was a remarkable testament to the value of terrorism.

The function and fortunes of terrorism in the region can be seen by examining how Syria, Iran, Iraq, and Libya have used it as a strategy for different reasons and with varying degrees of effectiveness. Syria can be considered the most successful in using terrorism as a strategy. This approach has helped it to control Lebanon (and to reduce Western influence there), to strike against Israel, and to influence the PLO and Jordan. While these efforts were by no means completely successful in achieving Syria's ambitions, terrorism clearly made a positive contribution to Syrian interests over a thirty-year period at a relatively low cost.

After playing a critical role during the mid-1960s in initiating Palestinian terrorism, Syria also used terrorism against the PLO when trying to control that organization. It created puppet groups, both in an effort to take over the PLO and to conceal Syria's violent operations against target countries and political forces. Syria usually acted cleverly and carefully. Seeking to avoid provoking Israel into war or even military retaliation, Syria did not strike directly against Israel through the Golan Heights but instead routed operations through Lebanon, Jordan, and even Europe.

Lebanon provided another test, again showing Syria's advantageous use of terrorism. After its army entered Lebanon in 1975, Damascus built up surrogate groups and allies that engaged in terrorist acts, including the Syrian Social National Party (SSNP) and the Palestinian al-Saiqa, Abu Nidal, and PFLP-General Command. After 1983, more Palestinian groups, including the Abu Musa splinter faction, were added to Syria's stable.

---

26 Barry Rubin, "External Influences on Israel's 1996 Election," in Dan Elazar and Shmuel Sandler, eds., *Israel's 1996 Election* (London, 1998).
27 See Chapter 8 of this volume.

The principal use of Syrian-sponsored terrorism in Lebanon was to force the withdrawal of Israeli, U.S., British, and French troops during the 1982–84 period. Although the actual work was largely performed by Iranian-backed Islamic fundamentalist groups, Syria gave them freedom to train, operate, and transport arms through Syrian-held territory. Having forced a U.S. pullout from Beirut, Syrian intelligence then turned its attention to southern Lebanon. Again, while much of the armed activity was organized by Shi'ite extremist groups tied to Iran, Damascus assisted Palestinian factions that it controlled, as well as Hizballah, to attack Israel.

Damascus apparently ordered the murder of Druze leader Kemal Jumblatt in 1977, because he was too independent-minded, and the assassination of President Bashir Gemayel in 1982, because of his dynamism and his alliance with Israel. Critical coverage of Syrian domestic politics and foreign policy was silenced by terrorizing Arab and Western journalists. In 1980, one of the most outspoken editors, Salim al-Lawzi, was kidnapped, horrendously tortured, and murdered. Syria recruited suicide bombers to attack the Israelis and allowed Iranian-backed forces to operate freely in attacking the U.S. embassy and Marines in Beirut.

Some suicide bombers were even more closely tied to Syria. In July 1985, for example, a twenty-three-year-old Lebanese named Haytham Abbas blew himself up in his car at a checkpoint of the Israeli-backed South Lebanese army. The previous day, Abbas, a member of the Lebanese branch of Syria's ruling Ba'th Party, had given a television interview praising Syrian President Hafiz al-Asad (whose picture was on his desk and wall), calling him "the symbol of resistance in the Arab homeland and the first struggler."[28] Other suicide terrorists belonged to different Syrian-controlled Lebanese groups.

When it appeared possible that Jordan might negotiate with Israel during 1982–83 and 1985–86, Syria organized numerous attacks on Jordanian diplomats and airline offices to deter any progress. In 1983, a wave of attacks by Syrian-sponsored groups killed Jordanian diplomats in Spain and Greece, and the Jordanian ambassadors to India and Italy. In 1985, a rocket was fired at a Jordanian airliner taking off from Athens; the Jordanian airline's office in Madrid was attacked; a

28 Damascus radio, July 16, 1985, in FBIS, July 16, 1985.

diplomat was killed in Ankara; and a Jordanian publisher was murdered in Athens. As soon as King Hussein gave up the idea, the assaults ceased.

Syria wanted to eliminate relatively moderate PLO officials, in order both to influence the organization's policies and to promote its own claim to be the Palestinians' patron. In 1984, a PLO Executive Committee member, Fahd Qawasma, who took a softer line on cooperation with Jordan, was killed in Amman. In 1985, another moderate, Isam Sartawi, was shot dead in Portugal. The 1986 murders of Palestinian moderates Aziz Shahada and Nablus Mayor Zafir al-Masri, a friend of Arafat's, were traced to PFLP operations from Damascus. Syrian-backed groups continued to work at subverting the peace process and intimidating Jordan in later years.[29]

While Syria was weakened by the USSR's collapse, it neutralized this problem by joining the anti-Iraq coalition during the Kuwait crisis, participating in negotiations with Israel, and engaging in some minimal cooperation with the "anti-terrorist" coalition following the September 11, 2001, attacks. In the end, these actions actually preserved Syria's immunity to punishment despite its own sponsorship of terrorism. The exception here was Turkey, whose threat to use military force in 1999 pressured Damascus into stopping support for the Kurdish PKK, a rare case in which the victim of a terrorist campaign had the leverage and willpower to bring it to an end.[30]

Still, the balance sheet for Syrian terrorism, despite failures, recorded many successes. First, Damascus used terrorism for limited, well-defined goals: gaining hegemony in Lebanon, breaking U.S. and Israeli leverage there, subverting the Arab-Israeli peace process, and blackmailing wealthy Arab oil-producing states into providing subsidies.[31]

Second, as noted earlier, Syria integrated terrorism into a broader strategy incorporating diplomatic and military leverage in order to increase its influence in Lebanon, place constraints on Jordan, and damage Israel.

29 Text of testimony by Phil Wilcox, State Department coordinator for counter-terrorism, House International Relations Committee, July 25, 1996. On King Husayn's charges against Syria, see *Palestine Report*, August 16, 1996.
30 Ami Ayalon, *Middle East Contemporary Survey, 1994*, Vol. 18, (New York, 1996), p. 489.
31 Jim Hoagland, "A Clean Slate for Syria?," *Washington Post*, September 19, 1987.

Third, despite some errors, Syria was more cautious than Libya and Iran in covering its involvement. Its combination of threats and deft handling of terrorist sponsorship discouraged Western states from applying sanctions. The only penalties that Syria faced were inclusion on the U.S. list of terrorism-sponsoring countries (which restricted some trade and loans) and occasional breaks in diplomatic relations (usually the brief withdrawal of an ambassador).

Finally, Syria was strong enough in its own right, as well as close enough to the USSR during the 1970s and 1980s, and to U.S. policy during the 1990s, to deter retaliation, a luxury that Iran and Libya did not enjoy.

Sponsorship of terrorism by Iran sought to achieve several aims: to spread Islamic revolution (at a relatively low risk to the Tehran regime), to seek hegemony in the Gulf, and to destroy Israel and stop the Arab-Israeli peace process. Terrorism abroad was also used to promote the more radical faction's standing at home, to subvert moderate initiatives to rebuild relations with the West, and to eliminate the regime's exiled opponents. For such ends, Iran employed terrorism, starting with holding U.S. diplomats as hostages in 1979. The more radical faction in the leadership used the ensuing crisis in an extremely practical way to displace moderates from power, unite the country around itself, and destroy U.S. influence within Iran.[32] By the 1990s, Iran was still, in the words of a U.S. State Department report, "the world's most active supporter of international terrorism."[33]

In trying to spread revolution, Iran worked mainly in the Gulf (mostly in the 1980s), Lebanon (supporting Hizballah), and Iraq.[34] In December 1981, the Iraqi embassy in Beirut was bombed as part of Iran's war effort against Baghdad. Thirty people, including the ambassador, died. The Iranian-backed Islamic Jihad bombed the French embassy in May 1982 in order to punish that country for selling arms to Iraq, Iran's enemy. Iranian-backed groups used suicide bombs with devastating effect against the U.S. embassy and Marine barracks in Beirut, and against the Israeli headquarters in Tyre in 1983. Evidence indicated

---

32 See Barry Rubin, *Paved with Good Intentions: The American Experience and Iran* (New York, 1980).
33 U.S. State Department, *Patterns of Terrorism* (Washington, DC, 1996).
34 Nizar Hamzeh, "Islamism in Lebanon: A Guide," and Eyal Zisser, "Hizballah in Lebanon: At the Crossroads," *MERIA Journal*, Vol. 1, No. 3 (September 1997).

that explosives for all of the bombings in Kuwait and Lebanon were furnished by Iran and transported through Syria.[35]

With less success, Tehran tried to build links to revolutionary groups in Egypt and other Arab countries. Iran always used Lebanese, Iraqi, or Kuwaiti Shi'ites to cloak its involvement in such attacks. During the 1990s, efforts were stepped up to forge alliances with anti-Arafat Palestinians – Hamas, Islamic Jihad, dissidents in the refugee camps of Lebanon, and the Popular Front for the Liberation of Palestine-General Command (PFLP-GC). Terrorist groups in Turkey also received help and training.[36]

On the Gulf front, Iran used terrorism as an extension of its war against Iraq and to strike at neutrals supporting Iraq. Kuwait gave vital transport and financial help to Baghdad. On December 11, 1983, Iranian-based Islamic Jihad terrorists used explosives against the U.S. embassy, a foreign residential complex, the airport, an industrial park, and a power station in Kuwait City. A great deal of hostage taking and terrorism ensued in the attempt to free seventeen Shi'ites imprisoned for these crimes in Kuwait.

In May 1985, Iranian-backed terrorists tried to assassinate Kuwait's emir. Six bystanders died. On May 17, 1986, Islamic Jihad attacked the al-Ahmadi and Mukawwa oil refineries.[37] In July 1987, two Kuwaiti Shi'ites were killed while trying to place bombs in a shopping area. The men had disappeared nine months earlier while fishing in the Gulf and had been trained as saboteurs.[38] The imprisonment by Kuwait of captured terrorists led to new kidnappings and attacks demanding their release.

The taking and releasing of hostages in Lebanon by Iranian-backed groups (in some cases the hostages were taken to Iran) was also used to further Iranian interests. In 1988, France obtained the release of two of its citizens held hostage in Lebanon by repaying a $330 million shah-era loan, letting an Iranian embassy official wanted for involvement in terrorism leave the country, and expelling anti-Khomeini activists.[39] The best-known such affair was the secret U.S.-Iranian arms dealings of 1985–86.[40]

---

35 See, for example, *New York Times*, October 5, 1984.
36 Ely Karmon, "Radical Islamic Groups in Turkey," *MERIA Journal*, Vol. 1, No. 4 (December 1997).
37 *Al-Dustur*, June 30, 1986.
38 *Arab Times*, July 18, 1987, p. 1.
39 *Washington Post*, December 1, 1987.
40 Barry Rubin, "The Reagan Administration and the Middle East," in Ami Ayalon, ed., *The Middle East Contemporary Survey*, Vol. 10, 1986–87 (Boulder, CO, 1989).

Iran remained Hizballah's patron, supplying it with money, arms, and training. Tehran also backed Palestinian groups – most notably Islamic Jihad but also, increasingly, Hamas – that used terror to oppose the Arab-Israeli peace process. Arafat claimed that Hamas received $20 to $30 million from Iran.[41] Iranian-financed efforts sought to persuade Palestinian refugees in Lebanon to support such groups, including PLO defectors opposing Arafat's policy.[42]

Even with the election of a more moderate government in 1997, radical factions sought to maintain such activities. Tehran's détente with Saudi Arabia and other Gulf states during the 1990s inhibited its operations in the Gulf. Yet even as Iran reduced its support for attacks overall, it still continued the same basic strategy regarding terrorism as a useful tool serving its national interest. Indeed, allowing such activities was a potential bargaining chip that Khatami could use to avoid internal conflict and to trade for radical concessions regarding his proposed domestic economic and social reforms. Conversely, radicals could use terrorism to sabotage Khatami's attempts to promote détente with the West.

Iranian-backed terrorism did not bring Islamic fundamentalist regimes to the Gulf or Lebanon, destroy Israel, or defeat Iraq. But terrorism was integrated into Iranian foreign policy, helping Iran to gain a foothold and weaken Western influence in Lebanon, intimidate Gulf Arabs, and regain assets from the West. In Tehran, at least, it seemed that the Islamic republic had confronted great powers on an equal basis, raised its prestige in the Islamic world, and foiled plots against it.

On the negative side, Iran's backing for terrorism was a major contributing factor in U.S. sanctions, which damaged the economy. These costs played a role in the election of a more moderate president and in increasing support for changes in Iranian policy. Sponsorship of terrorism then became the instrument of the radical faction, but the fate of this strategy transcended the evolution of the domestic power balance in Tehran.

Iraq, too, used terrorism for very specific purposes: during the 1970s and 1980s against dissidents abroad, in efforts to take over the PLO,

41 Regarding his views, see, for example, his interview in *al-Sharq al-Awsat*, July 26, 1995, translated in FBIS, July 27, 1995, p. 10.
42 "Lebanon: Fundamentalists Replace the PLO," *Intelligence Newsletter*, No. 245, July 26, 1994.

and to hit at Israel, Iran, and other enemies, as well as to pressure Gulf Arab monarchies to provide financial help. Yet President Saddam Hussein put a higher priority on direct military action, launching attacks against Iran (1980–88) and Kuwait (1990–91). The results for Iraq were disastrous.[43]

An especially significant operation, setting off larger political events, was led by Nawaf Rosan, an Iraqi intelligence colonel who also served as Abu Nidal's deputy. Rosan led a three-man hit team that seriously wounded Israeli Ambassador Shlomo Argov in London on June 3, 1982. Three days later, Israel invaded Lebanon, and four days after that, Iraq offered a unilateral ceasefire in the Iran-Iraq war, arguing that the Arabs and Iranians should unite against Israel. Rosan was a Jordanian officer recruited by Iraqi intelligence. In London, his group reconnoitered and prepared to attack the embassies of the United Arab Emirates, Jordan, Saudi Arabia, Egypt, and Kuwait, if Iraqi interests so dictated. The attack on Argov was designed to provoke an Israeli attack on Syrian forces in Lebanon. Syria, Iraq's enemy and an ally of Iran, would suffer, while a new crisis would give Baghdad a good excuse to demand – unsuccessfully, however – that Iran end the Iran-Iraq war.[44]

In Iraq's case, terrorism was also deployed domestically, since at times the government viewed the Kurdish and Shiite communities virtually as foreign entities to be conquered. For example, fearing that they would support Iran or Islamist revolution, Iraq deported over 200,000 ethnic Persians and shot about 600 clerics and activists, including the popular Ayatollah Bakr Sadr and his sister, in 1978. In 1988, it used poison gas and mass shootings against its Kurdish citizens and forcibly resettled hundreds of thousands of others.[45]

Nevertheless, in retrospect, it could be argued that Iraq did not use terrorism enough. If it had employed terrorist operatives even more to subvert Iran, to intimidate Kuwait into concessions, or to coerce payments from the Saudis and others, Iraq would have been far better off than it was using conventional warfare. The lack of surrogate terrorism was especially noticeable during the 1990–91 Kuwait crisis. (The later,

---

43 For an assessment of Iraq's policies and the consequences, see Amatzia Baram and Barry Rubin, *Iraq's Road to War* (New York, 1994).

44 Ian Black, "Iraqi Intelligence Colonel Led Terrorists in Bid to Kill Envoy," *Guardian*, March 7, 1983.

45 This story is documented in Kanan Makiya, *Cruelty and Silence* (New York, 1993).

Iraqi-sponsored attempt to kill former U.S. President George Bush was an exception that stood out by its uniqueness.) By the late 1990s, Iraq's inactivity and weakness had cost it (perhaps temporarily) many of its foreign terrorist assets.

Compared to Syria, Libya's Muammar Qadhafi failed because he used terrorism in a grandiose, unfocused manner while being in a far weaker position to defend himself afterward. His list of targets included exiles, the PLO leadership, Israel, the United States, and a variety of other states including Egypt and the Maghreb countries, states in sub-Saharan Africa, the Philippines, and Ireland. He openly campaigned to murder opponents abroad, telling students in a May 1980 speech that such émigrés "should be physically liquidated."[46] Eleven were killed in 1980 and 1981, and five such assassination attempts occurred in 1985. In March 1984, a bomb planted against Libyan émigrés injured twenty-four people in England. The following month, Libyans fired from the embassy building in London at a peaceful demonstration. A British policewoman was killed, and eleven exiles were wounded. Due to Libyan pressure, the suspects were allowed to leave Britain.

After two efforts to murder Libyan exiles in Egypt, the Egyptians, in 1984, faked pictures of a bloody "victim" and gave them to Libyan agents. Libya's official media celebrated the murder, only to be confronted with Egyptian audio/video tapes and confessions from four arrested Libyan agents. Another hit team planning to kill Mubarak and others, including U.S. diplomats, was captured in Cairo in November 1985.

Abu Nidal also had Libya as a patron. In December 1985, his men launched simultaneous attacks at the airports of Rome (twelve killed, including five Americans, and seventy-four wounded) and Vienna (two killed and over forty wounded). Libya's official news agency praised this as "heroic." Tunisia reported that Tunisian passports used by the Vienna terrorists had been confiscated by Libya from workers it had expelled earlier that year. "By providing material support to terrorist groups which attack US citizens," Reagan said after the shootings, "Libya has engaged in armed aggression against the United States under established principles of international law, just as if he had used its own armed forces."[47]

---

46 Amnesty International, *Political Killings by Governments* (London, 1983).
47 *Washington Post*, January 8, 1986.

U.S. intelligence found a similar trail in the bombing of a discotheque frequented by American servicemen in West Berlin in March
1986, and in the murder of an American hostage, Peter Kilburn, in
Beirut the next month, shortly after the U.S. reprisal raid on Libya. A
Libyan military attaché in Syria had arranged for a Libyan-financed
group to purchase Kilburn from his kidnappers and then to kill him.
The U.S. bombing of Libya in 1986, while it made Libya more cautious
in covering its tracks, may have led to the Libyan-sponsored attack destroying a Pan American passenger plane over Lockerbie, Scotland, in
1988. Both American and British courts indicted Libyan officials, one
of whom was tried and convicted. According to the U.S. State Department, senior government officials involved in previous terrorist attacks
around the world orchestrated the operation. Forensic evidence indicated that the bomb's timer was unique to Libyan inventories, and an
official of the Libyan national carrier, Libyan Arab Airlines, used his
credentials to circumvent security procedures in Malta in order to assist
in the operation.[48]

Merely to list Libyan-sponsored attacks reveals a remarkable variety
of activities: the May 1990 Palestine Liberation Front seaborne raid on
Israel (training, arms, and the mother ship used), the Abu Nidal group's
attack on the Greek ship *City of Poros* in July 1988 (weapons and
base), the bombing of UTA Flight 772 over Africa in September 1989
(as charged by a French court in January 1998, naming Qadhafi's
brother-in-law, Muhammad al-Sanusi, as mastermind of the attack),
and a 1990 bombing attempt in Ethiopia intended to kill the Israeli ambassador there. Groups trained in Libya included the Abu Nidal organization, PFLP-GC, the Palestine Liberation Front, Palestinian Islamic
Jihad, the Provisional IRA, the Philippines New People's Army (NPA),
and even some Latin American organizations. Libya continued to assassinate or kidnap dissidents abroad – in places as far-flung as the
United States and Indonesia – and ran a number of training camps for
various terrorist groups.[49]

Yet Libya could show no gain from any of these activities. At the same
time, losses as a result of international sanctions on Libya are estimated

---

48 U.S. Department of State, "Libya's Continuing Responsibility for Terrorism," in *Patterns
    of Global Terrorism: 1991* (Washington, DC, 1992).
49 Ibid. The U.S. State Department, in *Patterns of Global Terrorism: 1989* (Washington,
    DC, 1990), reported that Qadhafi had aided thirty different groups.

at over $10 billion for the period between April 1992 and the end of 1994 alone.[50] Despite the ongoing sanctions against Libya for its sponsorship of terrorism, Tripoli continued to harass and intimidate Libyan expatriate dissidents in 1997. Libya is also believed to have abducted prominent Libyan dissident and human rights activist Mansur Kikhia in 1993 and to have executed him in early 1994. Kikhia, a U.S. green card holder, was married to an American citizen.

Libya continues to be held responsible for other past terrorist acts that remain of interest. Germany in November 1997 began the trial of five defendants in the 1986 La Belle discotheque bombing in Berlin, which killed three persons, including two U.S. servicemen, and wounded more than 200, many of them seriously. In opening remarks, the German prosecutor said that the bombing was "definitely an act of assassination commissioned by the Libyan state." German authorities issued warrants for four other Libyan officials, who were believed to be in Libya, for their role in the case. Libya also continued to provide support the most extreme Palestinian terrorist groups, including the Abu Nidal organization, Palestinian Islamic Jihad, and the PFLP-GC.[51]

Sudan served as a haven, meeting place, and training hub for a number of international terrorist organizations and funneled assistance to various groups. The U.S. State Department in November 1997 announced new comprehensive economic sanctions against Sudan, ordering the departure of terrorist financier Usama bin Ladin. The UN Security Council's demands included that Sudan turn over the three Egyptian Islamic Group fugitives linked to the attempted assassination of Egyptian President Mubarak in Ethiopia in 1995. Sudan's support for terrorist organizations included paramilitary training, indoctrination, money, travel documentation, safe passage, and refuge in Sudan.

Usama bin Ladin was one of the most significant sponsors of Sunni Islamic terrorist groups. The youngest son of the Saudi construction magnate Muhammad bin Ladin, he joined the Afghan resistance almost immediately after the Soviet invasion in December 1979. He played a significant role in financing, recruiting, transporting, and

50 Bruce Maddy-Weitzman, *Middle East Contemporary Survey, 1995*, Vol. 19 (New York, 1997), p. 479.

51 U.S. Department of State, "Overview of State-Sponsored Terrorism," in *Patterns of Global Terrorism: 1997* (Washington, DC, 1998). http://www.state.gov/www/global/terrorism/1997Report/1997index.html.

training Arab nationals who volunteered to fight in Afghanistan. During the war, bin Ladin founded al-Qa'ida – the Base – to serve as an operational hub, predominantly for like-minded Sunni Islamic extremists. The Saudi government revoked his citizenship in 1994, and his family formally disowned him. He had moved to Sudan in 1991, but international pressure on that government forced him to return to Afghanistan in 1996.

In August 1996, bin Ladin issued a statement outlining his organization's goals: drive U.S. forces from the Arabian peninsula, overthrow the government of Saudi Arabia, "liberate" Muslim holy sites in "Palestine," and support Islamic revolutionary groups around the world. To these ends, his organization has sent trainers throughout Afghanistan, as well as to Tajikistan, Bosnia, Chechnya, Somalia, Sudan, and Yemen and trained fighters from numerous other countries, including the Philippines, Egypt, Libya, and Eritrea. Bin Ladin also has close associations with the leaders of several Islamic terrorist groups and probably has aided in creating new groups since the mid-1980s. He has trained their troops, provided safe haven and financial support, and helped them with other organizational matters.

Beginning in August 1996, bin Ladin was very vocal in expressing his approval of and intent to use terrorism. He claimed responsibility for trying to bomb U.S. soldiers in Yemen in late 1992 and for attacks on them in Somalia in 1993. Reports suggest that his organization aided the Egyptian Islamic Group in its assassination attempt on Egyptian President Mubarak in Ethiopia in 1995. In November 1996 he called the 1995 and 1996 bombings against U.S. military personnel in Saudi Arabia "praiseworthy acts of terrorism" but denied having any personal participation in those bombings. At the same time, he called for further attacks against U.S. military personnel, saying: "If someone can kill an American soldier, it is better than wasting time on other matters."[52]

While it is not clear that bin Ladin was sponsored by any state, he played a central role in the paradigm debate of the 1990s, particularly after his group's successful attacks against the U.S. embassies in Kenya and Tanzania in 1998, its assault on the USS *Cole* in Yemen in 2000, and

---

52 Interview, May 1, 1998, with ABC journalist John Miller. http://www.homelandsecurity.org/quotes/quote.cfm?Authorid=26.

finally its September 11, 2001, operation against the World Trade Center and the Pentagon, the bloodiest single terror attack in world history.

In many ways, bin Ladin's activities fell into the traditional pattern of Middle Eastern strategy. He aimed to show that Islamist revolution could succeed, that America could be defeated, and that hatred of the United States could be a useful tool for mobilizing the masses in support of a cause. By arguing that his terrorism had accomplished more than conventional Arab armies, bin Ladin was reinforcing a key theme in the use of violence by regional states. By reinterpreting Islam and upholding the righteousness and potential success of radical violence, he and others fought against the paradigm for change and pragmatism in the Arab world. While explicitly rejecting his leadership and call for a war on America, regimes, intellectuals, and the Arab media used these arguments for parallel purposes and attempted to exploit the resulting incitement and hatred. Even the Taliban's fall and bin Ladin's apparent defeat did not overturn the triumphant intellectual system they represented. Though Islamist movements were in a struggle to overthrow the status quo, in fact the rulers successfully exploited this apparent threat for their own benefit.

7

THE BATTLE FOR THE
SOUL OF ISLAM

For decades, and especially since the Iranian revolution, there has been a tremendous battle for the soul of Islam among adherents of that religion holding very differing views. Radicals raised new interpretations that they claimed to be in accord with true Islam as it was originally meant to be. In fact, though, their worldview – which was at odds with how Muslims had practiced and thought about their faith for a thousand years – constituted an attempt to transform that religion. While the Islamists face an uphill battle – and are more likely to make trouble than they are to make successful revolutions – they certainly have a better chance to succeed in revising Islam than do the far weaker liberal Islamic forces.[1]

Many Arab governments hoped, however, to use the movement for their own purposes, channeling its anger against others. The regimes and their media told the West that the Islamists were not against "us" because of our mismanagement, incompetence, corruption, and repression, but against "you" because of your foreign policy. The regimes wanted to transform the Islamists from being a revolutionary movement to being an effective lobbying tool vis-à-vis the West. Moreover, a radical Islamist movement that put the emphasis on hating the West and Israel was much more useful for Arab regimes than a revolutionary Islamist movement that was firing machine-gun bullets at its officials. The solution, then, was not to change the system or quality of government in the Arab world, but for the West to give the rulers more respect, money, and concessions.

---

1 For a survey of Islamist movements, see Barry Rubin, ed., *Revolutionaries and Reformers: Contemporary Islamist Movements in the Middle East* (Albany, NY, 2003).

To those among their own citizens who found the Islamist message attractive, the regimes insisted that they were really on the same side. Governments wanted to show that they were pious and respectful of Islam, at least through symbols and lip service. They were eager to demonstrate that they fought its battles at home and abroad. The attacks on America of September 11, 2001, did not change this situation; they reinforced it. The regimes preferred to redefine the movement itself as anti-American and based on frustration over the Palestinian issue, not as a revolutionary effort to overthrow the governments themselves based on domestic issues.

In the broadest sense, then, the Islamist movements – unintentionally, of course – did more to reinforce than to destroy the existing systems in their countries. Facing such an internal threat, the regimes had a rationale for maintaining states of emergency and other tight controls. If radical Islamists could more easily take over the country using democracy and human rights as tools, then such things were dangerous luxuries that the rulers would reject. Many who might otherwise have been advocates of democracy were dissuaded by fear that more freedom might lead to a far worse situation. Simultaneously, though, Islamists themselves pushed public opinion even further away from moderation, helping to undermine any chance of peace with Israel or closer relations with the West. The Islamists did not defeat the governments in their countries, but they did deal a deadly blow to any hope for liberal reform. The Islamist revolution lost, but the Islamists helped the reactionary counterrevolution to win.

Their original expectations, of course, had been quite different. In the aftermath of Iran's revolution, it had seemed possible that several imitators would similarly transform the whole region. The American and French revolutions had encouraged a wave of democratic revolutions throughout Europe and elsewhere. The Russian revolution had inspired the formation of communist parties that struggled to imitate it for many decades. The Chinese and Cuban revolutions had launched lots of movements that imitated their rural guerrilla warfare strategies, believing that those victories could be duplicated elsewhere.

Iran's revolution should be seen in a similar historic perspective, though the fact that the world's first revolutionary Islamist state was neither Arab nor Sunni Muslim deterred even wider support among Arabs. Later, as had happened with its Arab nationalist counterparts,

Iran's own clearly visible failures and internal problems discouraged the idea that an Islamist revolution would solve all problems. Of course, the Iranian factor did not create the movement. It had already existed independently and had deep roots in several Arab countries. But even the existing groups were galvanized and strengthened by the seizure of power by their Iranian counterparts, which also inspired many fresh recruits and the formation of new Islamist organizations. At least the Iranians showed that it could be done. Their claim to have the workable and correct answer for their countries' problems and the people's burning grievances now had more legitimacy.

The militants who favored this new political Islamism could mobilize anger and frustration at just about every aspect of social life, domestic politics, and the international situation. Horrendous living standards, no jobs, an indifferent government bureaucracy, and lack of any reason to believe that things would get better were major factors in their appeal. As an Algerian scholar explained,

Opposition to the regime appeared as a reaction to disillusionment with the post-independence state, an entity in which Algerians had placed a heavy emotional investment after many years of hardship and sacrifice under colonial rule. . . . The political ideology of the Islamists corresponds to the political culture and ideas of the average Algerian, who blames the regime for its inability to fight corruption. As he sees it, the government is incapable of improving the conditions of everyday life (jobs, housing, transportation, and so on) and is dominated by people who seek only to enrich themselves and their relatives. . . . If those in power fear God and obey Holy Writ, they will not become corrupt. . . . [They] appeal to God in order to limit the arrogance and arbitrariness of the current government.[2]

The Islamist creed said that the Arabs were behind not because they were insufficiently Arab nationalist – for that idea, too, was a Western importation – but because they had lost contact with their own roots. They insisted that only Islam could unite the society, mobilize the masses, overturn the present unsatisfactory rulers, destroy Israel, make the Arabs equal to or even greater than the West, and provide all the answers for ordering the ideal society to be created thereafter. It was not an illogical response, since when all else fails, only God seems to be the

2 Lahouari Addi, "Algeria's Tragic Contradictions," *Journal of Democracy*, Vol. 7, No. 3 (1996), p. 104.

answer. But to determine God's political views, and especially to persuade everyone else that you – and only you – have properly interpreted them, is a far more difficult matter.

Radical Islamists insisted that they were fundamentalists because they were returning to the historic essence and proper interpretation of Islam. In practice, though, they represented an attempt to reinterpret Islam through modern ideas and new perspectives. They were moved less by theological reflections than by an urgent need to find a different way to solve the political problems that had long perplexed Arab nationalism: why the Arabs and Muslims were behind the West, why they had failed to achieve their goals, how they could create an ideal society on Earth. In practice, then, the Islamists were saying that they were better able to modernize their societies – albeit their own, very selective type of modernization – than nationalism or Westernization could. Even when they gave such things a lower priority, Islamists did not reject technological advancement, material betterment, social change, and other things associated with progress. Instead, they were convinced that only old ideas could achieve such progress successfully.

They found little competition from the sector that many in the West assumed would be the wave of the future: the secular-oriented Arab liberal intellectuals and democracy advocates, who were far too weak to play a leading role in any country. Equally, the Islamists' favorite self-defined enemies, the United States and Israel, played virtually no role in the struggles over power in the various Arab states.

But their real enemies had plenty of assets. In fact, the radical Islamists' chief rival was traditional Islam itself, as preached by most clerics and practiced by most Muslims. The refusal of most Muslims to accept the new Islamist vision lies at the root of the movement's failures to gain hegemony in the region. On many specific issues, the classical texts and customs were obviously different from the claims made by radical Islamists. Islam as traditionally practiced was a conservative creed, designed to coexist with society as it was and to accept its rulers, at least if they were Muslim ones, not to challenge them. Thus, in some ways Islamists wanted to revise their faith in light of the latest political developments and analyses, while in other ways they sought to leap over roughly 1300 years of history to return to Islam's earliest revolutionary phase.

To accept the idea that the revolutionaries' brand of Islam was really right for today – indeed, the only valid form of Islam – the Muslim masses would have to decide that their own beliefs and practices were wrong, despite the fact that they and their ancestors had always lived according to those precepts. Why had they to discover suddenly that the principle of jihad required them to fight the West, that their own rulers were enemies of Islam who must be overthrown, or that suicide terrorism intended to kill civilians was properly Islamic?

Thus, many Muslims concluded that the radicals were attacking them rather than battling on their behalf. Their views would not be swayed by theological debate as such, but only by a concerted propaganda campaign whose passion might overwhelm memories and better judgment. After twenty years of largely unsuccessful efforts to stage revolutions within Arab states, many radical Islamists concluded, like bin Ladin, that only hate-filled xenophobia had a chance to overcome these obstacles. The revolutionary Islamist movement became what might be called the jihadist Islamist movement, focusing its attention and doctrine on fighting non-Muslims.

Just as radical Islamists ran up against the prevailing practice of Islam, they also collided with the reality of the particular nation-states where Muslims lived. While radical Islamists might see the existence of separate countries as obstacles to the creation of a united Muslim state under a caliph, such factors were too powerful to ignore. Each radical Islamist movement had to develop a strategy and tactics appropriate for its individual country and to combat a specific ruling regime. Consequently, the groups grew in different directions, each with its own leaders, doctrines, and timetables. In creating al-Qaida as a multinational group with allies in different countries, bin Ladin was trying to solve this problem.

Further, while Islamist groups insisted that all good Muslims were really united, they often owed their existence and their support base to the fact that they were representing ethnic or national groups. In Lebanon, Hizballah is essentially a Shi'ite communal party opposing Christian and Sunni Muslim hegemony, a situation guaranteeing conflict with the country's other communities. In Syria, the Islamists represent a Sunni majority, the country's traditional rulers, who oppose an essentially non-Muslim (Alawite) government. In Iraq, the movement represents a Shi'ite majority that is dissatisfied with a largely Sunni ruling elite. With the partial exception of the Muslim Brotherhood network – which encourages some cooperation among the Egyptian, Jordanian, Palestinian (Hamas), and Syrian Muslim Brotherhoods – each movement stands mostly on its own, battling a relatively well-financed and well-armed local government.

Government propaganda against the Islamists often built very successfully on the idea that Islamists were enemies of traditional Islam and traitors to the nation. In addition, the regimes had many assets, including Islamic ones, that could be used to wage this struggle. Not only did the rulers control money, patronage, and repression, but often they also had a significant degree of control over mosques, religious schools, mullahs, and the media. Their tactics to counter revolutionary Islamists included expropriating Islamic symbols, co-opting large elements of Islamic institutions, promoting patriotism and Arab nationalism, and unleashing repression.

Repressive regimes or those feeling their survival threatened by revolutionary Islamists, such as those in Syria, Iraq, and Saudi Arabia, have been quite prepared to kill or imprison activists and to ban their movements. In many cases, a government's willingness and ability to apply massive force has crushed Islamist insurgencies. Saddam Hussein murdered a number of leading Shi'ite clerics. His Syrian counterparts wiped out much of Hama, one of the country's biggest cities, in 1982, killing between 10,000 and 30,000 people in order to eliminate a center of supporters for the Islamist movement.

Repression has also been successfully combined with a government's attempts to use and control Islam for its own purposes. Saddam's secularism and ferocity against pious Muslims did not stop him from garnering Islamist support for his 1990 invasion of Kuwait as a holy war, or even for adding the Muslim slogan Allahu Akhbar ('God Is Great') to Iraq's flag. The kings of Jordan and Morocco – who claim descent from the family of the founder of Islam – and of Saudi Arabia, the leader of the Wahabi sect and guardian of Mecca and Medina, possess considerable Islamic credentials of their own. At one politically sensitive moment, the late King Hussein grew a beard in order to court this constituency. In Egypt, the government controls a huge Islamic sector, ranging from local mosques to the prestigious al-Azhar religious university. Preachers and teachers in Islamic schools are government employees. Arafat was also ready with an appropriate Islamic reference or

Quranic quote in every speech. He created his own satellite Islamist party, gave high posts to Islamist activists who supported him, and maintained a clever balancing act, sometimes keeping Hamas in line while at other times using its terrorist violence to serve his own strategy.

The radical Islamists' defeats can be traced to both a lack of popular support and the effectiveness of government countermeasures. As a result of the domestic Muslim and regime resistance to their message, radical Islamists were unable to stage successful revolutions. True, Iran's regime survived, but it became increasingly unpopular at home. Khatami favored the survival of Islamist Iran but on terms quite contrary to what the hard-liners who really ruled the country or their would-be imitators elsewhere wanted. Revolutionary Islamist doctrine and groups did become the principal opposition force throughout the Arab world, but, contrary to their preferences, they remained in opposition.

By the late 1990s, most traditional Muslims still rejected radical Islamism, though more of its ideas were filtering into their thinking. Arab nationalism also continued to exercise a powerful (even if reduced) appeal, and incumbent regimes cooked up a clever mix of repression and co-optation aimed at suppressing these groups. Uprisings in Egypt and Algeria had been defeated. Although Lebanese and Palestinian Islamist groups could claim successes in individual attacks against Israel or in that country's withdrawal from Lebanon, this had not brought them any closer to defeating Israel or to gaining leadership over their own peoples. The Islamist revolution was not succeeding.

Thus, the emergence of a movement around Usama bin Ladin was not a result of the radical interpretation's success in winning over the masses; rather, it was a desperate reaction to its failure. Having lost in every other way, bin Ladin and his followers tried to play the anti-American card, downgrading their opposition to the Arab regimes to the point where they might tolerate bin Ladin and his movement as an asset, or at least not as a threat. On September 11, 2001, however, they were too successful in attacking the United States. At first, this made them very popular in the Arab street, and regimes rushed, each in its own way, to profit indirectly from the event. But America was too angry for Arab states or even Iran to risk its wrath by explicitly endorsing or protecting al-Qa'ida groups. Nonetheless, as the debate continued, and whatever his own movement's fate, bin Ladin had struck a powerful doctrinal blow for a further radicalization of Islamist thought.

At the start, radical Islamists had made three main arguments in launching their political movements:

1. Islam is the answer to the problems of Muslim society in every country of the region. The relative weakness of Muslims and of Arab societies compared to the West, their slow or stagnant economic development, their failure to destroy Israel, domestic and inter-Arab disunity, inequality and injustice, and other such problems are caused by the failure to implement Islam properly.

Many Muslims who might tend to agree with the first sentence nevertheless find other sources of doctrine and explanations for their current unhappy situation equally or more acceptable. For example, large proportions of Muslims embrace Arab and Turkish nationalism and other non-Islamist political ideologies. The virtual single-factor explanation of shortcomings, grievances, and solutions does not dominate their thinking, even if they accept some Islamist ideas.

A Western analogy would be that while communist movements claimed to speak on behalf of such large entities as workers, oppressed minorities, and progressive thinkers, these same groups usually rejected that purported leadership. While there were many who endorsed those elements of the Marxist parties' arguments demanding social justice, strong trade unions, and a redistribution of economic power, far fewer accepted that doctrine's systematic ideology or decided to join Communist parties.

2. Implementing Islam and resolving the huge problems of the Arab and Iranian peoples or countries require that radical Islamist groups seize and hold state power. The best-known, though hardly sole, proponent and architect of this premise was Khomeini, though not all radical Islamists echo his view that Islamic clerics should rule.

In many Arab countries – and to some extent even in Iran – the leading clerics favor conservative Islamic views that involve accepting existing Muslim rulers, a division of authority between state and religion, and avoiding the use of violence against other Muslims. By contrast, the radicals interpret the need for Islam to be in full and direct political power as a core value of Islam. Any view of Islam that does not accept this tenet is illegitimate. In historical terms, the problem is that Islam existed for many centuries dominated by a completely opposite idea:

A ruler should be properly pious, but the state need not be ruled and shaped by Islam. In addition, while there have been many exceptions, Islam has usually adopted tolerant pluralism among its own adherents.

The radicals claim they are going back to the religion's origins in the seventh century (hence returning to fundamentals), but in fact theirs is a deviant, even heretical, viewpoint not accepted by the majority of Muslims or clerics. Even in Iran, there were and are many respected senior clerics who reject Khomeini's views. Indeed, again, those who oppose radical Islamist doctrine are often more respected and have better scholarly credentials than those who embrace it. For example, the leadership of the al-Azhar University in Egypt and the top clerics in Saudi Arabia all reject this view. The radicals try to portray them, with varying degrees of success, as puppets of the regimes.

While some revolutionary groups draw on one or more respected Islamic clerics, they are often few in number or marginal ones whose credentials are far less impressive than those of the state-appointed clerics who portray the revolutionaries as charlatans or heretics. The radicals' response is to claim that lay people with the proper political line, like bin Ladin himself, are entitled to interpret Islam and to issue decrees. Another tactic is to find relatively obscure, low-ranking clerics – such as Shaykh Umar Abd al-Rahman in Egypt and Mullah Umar in Afghanistan – and build them into charismatic leaders. The Islamists are equally ready to use the most modern tools of all, such as cassette tapes, to circumvent the traditional clerical hierarchy and reach a mass audience.

These tactics are in line with a broader trend in the Islamic world. As Dale Eickelman has noted: "What distinguishes the present era from prior ones is the large numbers of believers engaged in the reconstruction of religion, community, and society. Today, the major impetus for change in religious and political values comes from below." This poses a challenge to the system in which professional clerics with a "mastery of fixed bodies of religious texts" hand down rulings. "No one group or type of leader in contemporary Muslim societies possesses a monopoly on the management of the sacred." But while some of those taking advantage of this opportunity are liberals, those most likely to win big audiences for their reinterpretations of texts and ideas are radical Islamists.[3]

3 In Rubin, ed., *Revolutionaries and Reformers*.

3. The only proper interpretation of Islam is the one offered by a specific political group and its leaders. This premise also poses a serious problem. For if the majority of people do not accept the doctrine as a whole, even more of them will reject at least some of the specifics of a given group's ideology, program, tactics, and strategy.

Here again, a Western parallel can be found in the Marxist-Leninist movement's demand for a dictatorship of the proletariat and the sole rule of the Communist Party, coupled with the ferocious denunciation of all who disagreed – especially labor leaders and social democrats – as lackeys of the capitalist regime. Such radical movements are almost inherently intolerant, because they claim to speak with the voice of God, while their opponents' views are denounced as traitorous or even satanic. This approach generates fiery propaganda and passionately dedicated recruits, but also makes many enemies and is incapable of convincing the majority. Moreover, since the radical sects believe that there is only one correct line, they often quarrel among themselves. There is rarely room in any organization for more than one charismatic leader. Factions and splits are inevitable, thus weakening the movement and sometimes leading to infighting.

Despite their handicaps, the radicals did have some advantages. They were directly bidding to have a monopoly on one of the most important trump issues, the political and social uses of Islam. Traditional Islam is less overtly political and more focused on individuals and their behavior, while radical activists are more energetic and visible in the public arena. The radical Islamists also enjoyed tactical flexibility, including the ability to use violent and nonviolent methods simultaneously. They were able to win adherents by providing grassroots social services, at a time when neither governments nor rival movements worked so closely and creatively to help the masses in this way. At the same time, since terrorism is an activity requiring a relatively small but highly motivated cadre – and is often adopted as a strategy precisely by such small groups – it was well suited to the radicals' situation of having fewer but very dedicated supporters.

Further, even on issues where the radicals deviated from Islam as it had been taught, believed, and practiced, their passion and example on many points significantly moved the debate and the community's beliefs closer to their views. There are many examples of these shifts. The radicals preached hatred of Jews and sometimes of Christians, while traditionally Islam professed to respect these two religions. Hatred of Jews – based on the conflict with Israel but not restricted to it – has now penetrated mainstream thinking. The radicals advocated and practiced suicide bombing and the deliberate killing of civilians, while traditional Islam rejected this type of behavior. A major debate over this issue has developed, with some conservatives now accepting, at least conditionally, the radical argument. The radicals reinterpreted the duty of jihad as requiring Muslims to make Islamist revolutions in modern times, to reject governments led by Muslims, and to kill Muslims who were officials in such regimes. Traditional Islam rejected these ideas, but many rank-and-file believers were won over to them.

In trying to maximize their advantages and overcome the many obstacles they faced, Islamist organizations basically used three different strategies: revolutionary, national liberationist, and reformist.

The revolutionary strategy seeks to overthrow an existing Arab government through armed struggle, as was attempted in Algeria, Bahrain, Egypt, Saudi Arabia, Syria, and Iraq. Except in Algeria, where Islamists turned to revolution after their electoral victory was blocked, these revolutionary groups were all relatively small organizations. They had little chance of winning a confrontation with the authorities. Rather, they wrongly expected – like many leftist insurrectionist groups in European and Latin American history – that violence itself would inspire and mobilize the masses to support them.

Four of these six "pure" revolutionary groups were also largely representatives of communities – Shi'ite in Bahrain, Saudi Arabia, and Iraq; Sunni in Syria's case – that are as much ethnic as they are theological groupings. Yet since their enemies were also Muslims, they could not explicitly identify themselves as fighters for a specific community, since such sectarian and nationalist definitions conflict with their Islamist ideology. At any rate, the movements were unable to mobilize solid support even within their own ethnic communities.

In the most despotic states, these revolutionary groups embody grievances that have been completely barred from expression, much less solution, by any other means. Yet the more repressive the state, the more easily it has suppressed the revolt. At any rate, all of these efforts, along with smaller such groups elsewhere, failed completely to seize state power.

One response to this defeat was to turn to even more extreme violence, as if to punish the people for not supporting them. The toll was horrendous, as shown by some examples from the month of December 1999 alone. In the final days of the twentieth century, twenty-one people, nineteen of them Christians, were killed in attacks by Islamist extremists in the town of Kosheh in Egypt. In Algeria, twelve school-children were killed by a radical Islamist attack on a schoolbus in the town of Milyana. In Turkey, the bodies of forty-five people tortured and murdered by the Turkish Hizballah group, including an Islamist feminist who was killed for not having the proper political line, were discovered.[4]

In truth, terrorism is not the weapon of the poor or oppressed, but a carefully thought out revolutionary tactic. Like those who used similar violence in Europe a century earlier, when it was called "the propaganda of the deed," radical Islamists believed that terrorist bombings and assassinations would delegitimize and demoralize their enemies. The result was expected to be the collapse of the government from within and an uprising of the masses, which would see the regime as vulnerable and the Islamists as their vanguard. When these measures failed, the violence was often escalated further, until or unless the revolutionaries were suppressed. Ultimately, such a terrorist strategy is the last refuge of failed revolutionary groups that can find no other way to build a mass base or to gain power.

The national liberationists, however, were the category of Islamist group most successful in gaining support from their constituencies, though none of them staged a successful revolution either. These organizations claimed that they would lead the Muslims against foreign, non-Muslim enemies. This approach was on safer traditional and theological grounds

---

4 On Kosheh, see Nagi A. Kheir, "Human Rights Report on Egypt's Kosheh Tragedy and Proposed Plan of Action," Advocates International, Virginia, January 10, 2000, http://www.advocatesinternational.org/kosheh.htm; "An Appeal to the Egyptian Nation," *Ibn Khaldun Center for Development Studies*, Vol. 9, No. 98 (February 2000). On Milyana, see "Algeria: Amnesty International Condemns Massacres of Civilians," Amnesty International Index MDE 28/017/2000, News Service No. 241, December 21, 2000. http://web.amnesty.org/ai.nsf/Index/MDE280172000?OpenDocument&of=COUNTRIES%5CALGERIA. On Turkish Hizballah, see Nilufer Narli, "Death of a Fundamentalist Feminist," *One World*, March 10, 2000, http://www.oneworld.net/cgi-bin/index.cgi?root=129&url=http%3A%2F%2Fwww%2Eoneworld%2Eorg%2Findex%5Foc%2Fnews%2Fturkey1100300%2Ehtml.

and had the advantage of not immediately dividing the community into good (Islamist) and bad Muslims.

This approach was used by the Islamist groups fighting the Soviets in Afghanistan, as well as by the Lebanese Hizballah, and the Palestinian groups Hamas and Islamic Jihad fighting against Israel. Yet even this stance did not necessarily guarantee Islamist forces leadership over all Muslims, much less victory over their opponents. There were always competing, usually nationalist, forces who could muster more supporters. Even Hizballah and Hamas, playing on highly popular anti-Israeli themes, could not gain hegemony, respectively, over Amal (the nationalist-oriented Lebanese Shi'ite group) and the Palestinian Authority, controlled by the nationalist Fatah group. In Afghanistan, the Taliban movement did temporarily gain control of the country, albeit only with significant financial help from Saudi Arabia and bin Ladin along with logistical support from Pakistan.

Like Third World Communist parties in earlier decades, these Islamists cooperated on broader fronts against the foreign enemy, while also trying to seize control of the overall movement and to establish their preferred form of state after victory. Acting as a vanguard in battling the infidels, they tried to show themselves both braver and more politically correct than the nationalists.

This strategy also required them, however, to ensure that the struggle did not end. When Israel withdrew from southern Lebanon in May 2000, Hizballah could and did claim victory. But this development also meant that Hizballah would no longer be seen in Lebanon as a heroic force allowed to stand above the law because it was waging a holy war. Instead, it would have to face the non-Islamist Shia groups, the non-Shia Lebanese communities, the Lebanese government, and the country's Syrian masters, all of whom had tolerated or helped its attacks against Israel but totally opposed Hizballah's program to make Lebanon an Islamist state. Of course, Hizballah was already functioning in its reformist mode as well, competing in elections and holding seats in parliament. But there it was not a heroic resistance movement but merely another small party with little influence and no prospects for growth.

Hizballah's solution to this problem was to ensure that, as the *Beirut Daily Star* put it – despite Israel's withdrawal from the south, and ten years after the Lebanese civil war had ended with the disarmament of private armies – "[t]here is a part of the country where militias [still] rule." Hizballah's leader, Shaykh Hasan Nasrallah, suggested that the Lebanese government let Hizballah rule the south and continue to fight Israel, since his movement had "more freedom to act without being dragged into dangerous situations." But, the newspaper concluded, Hizballah was no longer "an embodiment of the national unity behind the resistance" but rather a domestic political force seeking its own interests.[5]

Similarly, Hamas and Islamic Jihad needed to use violence to block any diplomatic solution to the Israel-Palestinian issue, since such an outcome would reduce the Palestinian motivation for continued struggle and put the Islamists themselves at the mercy of a nationalist regime. In short, the national liberationists did not want to have to transform themselves into playing the far more difficult role of revolutionaries or the far less exciting one of reformists. As long as the battle went on, though, the Lebanese government and the Palestinian Authority each had its own reasons for letting such groups operate freely.

The reformists are the third type of Islamist group. The most open Middle Eastern regimes, such as those in Egypt, Jordan, Kuwait, Morocco, Turkey, and Israel, let Islamist parties function openly and participate in elections. These governments are confident that they can survive an Islamist challenge, and some of them – for example, Egypt and Jordan – are also ready to manipulate voting results to ensure that Islamists are always kept in the minority. In Turkey, an Islamist party was even allowed to hold executive authority briefly. At the same time, Islamists are encouraged to stay within the law, since violent efforts are dealt with severely. The Islamists themselves, or at least their majorities, are ready to accept the rules of the game, because they judge any attempt to seize power as suicidal.

If this trend were to continue, eventually Islamist parties could become the equivalent of the Christian Democratic parties of Europe and Latin America, or of Israel's Jewish religious parties. This means they would become parties focusing on advocacy regarding specific issues and protecting the interests of their supporters and institutions, rather than on seeking to transform society as a whole. In turn, these movements could

5 Michael Young, "What Red Lines for Hizballah," *Beirut Daily Star,* July 6, 2000.

become interest groups within society rather than standing in opposition outside the system with the principal goal of overturning it. They could bring about some changes, such as making society more religiously observant. Equally or more important, they could build a vast social and educational apparatus of institutions and thereby create a permanent community of supporters.

Islamist politicians, many of whom are by no means eager to give their lives for the cause, have an incentive to accept the system's rules. Agreeing to be the loyal opposition keeps them out of jail, safeguards their property, and gives them a chance to gain more wealth, patronage, and prestige. Reformism does not arise from venal considerations alone, but such personal benefits can certainly make such a choice more attractive, as does the lack of a viable alternative strategy. Movements that eschew violent tactics can try to move society toward a more Islamic identity, hoping that this will some day let them transform it altogether.

The appeal can be in terms of practical politics with little connection to ideological or theological factors. In Morocco, the leader of a major left-wing party explains that the poor turn toward the Islamists because "[w]e have adopted middle class values. We've lost contact with the people. We must regain the poor neighborhoods. The Islamists have seduced our natural electorate and promised them heaven on earth." A woman Islamist activist there explains the approach in these terms:

We help people in practical ways. We visit the sick, help them to buy medicine, contribute to funeral expenses, organize evening classes for the schoolchildren and support single women, widows and divorcees. We also contribute to the cost of [religious] pilgrimages and provide legal aid for the victims of recognized abuse. Our work is not just spiritual; it is practical, helping people with their everyday problems. With the shortcomings of the state and the tough conditions of daily life, people discover, thanks to us, solidarity, mutual assistance and fraternity. They realize that Islam is about people. Our aim is to gain power peacefully, by persuasion and education. We are against violence.[6]

---

6 Ignacio Ramonet, "Morocco: The Point of Change: New Hope, Old Frustrations," *Le Monde Diplomatique*, July 2000. http://www.monde-diplomatique.fr/en/2000/07/01ramonet.

The party tries to get budgetary support from the government coffers; its constituency obtains patronage and services from the party. Its leaders receive various privileges, including financial benefits, power, and prestige that might be lost if they were to challenge the government. They are able to create a wide range of organizations as well as to take over professional associations and student councils through institutional elections, even in countries where the regime manipulates parliamentary elections.

The reformists' problem, however, is that they will not be allowed to take power, since the current regimes – as well as the leaders of other parties and communities – assume that an Islamist party that did gain power peacefully would never surrender it peacefully or democratically. To accept that fact of permanent exclusion from ruling power would be to abandon their transformative vision; to reject it would mean their suppression and the destruction of all the institutions they have built up.

In response, reformist Islamists argue that their techniques will win many followers among conservative Muslims who would never support armed struggle, and will provide a springboard for taking power in the future. But if people are able to live an Islamist lifestyle, they may feel less need to transform an entire society. In Turkey, the Islamist party split in 2001 into radical and moderate elements, with the latter realizing that the movement could never make much progress until it persuaded other Turks that it does not seek to establish an Islamist state. Yet the most successful liberal Islamic movement, that of Fetullah Gulen, was ultimately suppressed by the Turkish military, which saw it as a revolutionary Islamic group in disguise.[7]

Those lacking patience or faith in this method conclude that the old leadership has grown too soft or even traitorous and they split away to form revolutionary groups.[8] This happened in Egypt, where the government let the main Islamist group, the Muslim Brotherhood, participate in electoral politics, hold parliamentary seats, and function as a movement. But permissible limits were clearly set. Periodic arrests and vote rigging served to remind the Brotherhood that it would be crushed if it ever appeared able to seize power. Revolutionaries left the group

7 Bulent Aras, "Fetullah Gulen and His Movement," in Rubin, ed., *Revolutionaries and Reformers*; Birol A. Yesilada, "The Virtue Party in Turkey," in Barry Rubin and Metin Heper, eds., *Political Parties in Turkey* (London, 2002).

8 An interesting comparison could be made to Latin America, where reformist communist parties lost cadre to new Cuban-influenced and Maoist groups that launched armed struggles.

because they thought it too timid, and these smaller and badly divided groups were ultimately defeated by the government.[9]

King Hussein of Jordan also showed how Islamist forces could be outmaneuvered. He let Jordan's Islamists participate in parliament but denied them real policy-making power. On the one hand, he adopted tough restrictions and threatened the Islamists with fierce repression. On the other hand, he made symbolic concessions, such as strengthening Islamic norms in Jordan and even letting the movement drag him into supporting Iraq during the Kuwait crisis.

By contrast, the Algerian regime's openness let the Islamists get too close to success. When they were on the verge of electoral victory, the army staged a coup to stop them. Faced with the choice between surrender and revolution, the previously peaceful Islamic Salvation Front (FIS) fought back, and the result was a bloody civil war that left tens of thousands of people dead. Other Arab governments are unlikely to repeat this mistake. If the legal route will not lead the Islamists to power, then this method too could be regarded as unsatisfactory. In short, like the Communist parties in Europe, accepting the reformism route requires a true revision of the movement's worldview and purpose that is hard but not impossible to make, but that can break an organization in the long run.

For the Islamists and their supporters, however, the struggle would continue as long as there is hope of victory. If success could not be achieved through successful takeovers of governments, they would gain encouragement from large demonstrations, terrorist attacks with large numbers of casualties, victories in student government and professional association elections, grassroots organizing, mosque sermons, and hearing their views repeated in the media. But if merely belonging to such a movement satisfied people, it could also mean that political Islamism itself, as Islam had traditionally been, was a political opiate for the masses, satisfying needs and making people less – not more – likely to revolt. In this case, which is already the situation in several countries, Islamism becomes a new pillar for the dominant system while making liberal reform even more difficult.

But if the radicals have major problems competing with the traditionalists, the liberal Muslims are in the worst situation of all. While

9 Barry Rubin, *Islamic Fundamentalists in Egyptian Politics*, second revised edition (New York, 2002).

liberals openly argue that they are trying to adjust doctrine to modern conditions – regarding the role of women, for example – the radicals have an advantage in claiming that their own views are merely a return to the original, proper interpretations. While the liberals argue a right of interpretation – which means others can offer different interpretations – the radicals deny they are doing this, insisting that theirs is the only conceivable standpoint. The radicals play on passionate hatreds and the very misperceptions fostered for decades by the regimes. The liberals try to use reason and believe they can learn from the West regarding tolerance and the modernization of religion. Finally, the already small liberal Muslim camp loses many potential recruits who become secularist, or at least religiously inactive.

Compared to the flourishing variety of Islamist groups, philosophies, and charismatic personalities, the liberal response is quite feeble. They could accurately warn, as did an Algerian scholar: "The Islamist opposition seeks to put in place a regime with the very same architecture as the one it is now fighting; the only change would be one of personnel." But how many people would accept the idea that "the true opposition is the one mounted by the democrats, who are trying to further the project of removing legitimating power from the hands of the army and founding a system run according to the principle of alternation in power by means of elections"?[10] Indeed, this explanation provides reasons for the army and the ruling establishment to fight against such an alternative.

One of the most articulate liberal analyses of the problem was penned by Ahmad Bishara, the leader of Kuwait's National Democratic Movement. Bishara said that Islam, like other religions, viewed God "[a]s a force of love, peace, compassion and a motivating force to the individual." But now Muslims needed a war "to save their faith . . . [from] fanatical cults and muftis who have hijacked Islam for their own ends." He called for a "body of enlightened clergy" to serve as "the sole interpreter of the faith," banning "the practice of obscure individuals issuing haphazard fatwas on behalf of all Muslims." Secular authorities and "enlightened Islamic scholars" should root out materials "prejudiced [against] women, insensitive to human rights and intolerant to other faiths and cultures" from religious school textbooks and the media. Instead, the emphasis in Islamic education and sermons should be

10 Addi, "Algeria's Tragic Contradictions."

on "the ideals of peace, tolerance and coexistence if Muslims aspire to fit in a multi-cultural and multi-ethnic world." [11]

"Many well-meaning Muslims think Islam is misunderstood in the West," Bishara explained. "Well, maybe to some extent that is true. But it is the failure of Muslims to understand the fundamental message of their own religion, practice it properly and accommodate it to the modern world that is at stake." He coupled this argument with a political prescription: "With the rise of the modern state . . . religion was increasingly removed from state affairs and relegated to a personal conviction. No society has since succeeded without this model. None will ever, either. Muslim societies cannot continue a self-deception that they are different. . . . They are not." Modern society was simply impossible without a separation between religion and state, including "Democratic governance, separation of powers, human rights or most basic international relations. Muslims and Muslim countries must accommodate themselves to this reality."

These were noble sentiments, but they also contained within them the reason why they would not be heeded and why liberal Islamist secularists have so few attractive alternatives. How could Bishara call for the supervision of religion by governments without keeping religion as just another arm of the state? The clear answer was that the regimes did not want to give up their control over religion because it was an important mechanism of control. Moreover, the government could make the popular and reasonable argument that to do so would give the extremists a free hand.

In addition, Bishara's approach also represented a threat to the leaders of traditional Islam, the governments' main allies in defeating the Islamists, as well as significant forces preserving the status quo. And there is another, more subtle, problem in Bishara's views. He invoked a foreign, non-Arab model of development as being the only one possible. In short, he was proposing imitation of the West, itself a taboo concept in the Arab world's public discourse, no matter how often critics admitted precisely this point in private. Thus, the sum total of supporters for the liberal argument would be a small minority of the intellectuals and clerics who faced the opposition of the state, traditionalist and radical Muslims, and the great majority of the population.

11 Ahmad Bishara, "After Afghanistan: Liberating Islam," *Arab Times*, September 17, 2001.

Similar sentiments were put forward by other Arab liberals – for example, by Alia Toukan, a businesswoman in Jordan. While criticizing the West, she also noted, "Many governments in the Muslim world bear a direct responsibility for pushing ... some of their people into political and religious extremism." Their shortcomings in this sense include "lack of democratization and political legitimacy ... rampant corruption, absence of accountability, and feelings of powerlessness. Islamist parties stepped in to fill the gap by taking over civil society and becoming the real leaders of the masses."[12]

The fact that "a fanatic has come from our midst and claims to speak on our behalf," she continued, required that "every Muslim and Arab ask him/herself what has gone wrong? How is it that our religion and culture have been so shamelessly hijacked by zealots who don't seem to respect the most basic of Islamic principles espousing religious tolerance and acceptance?" This extremist minority had prevailed because the moderate majority remained silent. Since extremists spread their ideas through mass organization and grassroots education, the moderates must do the same. She particularly recommended voting for moderate candidates for parliament and professional associations and alliance with moderate religious leaders.[13] Such a strategy, which was not even possible in most countries, was not exactly a devastating threat to the regimes and militant Islamists.

Moreover, this pair of liberal articles – and most, though not all, others of this type – has two significant things in common. Both were op-ed pieces published in English-language newspapers. In Arabic and in articles written by reporters and regular columnists, they were dwarfed by a tidal wave of quite different utterances. In addition, these two articles called on governments to fight extremism by becoming more democratic and less corrupt, advice most Arab regimes would not be eager to heed. Moreover, the articles were written in Kuwait and Jordan, the two Arab countries where there was perhaps the greatest chance for the emergence of strong liberal and moderate Islamic movements. Still, that alternative vision – the one most vital for a peaceful and progressing region – held a distant last place in the Arab world's battle of ideas.

The progress of Islamist movements has been far from the triumphal march to power hoped for, and predicted, by the Islamists themselves.

12 *Jordan Times*, November 27, 2001.
13 Ibid.

Indeed, it is more likely that the only radical Islamist regime, Iran, will decline than that it will be joined by new comrades. The great majority of Muslim Arabs, at least of the current generation, will not join radical Islamist groups or support such revolutions in their own countries. The appeals of Arab nationalism and traditional Islam are still too great. What could be more ironic and revealing than the fact that those who wanted to launch global war on behalf of Islam – al-Qaida and the Taliban – were hunted down by some of the world's most pious Muslims. After killing their Islamist radical enemies, the Afghan soldiers, who called themselves *mujahadin*, went to pray.

Yet a broad trend toward moderation is equally unlikely. The existence of strong Islamist groups drags societies into a more rigid interpretation of, and a larger public role for, their religion. Reformist Islamist groups will enlarge their sphere of influence, including their ability to set the social and political agenda. This situation will make a liberal democratic approach to religion and politics even harder to accept. And for the radical Islamists themselves, periodic frustration at not being able to gain full power – or, conversely, government crackdowns to ensure they will not take over – will lead to violent episodes.

Perhaps the historical function of Islamist organizations is not so different from the role that similar reactionary religious and social movements have played historically in the West. Such groups and schools of thought, of which the fascist ones are only the best-remembered but hardly unique examples, formed as responses to the challenges of modernization, nation building, democracy, and capitalism. They raged against alien ways as undermining their societies' traditions and authenticity, stirred up communal hatred at home and aggression abroad, and blamed conspiracies of Jews, foreign imperialists, or others for all of their problems. Claiming to provide alternative routes to development, such groups looked to historic utopian models such as the ancient Germanic tribes, medieval corporatism, and early Christianity as ideal eras that they would recreate. Yet these "rejectionist" European groups lasted a very long time, were repeatedly reborn in different forms, and were responsible for killing many millions of people.

Only the outright defeat of the extremists, the success of modernization, and the reformulation of religious doctrine can end this historical episode. The Middle East seems far from reaching that goal, farther than any other part of the world.

In this complex of factors, one other point also stands out. While Islamist groups often seem to be a threat to the state, they are more often, in practice, tools of the state. Starting in the 1950s, Saudi Arabia made the promotion and export of its version of Islam a front line in its defense against Nasserism. In later years, Saudi money financed the Taliban directly and bin Ladin's movement through educational and charitable groups. The Egyptian and Jordanian governments also allied themselves with Islamist groups at times in their struggles against leftist movements.

Even radical secular states such as Iraq, Syria, and Libya sponsor Islamist terror groups abroad in order to promote their interests and strike at their adversaries. Iran and Sudan, as Islamist states themselves, certainly fall into this category. All Arab states have backed Islamist groups using terror against Israel, and Pakistan played the same game against India and in promoting its own influence in Afghanistan. The attempt by many Arabs to argue that the United States is really responsible for radical Islam, because of a very brief and limited use of such forces in Afghanistan, is no more than a typical example of the region's obsessive blame-shifting.[14]

But as always, the Islamists, like everyone else in the Arab world, faced the choice of whether to put the priority on the struggle to improve life at home or on the struggle to defeat those perceived as enemies abroad. Failing to make revolution at home, Islamists had an incentive to turn outward. With the breakdown of the peace process, regimes and their opponents were on the same side – a situation that had benefits for both of them – against Israel and at least rhetorically against the West. A Tunisian Islamist, Shaykh Rashed al-Ghanushi, has said that the current rulers "[a]re not the kind of regime that we want. . . . [They] are undemocratic and do not satisfactorily represent the will of our peoples." However, the current task means this issue should be ignored in order "to mobilize them in support of the Intifada and the liberation of Palestine." There is now consensus among the rulers, Islamist movements, Pan-Arab nationalists, and the people. "The mobilization of the [Arab] masses serve the regimes, because these regimes

---

14 Actually, the same relatively moderate Islamic groups that received the most backing from the United States in Afghanistan during the battle against the Soviets returned, in the form of the Northern Alliance, to become U.S. allies in battling the Taliban regime many years later in 2001.

are under immense pressure from the Americans and they need an excuse not to give in to them."[15]

What he could have added was that a reduced Islamist revolutionary challenge strengthened the regimes. By giving up their failed efforts to overthrow governments, the Islamists could function more freely and avoid repression. Probably, this alliance would not do much to advance the Palestinian cause, destroy Israel, or expel the West. But it would do a great deal to preserve the status quo within the Arab world itself. Once again, change at home was sacrificed for illusory triumphs abroad. In the end, the Arab societies would have no gain in either category.

Indeed, what the radical Islamists had done with the advent of bin Ladin was to copy an old technique of the Arab nationalists. Knowing that both revolutionary and reformist Islamist groups had failed, they sought to reorient themselves in the image of the most successful version of radical Islam: the national liberation movement. Instead of trying to lobby or overthrow Arab regimes, they would become the vanguard of the Muslim people in fighting the rest of the world. Such a transformation suited the governments' purposes very well. Even if they did not launch a single attack on America or Westerners – the sort of inactivity that many of the rulers preferred – this new version of Islamist ideology could be transformed from a threat into a type of involuntary ally. If these dangerous revolutionaries died as martyrs whose example would inspire increased xenophobia but who would not be around to bother the regimes, that outcome was all the better.

By the late 1990s, in the face of so many thorough defeats, the radical Islamist movement moved toward this new orientation, imitating their most successful counterparts in order to seek new categories of victims – non-Muslims – abroad and at home. Hizballah had done relatively well by attacking the Western presence in Lebanon and Israel. Hamas and Islamic Jihad were the first Sunni Islamists to use suicide attacks, posing as the vanguard in the anti-Israeli struggle. The Jihad group in Egypt and the Armed Islamic Group (GIA) in Algeria, which would soon join bin Ladin in an anti-Western alliance, had experimented, respectively, with attacks on tourists and assaults on French interests (both in Algeria and in France itself). Bin Ladin had participated

15 Interview on al-Jazira television. Translation in MEMRI No. 245, July 23, 2001.

in precisely such a struggle in fighting the Soviets in Afghanistan. Consequently, the Taliban, having come from this same background, became another ally of the new Islamist trend. Indeed, that was the only battle that Islamists could claim to have won in the twenty years following Iran's revolution. All that bin Ladin had to do was to shift these tactics from attacking the Soviets to going after the world's sole remaining superpower in New York and Washington.

Killing other Muslims, a questionable practice under Islamic law, had always been a problem for radical Islamists and a source of their unpopularity among fellow Muslims. The Islamists could only justify having Muslim victims if they could be completely dehumanized – the regime as anti-Muslim, the state as a traitor to Islam, and individuals as apostates, murderers, and enemies of God. Even then, such attacks often backfired in propagandistic terms. These criteria did not apply, however, to non-Muslims. Attacking foreigners and non-Muslims raised the revolutionaries' popularity among their own constituency, avenged popular grievances, and showed that these groups were fighting the people's battles better than any other group.

Some Islamists were very much aware of the value of this new approach. For example, an Egyptian Islamist and close ally of bin Ladin, Ayman al-Zawahiri, wrote that the Muslim masses would not join the revolutionaries unless they understood and accepted their slogans. The most popular of those were hatred of America and Israel. In addition, "[a] single look at the history of the mujahidin in Afghanistan, Palestine, and Chechnya will show that the jihad movement has moved to the center of the leadership of the nation when it adopted the slogan of liberating the nation from its external enemies and when it portrayed it as a battle of Islam against infidelity and infidels."[16]

Bin Ladin's great innovation, then, was to open up a new front against Americans and to give this strategy a justification. All of the basic ideas he needed, however, had already been expressed by a range of radical Islamist thinkers, from the Egyptian Sayyid Qutb in the 1950s to Khomeini in the 1970s, and by a score of Islamist thinkers thereafter. Killing Americans in East Africa (the 1998 attack on U.S. embassies in Kenya and Tanzania), in Yemen (the bombing of the USS *Cole*), and most spectacularly in America

16 Ayman al-Zawahiri, *Knights under the Prophet's Banner*. The text was published in *al-Sharq al-Awsat*, December 2–12, 2001. The book was translated by FBIS, December 2, 2001 (FBIS-NES-2001-1202-12).

itself (September 11, 2001) was very popular in the Arab world.[17] Even those who claimed to mourn the victims cheered the gestures. Such activities brought Islamists not one inch closer to successfully making revolution or to seizing state power, but did make them feel and appear to be more powerful and successful. Most important of all, this type of action appealed to tens of thousands of Muslims who would never dream of becoming personally involved in violence. Bin Ladin had updated the tactic of populist xenophobic terrorism. Yet this strategy, too, did not work. What could be more revealing than the fact that those who wanted to launch global war on behalf of Islam – al-Qaida and the Taliban – were hunted down in Afghanistan by some of the world's most pious Muslims, who were allied with the United States against them.

The Arab regimes' own failures and the towering barrier that their system posed to development helped to promote Islamism as the only acceptable alternative. In a terrible irony, though, these same states simultaneously used the existence of the Islamists as an excuse for not moving toward greater democracy, free speech, or human rights. Here are most vividly seen the paradoxes posed by the rise of Islamist movements. They could not solve the problems of the Arab world, but they could make the problems of the Arab world unsolvable. They could not bring victory to the Arab world over the West or Israel, but they could block good relations and peace. They could not replace the Western model of development, but they could discredit it. While posing as the solution, the Islamists in fact greatly intensified the problem.

17 Cameron Brown, "The Shot Heard Round the World: The Middle East Reacts to September 11," *MERIA Journal*, Vol. 5, No. 4 (December 2001), pp. 69–89, http://meria.idc.ac.il; and Barry Rubin and Judy Colp Rubin, *Anti-American Terror and the Middle East* (New York, 2002).

8

THE ARAB-ISRAELI
CONFLICT

Foundation Stone or Millstone?

For fifty years the Arab-Israeli issue often appeared to be the single most important feature of Middle Eastern politics. Seemingly unsolvable, it sparked seven major violent conflicts. Yet, gradually and reluctantly, most Palestinians and Arab states seemed to be reassessing their goals in order to accept a land-for-peace solution instead of seeking Israel's destruction. This shift, in turn, made possible changes in Israeli policies and public opinion that opened the way to a peace process.

Realizing the inability to solve the conflict through force should have been a major step toward reaching a peaceful resolution. Only when both sides perceived that neither Israel's destruction nor the Palestinians' permanent exile and political extinction would happen could the parties involved become ready for a two-state solution, giving each side a national framework. Equally, the conflict's apparent endlessness, incurring high costs with no prospect for absolute victory, made success at the bargaining table seem both plausible and desirable.

In general, the basis of the peace process was supposed to be the Palestinian and Arab conclusion that the conflict's costs exceeded its benefits and that a compromise, negotiated outcome was the best they could do. But were these assumptions true? If the conflict was a millstone around the Arab world's neck, then ending it made eminent sense. But if it was a foundation stone for the existing Arab system, it had a value going far beyond the immediate issues involved. In that case, no war, no peace was preferable to either war or peace.

During the period from the 1950s to the 1990s, the Arab world was unable either to defeat or to destroy Israel despite its vast superiority in money, territory, and population. Indeed, this effort damaged the Arab states more than it did Israel itself. No strategy worked. Arab states suffered from military defeats and wasted resources. The resulting instability fostered revolutionary Islamist movements, expensive arms races, and catastrophic civil wars. As Syrian Foreign Minister Sharaa put it later, describing the many failures, "We have faced setback after setback, stab after stab on the Arab body, and crack after crack in the Arab national plan. On the other hand, the Zionist plan kept advancing, thanks to the mistakes in the Arab plan."[1] Yet the issue was whether there were mistakes in the Arab plan that prevented it from being realized, or whether the plan itself was a mistake and a totally new plan was needed.

Starting in the 1980s, then, there was a reconsideration of Arab goals and tactics, which intensified after the Kuwait war, revolving around the need to explain why the Arabs were losing and whether it would be better to end the conflict. As Syrian Foreign Minister Sharaa explained it, the Arabs seemed to be "really cornered and faced with one of two choices. Either we have to accept a peace that is akin to capitulation and surrender, which can never be the peace we want, or we have to reject peace without a solid ground on which to base this rejection."[2]

The conclusions that might have been drawn should have been obvious. First, Israel prevailed because it was a real country representing a genuine nationalist movement that would not disappear. Second, Israel had adopted certain techniques that made it stronger – including democracy and a strong civil society – that the Arabs might benefit from imitating in their own manner. Third, since the battle could not be won, it made sense to end it on the best possible terms. That is how most Western observers viewed the issue, and they expected the Arabs to do the same. For them, getting this distraction out of the way would make possible a focus on other priorities.

In general, though, these were not the lessons drawn – at least publicly – by most Arab leaders, political movements, and intellectuals. Instead, they rejected all three assertions, continuing to assert that the conflict was worth fighting – indeed, that there was no alternative – and that it could be won. For the existing regimes, having the conflict to deflect attention away from democracy, economic reform, and civil liberties was of the

---

1 Speech of January 27, 2000, to the Arab Writers Union Conference in Damascus. The text is from *al-Usbu' al-Adabi*, February 12, 2000. http://www.awu-dam.com. Translation is from FBIS, February 12, 2000.
2 Ibid.

utmost value. The same basic consideration applied to opposition movements, which needed the conflict as a weapon in trying to gain power, arguing that the rulers' inability to win meant that Islamist governments were needed, while any moves by the rulers to make peace only proved that the Islamists should replace such traitors.

Within the Arab world, Israel's survival was attributed simply to U.S. backing or, in Islamist circles especially, to the pervasive and subversive international power of the Jews. These ideological views, when coupled with the advantages of continuing the conflict and the specific intransigence of Syrian and Palestinian leaders, ensured that the issue would not be resolved in the 1990s. On this issue, as on others, a powerful and utilitarian continuity prevailed.

During the 1948–67 period, the Arab side never considered implementing a two-state solution by turning the Jordanian-ruled West Bank and the Egyptian-controlled Gaza Strip into a Palestinian state. After Israel captured these lands, almost all Arab states as well as the PLO rejected a wide range of peace plans – Israel's 1967 offer to trade captured territories for peace, the 1977 Camp David accords, the 1982 Reagan plan, and many others – that might have been adopted, and adapted, to this end.

It took almost half a century to arrive back at a situation approximating the one offered at the very start. The basic concept of the 1990s' peace process – to create an Arab Palestinian state alongside an Israeli Jewish state – was the UN's original 1948 plan that had been accepted by Israel but rejected by the Arabs, who insisted that the only acceptable outcome was an Arab state occupying all the land between the Jordan river and the Mediterranean.[3]

The only option offered to Israel was to abandon national existence altogether, a clear roadblock to any political solution. Yet it was the Arab side whose strategic position steadily worsened. By 1948, the Palestinians could have obtained one-half of what they might have received in 1939; by 1967, 1979, or 1993 their opportunities had been halved again. Suffering the most in the long conflict, they were also the party that most perpetuated it, explicitly preferring deadlock to a solution requiring any real compromise.

---

3 But after fifty years of struggle, the size of the Palestinian state under discussion was smaller than what could have been easily achieved in 1948.

The PLO's basic strategy was in line with the 1971 statement of Abu Iyad, its most powerful leader after Arafat, that it had "no right" to negotiate a settlement but must keep struggling, "even if they cannot liberate a single inch," in order to preserve the option to regain all of Palestine someday. In 1984, he still thought so: "Our steadfastness and our adherence to our land is our only card.... We would rather be frozen for ten more years than move toward treason."[4] No matter the justice of the Palestinian claim, it was simply not realizable, and trying to achieve it prevented the Palestinians from getting anything at all for a very long time. Indeed, even today, Palestinian public opinion has difficulty revising this worldview.

The PLO's strategy also arose from a specific analysis of Israel. Assuming that its existence was an aberration, Palestinian leaders were sure Israel would collapse. They urged Arab states to go to war, staged terrorist attacks to demoralize Israelis, thinking the response would ultimately be flight or surrender, and continued to fight, believing time was on their side.

All of the Arab states had rejected Israel's creation in 1948 and maintained a position of total hostility toward it throughout the next thirty years, in which permanent rejection of peace with Israel was the most fundamental principle of inter-Arab politics. Breaking this taboo was extremely dangerous. Jordan's King Abdallah was assassinated in 1951 by the Palestinian leadership, which feared he might make peace with Israel. Egypt changed this situation by reaching a treaty with Israel in 1978. But despite some secret contacts (mainly with Jordan), no other Arab country followed this example for another fifteen years. Meanwhile, Egypt was isolated, boycotted, and ejected from the Arab League. President Anwar al-Sadat, who had decided to end Egypt's war with Israel, was assassinated in 1981. Lebanon's 1983 agreement with Israel was killed by pressure from Arab states and domestic forces. The man who made that deal, Lebanese President Bashir Gemayel, was then killed by the Syrians.

The Arab stance was originally based on an expectation of total victory. By the 1970s and the 1980s, when this prospect seemed increasingly unlikely, most Arab regimes were still constrained from making

4 Abu Iyad, *International Documents on Palestine 1971* (Beirut, 1972), p. 352; *al-Majalla*, March 10, 1984. Arafat used almost precisely the same words in December 1977 *International Documents on Palestine* (Beirut, 1973), p. 458 – and again in 1988, "Knowing the Enemy," *Time*, November 11, 1988, pp. 47–8.

peace by ideology, public opinion, and material interests. Obeying the Arab commandment of enmity toward Israel enhanced each regime's stability and ostensibly improved its position in the domestic and inter-Arab contest for power and survival.

For these reasons, the Arab-Israeli conflict was no typical international dispute that might be easily settled by some ingenious formula to split the difference. Equally, the decades-long deadlock was not due to a misunderstanding or mutual hostility but to the Arab side's rejection of compromise. As long as the Arabs viewed Israel's destruction as the only solution, there could no serious negotiation.

The conflict's burdens did, however, wear down Arab eagerness, and perhaps even willingness, to pursue it. These factors included frustration at the inability to destroy Israel and the lack of any reason to believe that this situation would change in the Arabs' favor, and the Arab defeats in the 1956, 1967, 1973, and 1982 wars, with accompanying losses of territory, money, prestige, and stability. Israel was strong enough to defend itself and to impose heavy costs on those who attacked it. Jordan expelled the PLO in order to end that group's threat to its stability and to avoid conflict with Israel. Syria barred direct terrorist attacks on Israel from it territory lest these provoke reprisals. Iraq saw its nuclear reactor destroyed; Saudi Arabia worried about possible attacks on its oil fields.[5]

Israel, Sharaa warned, was more powerful than all of the Arab states combined. The United States supplied Israel with advanced weapons, from rifles to rockets and planes, plus gigantic computers that even the Europeans didn't have. Israel was making advanced weapons of its own, exporting them even to China. New German-made submarines had arrived that could be equipped with nuclear missiles.[6] At the same time, Sharaa and his audience knew, Syria could not afford to pay top

---

5 For an overview of the conflict and of Arab politics during these years, see Avraham Sela, *The Decline of the Arab-Israeli Conflict: Middle East Politics and the Quest for Regional Order* (Albany, NY, 1997).
6 An interesting example of Arab perceptions was Syrian Foreign Minister Sharaa's claim that Israel's arms spending was twenty times that of Syria. In fact, according to the SIPRI website, http://projects.sipri.se/milex.html, Israel's 1998 defense budget was $8.5 billion, while Syria's was $3.1 billion. Even this gap, however, is misleading, since a large portion of spending was for soldiers' wages and benefits, which were far cheaper in Syria. In proportion to their gross domestic products, the two countries have similar levels of military spending: 9.5 percent for Israel compared to about 8 percent for Syria.

prices for the kind of weapons and spare parts that it had once obtained with Saudi aid, paying discounted Soviet prices.

Equally, Arab leaders and intellectuals could no longer entirely ignore other problems that competed for attention or were worsened by the conflict. These included lagging economic development and growing domestic opposition groups, the threat from Iran, and the danger of radical Islamism. Inter-Arab quarrels continued unabated and sometimes broke out into dangerous crises. The oil producers had less money to finance military spending. The gap between rhetoric and action was also increasingly visible; Arab states were passive, for example, during the Lebanon war and the Palestinian *intifada*.

At the start of the 1990s, these trends intensified, responding to both global and regional developments. Iraq's annexation of Kuwait showed just how dangerous the old game could be for Arab countries. By further subverting regimes' stability, the Arab-Israeli dispute could be considered for the first time in history as undermining rather than reinforcing their hold on power. The Cold War's end and the USSR's collapse made the United States the world's sole superpower, weakened radical Arab governments, gave moderate ones an incentive to improve relations with Washington, and reduced U.S. constraints on the use of its own power. For Arab states needing to ensure U.S. protection and aid, limiting the conflict and even making peace with Israel seemed a necessity.

Reflecting these historical lessons, Mubarak told an interviewer in 1989, in the most cogent critique of the traditional Arab view ever given, that:

God has granted us a mind with which to think. We fought for many years, but where did we get? We also spent 100 billion [sic] on wars, apart from thousands of martyrs until we reached the present situation from which we are now suffering. I am therefore not ready to take more risks. . . . Wars have generally not solved any problem. Regardless of the difficulties or obstacles surrounding the present peace process, our real effort focuses on removing these obstacles and bringing viewpoints closer.[7]

The PLO, too, suffered from its misadventures during the long conflict and from the changing conditions. For the PLO, the Arab states were both blessing and curse. They were an indispensable base of support without

---

7 Interview, Middle East News Agency, January 24, 1989, in FBIS, January 25, 1989, p. 15.

which the movement might have collapsed or been ignored, but they also injured and tried to dominate it. While Western observers insisted that the Arabs passionately supported the Palestinian cause, Palestinians themselves felt "that virtually every Arab state has stabbed them in the back at one point or another," as Yezid Sayigh wrote in 1984.[8] A PLO intelligence chief estimated that the Arab states were responsible for slaying three-quarters of the Palestinians killed in the struggle.[9]

Arab financial pledges often went unpaid. A 1978 inter-Arab agreement promised $250 million a year to the PLO and $150 million to a Jordan-PLO committee. Only Saudi Arabia paid its share. Nor did Arab states give much to UN relief efforts for Palestinian refugees. The United States paid over 40 percent of its budget. During the 1970s and 1980s, Saudi Arabia was the PLO's most reliable source of aid. But apart from a short-lived 1973 oil embargo, the Saudis and other Gulf Arab monarchies refrained from direct involvement in the conflict. In the latter 1980s, Saudi aid dwindled as the regime spent more money at home and diverted funds to help Iraq in its war against Iran. Saudi investments in the West discouraged actions against Western interests.

The real crisis came when Arafat backed Iraq's seizure of Kuwait, provoking a strong, bitter Saudi response. All Saudi aid to the PLO and Palestinian institutions was cut off. Kuwait, whose many Palestinian residents had always made it sympathetic to the PLO, went even further. After Iraqi forces retreated, Kuwait expelled most Palestinians from the country and virtually boycotted the PLO thereafter.

Arab states stood by, or even pushed, as the PLO was chased from Amman to Beirut, and from Beirut to Tunis. In this context, voting on UN resolutions, donating money, and even secretly abetting terrorism were low-risk propositions. But a PLO trying to drag them into another losing war with Israel or endangering their links to the West was a nuisance. A sympathetic historian wrote, "Few independence movements have been so heavily dependent on external assistance"; the PLO's survival required maintaining "unity at any price."[10]

---

8 Yezid Sayigh, "Fatah: The First Twenty Years," *Journal of Palestine Studies*, Vol. 13, No. 4 (Summer 1984), p. 115.

9 Ibid.; Walid Kazziha, *Palestine in the Arab Dilemma* (London, 1979), pp. 15–19.

10 Alain Gresh, *The PLO: The Struggle Within* (London, 1985), p. 246. See also Walid Khalidi, "The Asad Regime and the Palestinian Resistance," *Arab Studies Quarterly*, Vol. 6, No. 4 (Fall 1984), p. 265.

Buffeted by constantly changing Arab policies, Arafat tried to avoid becoming any ruler's enemy or puppet. This was a difficult task, as evinced by the 1970 Jordanian-PLO war, the post-1975 Syrian-PLO feud, and entanglements with Lebanon's civil war, Iran's revolution, and Saddam Hussein's takeover of Kuwait. The PLO also internalized the Arab world's fragmentation. It was, after all, a loose umbrella organization, and Arafat never made a serious effort to impose his will on the various ideologies, fiefdoms, and loyalties that kept the PLO together. Constantly toiling for consensus with Arab states and Palestinian groups, Arafat often gave veto power to the most militant of them, blocking any realistic policy.

Even without pressure from those more radical than he, Arafat had repeatedly brought his cause to the brink of disaster. While he escaped each time, Arafat had never even come close to the brink of success. In 1970, the PLO had been driven out of Jordan. A dozen years later, first Israel and then Syria threw him out of Lebanon. The Palestinian *intifada* of the late 1980s had stirred up a great deal of enthusiasm but produced no real results. Refusing to condemn terror, Arafat had thrown away his first dialogue with the United States, then backed Iraq's losing aggression. There had been a gradual trend in Palestinian debates toward realizing that some compromise with Israel was needed, but no decisive step had been taken.

Now this policy shift could no longer be postponed. After Saddam, his latest patron, suffered such a devastating defeat and discredit among the Arabs, Arafat also needed to find a way out of the mess. In the 1990s, one could believe that a majority of Arab rulers were sick of the conflict. Rather than being useful in demagogic and financial terms, maintaining the battle at its old intense level was clearly dangerous to the regimes' survival as well as to their countries' prosperity and stability. Rather than being eager – at least in rhetoric – to sacrifice themselves for the Palestinians, the Arab states were reluctant to do anything to help them and became more interested in distancing themselves from the Palestinian cause.

For these and other reasons, Arab states and the PLO began talks with Israel in 1991. In 1993, the PLO signed an agreement with Israel that brought it to the West Bank and Gaza as an interim government, the Palestinian Authority (PA), with the goal of finding a solution to all of the remaining issues. Next, Jordan signed a peace treaty with Israel.

Once the PLO had signed its own agreements with Israel, it could no longer deny other Arabs the right to do the same thing.

Arab leaders saw the decision as freeing them to choose whether to make peace with Israel, consider their obligation to the Palestinian struggle to be ended, or condemn Arafat as a sell-out. Syrian Defense Minister Mustafa Tlas called Arafat "the son of 60,000 whores" for making too many concessions.[11] Other Syrian leaders used less rude words but also showed their disdain. Most Arab governments took the opportunity to withdraw even further from the conflict and to reduce help for the Palestinians. Only about 5 percent of money pledged to the PA came from the Arab world. Indeed, Israel and the United States were now in the strange position of urging Arab states to help Yasir Arafat.

Meanwhile, moderate Arab states complained about Arafat's policy in order to excuse their minimal help for the PA, and radical regimes denounced the peace process. The 1996 Arab summit's final communiqué demonstrates this principle. The Arab leaders urged Europe, Japan, and other countries "to continue providing political and economic support to the Palestinian people and their National Authority." But there was absolutely no Arab pledge – not even a non-binding recommendation – to organize their own aid program for the Palestinians.[12]

Still, by June 1996 the Arab summit's final resolution called peace with Israel "a strategic decision."[13] Mubarak urged Israel's government "to cooperate with us so as to complete the peace process without slackness or hesitation." King Hussein noted that the Arabs always knew that peacemaking would be hard, but that the current process was "the only available option ... [and] possible means to bring the conflict to a just and lasting solution that can endure."[14]

Many thought that such a solution would be reached and would endure because it fulfilled Arab interests. The question remained, though, which set of interests would be paramount. U.S. National

---

11 Syrian Defense Minister Mustafa Tlass as quoted in the Lebanese newspapers *al-Safir* and *Daily Star*, August 3, 1999.

12 Official text of the resolution obtained at the summit. See also "Final Communique," FBIS, June 23, 1996, Vol. 2, p. 13; CNN, June 23, 1996, http://www.cnn.com/WORLD/9606/23/summit.transcript/.

13 Ibid.

14 Text of June 22, 1996, speech from Egypt's Ministry of Information, State Information Service.

Security Advisor Tony Lake argued, for example, that "progress in Arab-Israeli peacemaking helps place the extremists on the defensive and increases their isolation". This was an overoptimistic assessment, since accusing one's own or a neighboring ruler of selling out Arab nationalism or Islam to Western imperialism continued to prove a useful tool for domestic insurgents and regimes alike. The incumbent governments knew they were being asked to give up an issue that provided their best means of mobilizing internal support, ensuring national unity, and deflecting attention from local problems.

Lake also suggested that peace would make governments "concentrate on the economic well-being of their people, they will feel more secure in meeting their citizen's demands for greater political participation and accountability."[15] Yet as rulers felt pressed by economic problems or citizens' demands, they were likely to become more – not less – authoritarian. "Political participation" sounded like a recipe for creating more opposition and internal conflict; "accountability" was a nice way to imply that the leaders would be blamed for their incompetence and corruption.

The history of the 1993–2000 peace process is extremely complex, full of agreements, violent incidents, and complex details. Yet in the end, it is not serious to suggest that this effort's collapse – an effort so many decades in the making – came about merely because of small issues involving timing and personal interactions, the precise location of borders, or the exact degree of control over holy sites. The ultimate problem was that the Arab world had failed in practice to come to terms with making peace. Even those people, including Arab leaders, who wanted to do so were blocked by their own interests as well as by the framework of regional maneuvering and public opinion that they had done so much to create. Can one really conclude that for Lebanon, Syria, and the Palestinians peace agreements were impossible because of a dispute over 1 percent of the land, when Israel was ready to turn over the equivalent of 99 percent?

In Lebanon's case, Hizballah announced that peace was impossible, despite Israel's withdrawal from south Lebanon, because Israel was still holding a small portion of land along the border that everyone had

---

15 Anthony Lake, "Confronting Backlash States," *Foreign Affairs*, March–April 1994, and speech to Washington Institute for Near East Policy, May 17, 1994.

hitherto assumed belonged to Syria. In Syria's case, Damascus insisted that peace was impossible, despite Israel's willingness to return the Golan Heights, unless additional territory on Israel's side of the international border, seized by Syria in the 1950s, was also turned over.

In the Palestinian case, Arafat was supposedly ready to sacrifice hundreds of lives and the chance to have an independent state over a few square blocks in Jerusalem, when Israel was ready to hand over the equivalent of all of the West Bank, Gaza, and most of East Jerusalem. Clearly, the impediment was not these issues but something far deeper and broader: the difficulty of making peace on any terms and the problems that entailed, the risks involved, and the need to give up all the domestic and regional advantages of having the conflict continue.

For the Palestinians, who had the most to lose, a large element in this outcome was Arafat's problematic leadership. Whether it was owing to a miscalculation of the balance of forces, a failure of nerve, a fear of transforming himself from revolutionary to statesman, or an unwillingness to give up the idea of getting everything in the future, the result was the same. It was one more example, Ajami wrote, of the Palestinian "refusal to bow to the logic of things that can and cannot be, in its sublime confidence" that some force would come to their rescue and "sense of exemption from the historical laws of gravity. . . . The practical always yields in Palestinian thought and practice. It loses out to the wrath, to the persisting idea that the land as a whole . . . is still there to be claimed."[16]

Abdallah Laroui gave a haunting depiction of this sensibility that the hope of ultimate victory is too priceless to compromise for material betterment. "On a certain day," Palestinians believed, "everything would be obliterated and instantaneously reconstructed and the new inhabitants would leave, as if by magic, the land they had despoiled; in this way will justice be dispensed to the victims, on the day when the presence of God shall again make itself felt."[17]

A leader would have to tell his people that this kind of utopian outcome is impossible, but Arafat would not do so, any more than his counterparts would openly call for abandoning the Arab national or Islamist dream. Indeed, he followed the opposite course, building up

---

16 Fouad Ajami in *US News & World Report*, January 8, 2001.
17 Abdullah Laroui, *The Crisis of the Arab Intellectual* (Berkeley, CA, 1976), pp. 31–32.

further the hope that the Palestinians had a right of return and would do so someday. Even in order to achieve a state, he would not agree that such a solution would end the conflict. Arafat never made the kind of speeches that were routine for leaders elsewhere in the world – but hardly ever in the Middle East – preaching the virtues of education and economic enterprise, preparing the ground for democracy, encouraging civil society. Yet also like his fellow Arab leaders, no disaster wrought by his decisions ever damaged his power. As Ajami noted, he had "done so well for himself by sending his people down so many blind alleyways, so many historical dead ends."[18]

Except for King Hussein, no Arab leader was as eager for Arab-Israeli peace as was Mubarak. But conditions also imposed on him considerable constraints and reservations. Egypt's ambitions for Arab leadership both encouraged its mediation efforts and made it afraid to alienate those more timid or more radical. Moreover, Egypt worried that an Israel integrated into the Middle East would also be a more formidable rival, challenging Cairo's primacy and perhaps dominating the whole region.[19]

At the same time, Mubarak knew that a hard line made him more popular at home and that moderation could weaken him, giving additional ammunition to the Islamists already engaged in an armed revolt and a broad cultural war against his regime. Given Egypt's domestic problems, even he could not easily dispense with this valuable asset. Thus, Mubarak was both rationalizing and expressing real concern when he claimed that he could not improve relations with Israel lest Egypt's people tell him to "go to Hell."[20]

But Mubarak was also ordering his lieutenants to stoke the fires of such attitudes. In August 2001, for instance, the state-controlled newspaper *al-Akhbar* said in an editorial, "The cruel occupation forces conduct a psychological war against the Palestinians throughout the

---

18 Ajami in *U.S. News & World Report*.
19 Fawaz A. Gerges, "Egyptian-Israeli Relations Turn Sour," *Foreign Affairs*, Vol. 74, No. 3 (May–June 1995), pp. 69–78. The idea that Israel could challenge Egypt as a regional leader seems strange. Aside from the two countries having several common interests, the continued hostility of several Arab powers and popular opinion severely limit Israel's ability to play such a role. Nonetheless, this belief plays an important role in setting Egyptian policy, just as many Arabs want to limit cooperation with Israel because they think it will lead to its economic domination.
20 Interview with *Jerusalem Report*, March 19, 1997.

occupied land, in an attempt to sow fear in their souls and create in them the illusion that their struggle and their heroic operations of martyrdom [referring to suicide bombings] will bring catastrophe on them."[21] In other words, through violence the Palestinians would win. It was their best tactic, and anyone who spoke differently was just spreading Zionist propaganda.

For Mubarak himself and the entire system, the value of the enmity with Israel was extraordinarily high. In public, at least, the masses applauded a ruinous but spiritually satisfying strategy. And whatever their private qualms, activists and intellectuals cheered these choices, proclaiming that enough time and violence would bring total victory. This was the answer to a question raised by an Egyptian writer, Hassan Hafez, in a non-Islamist opposition paper: "I wonder why we blame Israel for every fault in [our] society. This is the logic of the weak, who seek a peg on which to hang all their mistakes in order to evade a true confrontation with reality." The same thing happened when an Egyptian airplane crashed, when Egyptian Muslims and Christians clashed, or when the economy did poorly.[22]

The alternative, Hafez concluded, is that "we have to grab those responsible for our failures by the collar instead of blaming Israel for all our problems like cowards. [Blaming Israel] causes us to look ridiculous before the world and it makes the small Israeli state look great. We have to be honest with ourselves before we blame others! When we blame others we are being untrue, we mock common sense and we scorn our people"[23]

Yet again, those who would be grabbed by the collar would prefer to avoid that unpleasant result. "None of us wishes to return to war and destruction nor seek to revert to the state of no-war, no-peace," Mubarak told the 1996 Arab summit.[24] But when Syria, Hizballah, and Arafat torpedoed the peace process, he went along with the crowd, no matter how bitterly or reluctantly. When the Palestinian *intifada*

---

21 *Al-Akhbar*, August 17, 2001. Translation in MEMRI No. 259, August 22, 2001.

22 Hassan Hafez in *al-Wafd*, February 26, 2000. Translation in MEMRI No. 91, May 5, 2000.

23 For some examples of this tendency see "Egyptian Reactions to the Egypt Air Crash Investigation," MEMRI No. 62, December 6, 1999; and "Anti-Semitism in the Egyptian Media Part III: 'International Jewish Conspiracies,'" MEMRI No. 79, March 20, 2000.

24 Text of June 22, 1996, speech from Egypt's Ministry of Information, State Information Service.

broke out in 2000, Mubarak's friends in the Egyptian press, such as *al-Gumhuriya* editor Samir Ragab, were writing how Mubarak had stuck to the Arab line, boldly supporting the Palestinian uprising, making sacrifices to help them "fight for their rights."[25]

Others were far more eager to destroy any chance of reaching a negotiated solution. Iran, Iraq, Libya, and Syria, each reflecting its different specific interests, had a great deal to lose if diplomacy succeeded. They did not want to see increased stability, a greater U.S. role, or the normalization of Israel's position in the region. Extremely dissatisfied with the status quo, they saw the Arab world's return to past militancy as a way to escape isolation and seize leadership. Otherwise, their hope of gaining (or keeping) influence over their neighbors and becoming the area's dominant power would be lost forever. The existence of a Western-oriented Palestinian state, which did not support their ambitions, and whose existence might even reduce tensions, would do nothing for them either.

In a July 17, 1997, speech, Saddam voiced the ideas held by all of the radical regimes and opposition groups:

Under Arafat's leadership the Palestinians must undermine Israel with full Arab state financial and diplomatic support.... Until Palestine is liberated, the Palestinians must avoid building a material base for the state that could become a heavy burden when the Zionist entity threatens to destroy it or actually does destroy it. The so-called self-rule area must be more of a base for revolutionary struggle than of a state structure.[26]

For Syria, peace with Israel would open the door for most other Arab states to have relations with Israel and to work with it on matters of common interest. But Israel would remain determined – and be far more able – to oppose Syria's ambitions to hold sway over Jordan, Lebanon, and the Palestinians. The United States would also use its stronger influence to block Syrian goals. An Israel-Lebanon agreement would follow any Israeli-Syrian accord, reducing Damascus's leverage in that country and bringing international pressure for a Syrian withdrawal.

These strategic losses would not be matched by any gains for Syria. An agreement with Israel would not bring much Western aid or investment. Freer access for foreigners and more open commerce and communications would weaken the dictatorship's hold over its own people. Syria

25 Quoted in *Ha'aretz*, October 26, 2000.
26 Translation by FBIS.

would lose prestige, aid, and deferral to its interests – the advantages that being a militant, confrontational state had once brought it in the Arab world. In short, Syria would be reduced to a secondary power. This was the meaning of the warning given by one pro-regime Syrian writer: "The Barak program, which has revived hopes for peace, is like a minefield; it conceals things that are not apparent on the surface."[27]

Yet while Arab liberals expressed their cynicism in private, few would associate their names with such ideas in public. "Conflict has been very important for the regime," explained one anonymous Syrian analyst. "When there were human rights abuses or corruption, the ultimate excuse was the conflict." Another Syrian added that the conflict had been used to legitimate regimes throughout the Arab world. "Syria must always have an enemy" to help create political cohesion. "No question, the fig leaf has been Israel," agreed a Lebanese analyst in Beirut. "The [Syrian] regime fabricated its legitimacy under that fig leaf. Asad used the discourse of war to block any discourse rejecting his policy. It worked." The retired Egyptian ambassador Tahseen Bashir explained, "Saddam Hussein uses the deep frustration of the Arab world to say that even his mistakes are justifiable, because he is fighting devils."[28]

Thus, as the Egyptian writer Amin al-Mahdi suggested,

History teaches us that the goal of Arab peace agreements with Israel has never been to attain a true peace that entails democracy, modernization, development and regional cooperation. The true goal has been, and continues to be, to solve [domestic] crises – to cover up the inability of the Arab regimes to adapt to modern life, and to justify territorial ambitions in the region.[29]

At times, especially during the 1990s, this rationale had weakened. Yet it was easier to revitalize it than to find a substitute. One Syrian pointed out, "People wonder: 'If you were really fighting Israel, then you wouldn't be importing all these Mercedes.' And the record of the regime is not commensurate with the sacrifices we have been asked to make. That's why after thirty years it sounds hollow."[30]

Yet although the overwhelming majority of writers, intellectuals, and others who make their voices heard in the Arab world might

27 Majid Mu'awwad in *al-Thawra*, July 9, 1999. Translation by FBIS.
28 *Christian Science Monitor*, July 12, 2000.
29 *Al-Hayat*, December 6, 2000. Translation in MEMRI No. 169, December 29, 2000.
30 *Christian Science Monitor*, July 12, 2000.

sometimes criticize a regime's steadfastness to the cause, they were far less eager to challenge the premises that made the issue so potent. Obviously, the view that Arab and Muslim interests are jeopardized is a powerful factor in itself, and so too is the demonization of Israel. For if Israel is as horrible, ruthless, and murderous a place as one would inevitably believe from the consistent claims of Arab media, governments, textbooks, clerics, and virtually every other institution – which suffer no contradiction or constraint – then how could peace be possible or desirable?

One exchange illustrating these points – genuine debates where two sides were represented were rare – was between the Syrian-Palestinian author Hisham Dajani and the famous Syrian poet Mamdouh Adwan. Dajani argued that most Syrian intellectuals supported peace, and he gave three basic reasons for doing so. First, a realistic examination of the situation showed that negotiations and compromise were the only way to get back the Golan Heights. "Due to the balance of power," Dajani explained, "we cannot regain our land unconditionally, and therefore, some concessions on the issues of water, security arrangements, and normalization of relations are unavoidable.... By now, there are no [more] illusions about the [possibility] of 'liberation' [of the Golan by force]. The only way to regain the Golan is through negotiations."[31]

Second, getting back Syria's territory would be sufficient. The destruction of Israel was not a necessary objective. "It is enough [if we] regain our land in its entirety," claimed Dajani. "This will also mean the return of our pride."

Third, Syria need not fear peace with Israel. "It is time," he noted,

we freed ourselves from any illusions. Israel will not swallow us after the peace just as it did not swallow Egypt, or even a small state like Jordan. The Syrian role in the region will be strengthened, not weakened after the peace. It is dependent to a large extent on our ability to succeed in the domestic battles: against corruption, for the modernization of legislation, for establishing civil society, and for the modernization of the political and economical infrastructure so that Syria becomes a state that moves ahead with time.[32]

31 *Al-Hayat*, February 9, March 2, and March 21, 2000. Translation in MEMRI No. 84, April 6, 2000.
32 *Al-Hayat*, February 9, 2000. Translation in MEMRI No. 84, April 6, 2000.

Especially worthy of note was Dajani's linkage – common among liberal Arabs – between peace, on the one hand, and reform, democracy, modernization, economic change, and the struggle against corruption on the other. Such ideas were not exactly music to the ears of the establishment and its supporters. But even aside from this problem, Dajani faced a distinctly uphill battle. After all, Adwan could simply reiterate the traditional Arab arguments, with all the passion and power they invoked. Despite the fact that Adwan had often been critical of Syria's government in the past, he knew the regime would support his viewpoint. Indeed, after his attack on Dajani, as a reward Adwan was allowed to write in the state-owned newspaper *Tishrin*, after having been banned for several years.

The return of Syria's territory, and even the creation of a Palestinian state, would not settle the issue because compromise was unjust, Adwan responded. Moreover, Israel would never be satisfied with peace and would strive to conquer the Arabs. "These are murderers and nothing more," Adwan insisted. "They – including those among them who now seem sympathetic to peace – are willing to treat us only as second-rate human beings that must be killed, or whose killing is not worth bothering about. They say: 'Let us stop the bloodshed. Let us rest for a while. We have tired of the killing. We have tired of killing you.'" Even if Israel were to make peace, it would only wait for another time to slaughter the Arabs.

Israel in any form could not be allowed to exist. The real goal was to reverse the Arab defeat of 1948, when Israel was created. In this context, the costs, the balance of forces, and the time that this would take were of no importance whatsoever. "I do not want to forget that Palestine in its entirety is Arab. . . . Some would say that this is the rhetoric of the 1950s and 1960s. I don't care if it is the rhetoric of the Stone Age. This is what I believe from the bottom of my heart." Even if intellectuals claimed that this was uncivilized behavior, or if politicians persecuted these views, Adwan's ideas would not change, and neither would those of most Arabs.[33]

In answering Adwan, Dajani used the type of rational, realpolitik, national-interest approach that won arguments elsewhere in the world, but not in the Middle East. Adwan, he explained,

speaks in the emotional language of a poet, and I, on the other hand, as a political publicist, cannot think in this way, because it is purposeless and it

33 *Al-Hayat*, March 2, 2000. Translation in ibid.

turns us into a nation that lives in dreams. . . . I deal with politics, the art of the possible, the art of the pragmatic. . . .

The historical enmity will subdue gradually, especially if Israel keeps the terms of the peace. Germany invaded France twice, murdered, slaughtered, and then was defeated. Today, Germany and France are allies. . . . There is no country in the world that suffered like Japan. Two large cities were wiped out and there were hundreds of thousands of casualties. . . . Today, Japan and the United States are allies. Why? Because the political leadership in Japan has dealt with politics and not with emotions. It left the emotions to the poets and turned to progress until it invaded the American and international markets.

The enmity [between Arabs and Israel] will dissolve with time. Your son is not as enthusiastic [to hate] as you. He did not witness the [Arab defeat in 1948] or the 1967 defeat, and your grandson will be even less enthusiastic than both of you. This is the logic of time. In reality, there is no such thing as eternal enmity. Just like there is no eternal friendship, only interests are eternal. . . . True, our generation at least cannot forget, but we cannot fight forever against those who are stronger than us and are supported by the entire West. . . .

Instead of sending our forces to lose the battle, let us turn them inward: to the battle for political and economic reform. . . .[34]

To a reader who asked whether Arab countries should be seen as extremists if they declare that they will liberate the land through war if negotiations fails, he answered: "Yes. . . . There is no one single Arab state that wants or is capable of fighting. The sole meaning of war has been more and more catastrophes and defeats Saddam style."

These were good arguments, but they were not winning arguments in the Middle East. No one was ready to force the Arabs to change their strategy if they simply chose to ignore the balance of forces. There was no force that could alter the internal functioning of these countries if their regimes refused to make any reforms. Continuing the conflict with Israel, even without taking any action except refusing to negotiate an agreement, was a viable option.

When Israel withdrew from south Lebanon, for example, the Beirut government would not or could not end the conflict. Syrian pressure, Hizballah's power, and domestic public opinion seemed to be more worrisome than the consequences of continued tension on the Israel-Lebanon

34 *Al-Hayat*, March 21, 2000. Translation in ibid.

border. Such a strategy could undermine reconstruction by forfeiting Lebanon's chances of attracting investment or gaining stability, but no one seemed to hesitate about making this choice. As a result, Lebanon refused to take control of its own territory. Even though the United Nations certified Israel's full departure from Lebanese soil, the Arab world refused to acknowledge this fact. Egyptian foreign minister Amr Musa, soon to be the Arab League's secretary general, proclaimed on October 24, 2000, that "Egypt and all Arabs [support] the resistance and Hizballah in their struggle to liberate the remaining occupied territories. Israel is the one that kept some territories and did not release prisoners. Therefore, it is responsible for what is happening." The UN and the United States did not lift a finger to change this situation.[35]

If the nationalists had such a hard time desiring, justifying, or making a transition, the Islamists were far less interested in such things. Even though they were not governing the Arab world, or leading the Palestinians, the Islamists had a tremendous cultural and ideological effect on Arab societies. And they had strong, clear answers rejecting any notion along the lines of Dajani's three points: that peace with Israel was necessary because the Arabs couldn't defeat Israel, that it was possible because the Arabs could accept it, and that it was desirable because it would be beneficial for the Arabs.

These issues were aired in a debate on al-Jazeera television in May 2001 between a Tunisian Islamist, Rashed al-Ghanushi, and the Moroccan liberal writer al-Saleh bu Walid. The position taken by Walid was to call not for Arab concessions but merely for the continuation of negotiations to reach a solution that would satisfy "the goals of the Palestinian people." Neither a war on Israel nor the *intifada* would succeed in winning victory. He also wanted to set Arab strategy in a way that would gain the support of Israeli and international public opinion.[36]

Ghanushi rejected all of these notions. Only struggle would work: "The Intifada is a natural, humane, and legitimate right" and has achieved "in the past eight months what the stupid and pointless

35 Report of the secretary-general, June 16, 2000. Secretary of State Madeleine Albright stated on June 18, 2000: "Those with authority in Lebanon now have a clear responsibility to ensure that the area bordering Israel is not used to launch attacks." But no foreign power or international body made Lebanon take that responsibility. Liat Radcliffe, "The Israeli-Lebanese Border Dispute and Resolution 425: Recent Declarations by the United States and the United Nations," *Peacewatch* No. 292, November 3, 2000.
36 Al-Jazeera television, May 23, 2001. Translation in MEMRI No. 245, July 23, 2001.

negotiations have not achieved in the past eight years. Oslo created illusions and sold false visions to the nation, and now it has been torn to pieces." Ghanushi believed that the balance of power was not set by Israel's strength or by the United States' sole superpower status. Instead, the Palestinian suicide bombers had "succeeded in creating a new balance of power." They had "taught the international system and the Israeli arrogance, supported by the United States, an important lesson." Why make peace if the Arabs were stronger and would inevitably win?[37]

The callers without exception also criticized Walid. "I am willing to negotiate from a position of strength, when I have put the enemy on his knees," said one from Saudi Arabia. "I am not prepared to sit with him when he has the upper hand." The Muslim readiness to become martyrs was the secret weapon that would defeat planes and tanks. "How did the Vietnamese get rid of the Americans? They sacrificed their sons and daughters as bombs sent to the American soldiers."[38]

Even the secular Syrian regime's media employed similar arguments proclaiming the impossibility of peace and the inevitability of victory. The problem was not just that Syria wanted a slight alteration in the border. As one article in the official *al-Thawra* newspaper put it, "The ones calling for normalization are ignoring the history of Torah Zionism, which turned the Almighty God into a real estate broker and a civil affairs officer in the service of the Israeli people whom God chose as an elite people from all mankind while throwing the remainder of humans into the bottom of the human pyramid!"[39]

These analyses may have been unrealistic for winning the struggle, but they certainly provided a rationale for not actively demanding peace and abandoning the struggle. The truth was that if they were willing to pay the price, the Arabs could continue the battle – all the more easily if confrontation was kept at a low level – for as long as they wanted. No one would stop them from doing so at either the international or the domestic level.

Such expressions were not the ravings of marginal figures; they were far more common than the voices of the liberals. And unlike the moderates'

37 Ibid.
38 Ibid.
39 Sabir Falhut in *al-Thawra*, July 13, 1999. Cited in James Perlin, "Syrian Media and Government on Barak and the Peace Process: On the Record," *Peacewatch* No. 222, August 12, 1999.

opinions, the most extreme concepts had the aura of official governmental approval. There is literally no case on record where the PA or any Arab government – with the exception of Jordan – punished or even criticized anyone for the militancy of their anti-Israel rhetoric or calls to battle.

On May 15, 2001, the topic on an al-Jazeera talk show was, "Is Zionism worse than Nazism?" Hayat al-Hwayek Atiya, who had translated books denying the existence of the Holocaust into Arabic, debated the liberal Tunisian intellectual Afif al-Akhdhar, representing the opposition to Holocaust denial in the Arab world. Atiya argued that Judaism had always been racist. During the program, over 12,000 viewers participated in a poll in which 84.6 percent said that Zionism was worse than Nazism, 11.1 percent said that Zionism was equal to Nazism, and only 2.7 percent said that Nazism was worse than Zionism.[40]

What was especially interesting about this discussion, however, was the exchange on Arab-Western relations and the treatment of liberal Arab viewpoints. Akhdhar argued that Arab claims – such as Holocaust denial and the assertion that Israel is worse than Nazi Germany – alienated the rest of the world and international public opinion. Such extremism, he insisted, actually hurt Palestinian interests, since only Arabs would believe it. "We cannot fight against international diplomacy, because then we will lose our cause. . . . We must learn from Israel and be realistic." To tell even the German people that "the Jews simply invented a massacre that never happened, and invented gas chambers that exist only in their imagination. This is a kind of stupidity and insanity."[41]

For Atiya, though, this was a brilliant tactic "because the Western conscience is particularly sensitive to the Nazis." As for Akhdhar, she suggested that his arguments – which of course were quite accurate – should be disregarded because such intellectuals only wanted to appease the West. Moreover, why should the Arabs pay any attention to the international media? It was Akhdhar who stood accused of lying and treason: "It is a shame that an intellectual should stand on the side of the strong and

40 Al-Jazeera program of May 15, 2001. Translation in MEMRI No. 225, June 6, 2001. But if anyone showed nostalgia for the Nazis, it was some on the Arab side. To coincide with Hitler's birthday, Ahmad Ragab, in his daily column for the Egyptian government-controlled *al-Akhbar* on April 20, 2001, exclaimed: "Thanks to Hitler, of blessed memory, who, on behalf of the Palestinians, revenged in advance against the most vile criminals on the face of the Earth. Although we do have a complaint against him for his revenge on them was not enough." Translation in MEMRI, April 18, 2001.
41 Al-Jazeera program of May 15, 2001. Translation in MEMRI No. 225, June 6, 2001.

not on the side of the truth. . . . President Bashar Asad said that Zionism is equal to Nazism. This is a courageous position that must be commended rather than be denounced in order to appease the West."[42]

Atiya had, however, accurately represented Asad's views, as declared by the leader of one of the Arab world's most powerful states to the assembled Arab rulers at their April 2001 summit. Asad also took up the theme of indifference to Western opinion and to any international balance of power. Why should the Arab leadership pay more attention to "advice that comes to us from foreign non-Arab countries" than to the Arab public. If the Arab governments stand their ground, "300 million Arabs . . . will support us morally and materially. If we don't, nobody, Arab or non-Arab, will stand by us and we will go from bad to worse." In short, what remained most important in domestic and regional terms was to retain Arab support by mobilizing the people and the regimes around the Arab-Israeli conflict.[43]

"Since we represent the Arab peoples," he continued, "it is only natural that we talk in a way that reflects the consciousness of the Arab citizen. We must not wait for definitions by the West, East, North, or South. We must make our own definitions and spread them." Then the Arab countries would not have to bow to "reality" but would create their own realities. "What is important," concluded Asad in a remarkable phrase, "is that if we act with determination we will get what we want."[44] The question, of course, is what the Arab leaders wanted. In terms of regime survival, the breakdown of the peace process meant the situation was excellent. But Asad was also rejecting the experience of the previous half-century.

His counterparts endorsed this approach. Egyptian Foreign Minister Musa had declared in October 2000 that the peace process as it had previously existed was finished. "Nobody among the Arabs, and especially among the Palestinians, will agree to return to the negotiating table on the basis of the old criteria and standards. Right now, the resolute stance taken by the Palestinian people, and its resistance to Israel's conquest, is the top priority." The Arabs, he said, would determine these new standards.[45] The Arab foreign ministers, meeting in January

42 Ibid.
43 *Tishrin*, March 28, 2001. Translation in MEMRI No. 202, April 2001.
44 Ibid.
45 Egyptian Foreign Minister Amr Moussa in *al-Safir*, October 25, 2000.

2001, insisted that the right of Palestinian refugees to return to Israeli territory was "sacred."[46]

Arab leaders competed with each other in pledging their devotion to the cause and their readiness to fight. The president of Iraq asked Israel's neighbors to give him land so that he could attack Israel. Syria called for annulling all Arab agreements with Israel, and the president of Yemen demanded a jihad to liberate Palestine. The head of one Egyptian political party declared that "Israel must be thrown into the sea," a statement altered by the Egyptian press to read: "Zionism must be thrown into the sea." One Fatah leader called for the export of the *intifada* "all over the Arab world in order to overthrow the traitorous rulers, so that Palestine may be liberated."[47]

The good old days had returned with a vengeance. None of the failures or crises were the Arabs' fault; Israel was the personification of evil; the Palestinians must be supported with all of the Arab world's resources (at least in terms of rhetoric); and if the West didn't like this, it could drink from the Nile. If the Arabs were steadfast, they would ultimately win everything they wanted. The reappraisal of the 1990s was erased.

This did not mean that the Arab leaders wanted to go to war with Israel. On the contrary, as in the previous several decades, excitement was to be whipped up and then restrained. But no one could easily dismiss the huge contradiction inherent in the regimes' propaganda. How could the Arabs go about their business when a Nazi-like regime, one that could easily be defeated with arms and determination, was committing genocide a few miles away? Why should any Arab states have good relations with the United States when it was, at the very least, supporting this evil and, at most, itself seeking to destroy Islam and the Arabs? Fortuitously, bin Ladin and the September 11 attacks came along to show that someone was fighting for truth and justice.

In October 2000, a scene symbolizing this gap took place in front of Cairo's central mosque. Shaykh Muhammad Seyyed Tantawi, head of al-Azhar University and one of the Sunni Muslim world's most important clerics, was confronted by an angry crowd of 200 people after his Friday prayer sermon, in which he had pleaded for calm. "You have to declare

46 Salah Nasrawi, "Arab Ministers Back Right of Return," Associated Press, January 4, 2001.
47 *Al-Hayat*, December 6, 2000. Translation in MEMRI No. 169, December 29, 2000.

war!" shouted one veiled woman. "We have to do something more serious. People are getting killed over there." The crowd called for mobilizing Egypt's army and for a jihad against Israel. "You want to fight?"
Tantawi responded. "No one is stopping you. But Egypt has already
fought four times and lost a lot. What is more helpful to the Palestinians,
to just say we declare war or to do real things like supplying them" with
donated blood, money, and weapons.[48]

Day after day, the statements made, articles written, and claims argued
were almost identical to those that had appeared in the late 1940s and in
every decade thereafter. "The Palestine Arabs will launch a relentless war
to repel this attack on their country," said an *al-Ahram* editorial in
1947.[49] Then, too, the Islamists had claimed that a willingness to sacrifice their lives would bring victory. In the words of the Egyptian Muslim
Brotherhood's leader, Hasan al-Banna, "You have always yearned for
this chance and now you have it. A wind is blowing from paradise sweet
with the smell of martyrdom."[50] And an Arab summit proclaimed, "The
world will see it is impossible to beat Arabs by force."[51]

Then, too, these fiery words were not matched by deeds. An Egyptian
newspaper mocked, "Among the young men who shouted 'Long live
Palestine!' We did not see a single one get a gun, put on a uniform, and say
'On to Palestine!'"[52] Saudi King Abd al-Aziz ibn Saud explained, "For a
Muslim to kill a Jew or for him to be killed by a Jew ensures him an imme-
diate entry into Heaven and into the august presence of God Almighty."[53]

And these were the attitudes and policies, it should be remembered,
that had led to the worst catastrophe in modern Arab history, the great
mistakes that were supposedly to be corrected a half-century later.
Nothing could be more appropriate to the new situation than the classic

48 Susan Sachs in the *New York Times*, October 14, 2000.
49 Christopher Sykes, *Crossroads to Israel* (Bloomington, IN, 1973), p. 325. It is now possible to see through (then-secret) diplomatic archives and other papers, that Arab leaders had grave doubts about the slogans they proclaimed publicly during the 1940s. It is
   quite possible that when these private statements are known in future the record will
   show the same gap between public discourse and their real thoughts. See Barry Rubin,
   The Arab States and the Palestine Question (Syracuse, NY, 1982).
50 *Al-Ikhwan*, December 10, 1947.
51 See British Foreign Office, 371 E11260/951/31, Campbell to FO, December 24, 1947.
52 U.S. Department of State Archives, Record Group, 59 890E.9111/4-2148, Pinkerton to
   Marshall, April 21, 1948; 890E.918/5-448, Pinkerton to Marshall, May 4, 1948.
53 British Foreign Office Archives, FO371 E7201/22/31, Walton to Rendel, October 25,
   1937.

assessment of the 1948 defeat made a half-century earlier by Constantine Zurayk, vice-president of the American University of Cairo, in his devastating book *The Meaning of the Disaster*:

> The representatives of the Arabs deliver fiery speeches in the highest international forums, warning what the Arab states and peoples will do.... Declarations fall like bombs from the mouths of officials at the meetings of the Arab League, but when action becomes necessary, the fire is still and quiet, and steel and iron are rusted and twisted, quick to bend and disintegrate.[54]

Yet the Arab states were also acting in response to Arafat's decisions to reject the peace proposals presented by Israeli Prime Minister Ehud Barak and President Bill Clinton during 2000 and then to carry out – whether or not he planned or initiated it – a war on Israel. Arafat's analysis of Israel and its withdrawal from Lebanon had made him expect that Israel would make more concessions, or even pull out of the West Bank and Gaza Strip unilaterally. Observing earlier events in Kosovo, he also seemed to think that the violence would trigger international intervention, peacekeeping forces, and eventually the return of the territory to the Palestinians.

If Arafat had signed a treaty with Israel, he would have been criticized by many in the Arab world and among his own people. If he had simply refused to make an agreement, his people would have been frustrated by the lack of change and he would have been criticized in the West for blocking peace. But, by rejecting peace and mobilizing violence, he became a hero to the former and a victim, at least for a while, to the latter. Domestic criticism was silenced. His support in the Arab and Islamic world hit all-time highs. The choice was politically brilliant on one level, but the price was the needless sacrifice of more than a thousand lives, much of the Palestinian infrastructure, and the chance to achieve Palestinian statehood on good – if not ideal – terms.

Even while Arafat had seriously contemplated a compromise solution during the Oslo process, he had never really challenged the basic goals and ideas that had shaped the movement over many years. Even as he met with Barak at Camp David, the constitution of his Fatah group continued to proclaim its goal to be the "[c]omplete liberation of Palestine and eradication of Zionist economic, political, military and

---

54 Constantine Zurayk, *The Meaning of the Disaster* (Beirut, 1956), p. 2.

cultural existence. . . . Armed public revolution is the inevitable method to liberating Palestine . . . a strategy and not a tactic. . . . This struggle will not cease unless the Zionist state is demolished and Palestine is completely liberated." Even as its leader negotiated, article 22 of the Fatah constitution opposed "any political solution offered as an alternative to demolishing the Zionist occupation in Palestine."[55]

These concepts were not merely relics of the past; they continued to influence the thinking and strategy of Palestinian leaders and activists. PA Minister of Information Yasir Abd Rabbo told his people over Voice of Palestine radio that Barak's offer to turn over the West Bank, Gaza, and parts of East Jerusalem to the Palestinians was a trick intended to "perpetuate their rule over us and turn us into a satellite state of Israel, which will come out of the settlement as the leading power in the region. No one can agree to that."[56] Yet any conceivable negotiated solution would arguably leave Israel as "the leading power in the region." The only thing that could prevent that outcome was the lack of any diplomatic settlement to the Arab-Israeli conflict.

The Clinton administration may have gone further than any previous American government to help the Palestinians, but to Arafat's own Fatah movement Clinton's effort to create a Palestinian state with its capital in East Jerusalem merely proved that "the Zionist group of the White House and the Zionist Lobby are controlling the future of the Palestinian people's cause." Making clear its real objection to the Camp David and Clinton proposals, Fatah explained that the right of all Palestinians to return (and, in a newly invented additional demand, to be both allowed to return and to receive compensation "for the years in which the occupation used these properties") would bring about the real solution. "The right of return does not aim to destroy Israel as Zionists claim; the right of return seeks to help Jews get rid of the racist Zionism that wants to impose their permanent isolation from the rest of the world."[57] In other words, the only outcome that Fatah would consider would be one that eliminated Israel on the basis of the PLO's 1974 program, which continued to dictate Palestinian strategy a quarter-century later.

55 Fatah's constitution is at http://www.fateh.org.
56 *Voice of Palestine*, October 9, 2000.
57 "Forty-four Reasons Why the Fatah Movement Rejects the Proposals Made by US President Clinton." Fatah Movement Central Publication, "Our Opinion," http://www.pna.gov.ps/ peace/44_reasons.htm <http://www.pna.gov.ps>.

As for the alleged willingness of Arafat's forces to suppress the radicals who would want to attack Israel and continue the conflict after a Palestinian state was established, Fatah saw this possibility as still another reason to oppose Clinton's plan. This proposal was in fact "the biggest trick," because accepting it "means moving the conflict into an internal Palestinian-Palestinian conflict that will destroy the intifada and into an Arab-Palestinian conflict."[58]

Rather than oppose the radicals, Arafat's lieutenants wanted to join them in their strategy and goals. For Fatah's young leaders, suicide bombing and terrorism were not just by-products but the very essence of the new strategy to overcome Israel's military superiority. They saw their key advantage as "the ability to transfer the battle into the enemy's territories."[59] Precisely because they were unable to take on Israel's army, their advantage lay in their ability to kill and maim Israeli civilians until that country gave up.

Some Palestinian leaders instead viewed violence as a clever tactic to gain more Israeli concessions; but they did not seem to realize how these actions were destroying any chance for a negotiated solution. Thus, Hani al-Hassan, a Fatah Central Committee member and an advisor to Arafat, told a Gaza symposium in October 2000, "The present Intifada enabled the Palestinians to change the old rules of the game, and thwarted Barak's attempt to place the responsibility for the stalemate in the peace process" on them.[60] As hundreds of Palestinians were being killed and the PA infrastructure was being destroyed, as terror tactics alienated the world and threw away all of the gains of the 1990s, Hassan could maintain that the *intifada* had strengthened the PA. As Israel easily won the military conflict and Israelis came to reject Arafat as a partner for peace and move toward electing Ariel Sharon as prime minister, Hassan proclaimed, "What we have witnessed in the Palestinian territories these past few days obliges our negotiators to raise the level of demands in the negotiations."[61]

Arafat in particular tried to incite the region to the heights of nationalist and Islamic passion at the October 2000 Arab summit. Speaking of Israeli opposition leader Ariel Sharon's one-hour visit to the Temple Mount, during which he entered no buildings, Arafat thundered,

58 Ibid.
59 Ibid.
60 *Al-Ayyam*, October 12, 2000. Translation in MEMRI No. 135, October 13, 2000.
61 Ibid.

"Sharon desecrated the al-Aqsa mosque and its compound. A new, religious, dimension was added to the Arab-Israeli struggle." He said that Israel's government was carrying out a "mass extermination campaign against our people" that it had been plotting for over a year. He accused Israel of using internationally banned weapons. Rejecting negotiation with Israel, he said that the problem could be solved only if Israel "is forced to submit to international legitimacy, implement the signed agreements, stop aggression," and so on.[62]

There was a curious contradiction in the Palestinian explanation of this struggle. On the one hand, it was the Palestinian war of independence, an offensive fought by heroic warriors to force Israel to yield to all of their demands. On the other hand, it was a defensive battle waged by helpless victims that was made necessary only by an unprovoked, carefully planned Israeli aggression intended to compel Palestinian submission.

Many Palestinian leaders could not conceal their absolute certainty that they would defeat Israel. PA Communications Minister Imad al-Faluji was exceptional in that he came from an Islamist background, but in this respect his views were typical. Speaking at the Ein al-Hilwe refugee camp in Lebanon during March 2001, he explained why the Palestinians could ignore the kinds of considerations that other political forces had to take into account: "The Palestinian people are the strong half of the international equation. It is the secret code and the key to any stability and peace not only in the Middle East, but in the world. . . . You can be sure that your stay here is temporary. We will not allow any force to raise any issue detrimental to the Right of Return to Palestine."[63]

Faluji's intoxication with exaggerated expectations of victory is not so different from the ideas expressed by Saddam Hussein, Bashar al-Asad, and many others among the Arab world's politicians, intellectuals, and average people alike. As Faluji put it,

Just as the national and Islamic Resistance in South Lebanon taught [Israel] a lesson and made it withdraw humiliated and battered, so shall [Israel] learn a lesson from the Palestinian Resistance in Palestine. The Palestinian resistance will strike in Tel Aviv, in Ashkelon, in Jerusalem, and

62 Speech at the Arab summit in Cairo, October 21, 2000. Translation in FBIS.
63 Alan Dowty and Michelle Gawerc, "The Intifada: Revealing the Chasm," *MERIA Journal*, Vol. 5, No. 3 (September 2001).

in every inch of the land of natural Palestine. . . . We will return to the early days of the PLO, to the 1960s and 1970s. . . . A new stage will continue until the rights are returned to their owners. . . .[64]

This absolute hatred was not just a propaganda ploy that could be shrugged off easily. Each accusation and distortion of Israel beyond its very real faults made it harder for the Palestinians to envision any possible compromise or for the Israelis to believe that they would ever do so. The official Palestinian news agency, Wafa, published stories claiming that Israel had started a new genocide against the Palestinian people by dropping poisoned bags of candy into Gaza from airplanes.[65]

Nader Tamimi, the mufti of the Palestinian Liberation Army, stated on al-Jazeera television that "the Jews have a sadistic mentality derived from the Torah which they have distorted as saying that man is 'a creature born from the seed of a horse.' The Torah says that all peoples that are not Jews must be killed." Suicide bombers were martyrs who would be married in heaven to seventy-two virgins. "I, the Mufti of those forces fighting in Palestine, say to them: your hand is blessed, brothers, when you kill; your hand is blessed, mother, who nurses this child who will one day become a martyr; your hands are blessed when you kill the enemy, blessed be you in Heaven, with the prophet Muhammad."[66]

Abu Ali Shahin, a veteran Fatah official who served in Arafat's cabinet, stated that "accepting the Oslo Accords was for the Palestinians, a betrayal of the historical legitimacy of the Arab right to Palestine." It was legitimate only because it was done "in order to gain a better position and to continue in liberation of the land." Syrian Vice-President Khaddam portrayed the *intifada* as the "countdown for the destruction of Israel."[67] And a Lebanese leader claimed that the present time offers "an exceptional historic opportunity to finish off the entire cancerous Zionist project."[68] "We were forced to leave Jaffa, Haifa and Tel Aviv," said a Hamas leader, "and recovering from that can only be achieved when war returns and forces the invaders out."[69]

64 *Al-Safir*, March 3, 2001. Translation in MEMRI No. 194, March 9, 2001.
65 Official Palestine news agency, "Israel Is Poisoning the Palestinians Candies," May 15, 2001, http://www.wafa.pna.net/EngText/21-05-2001/page014.htm.
66 Al-Jazeera program of May 23, 2001. Translation in MEMRI No. 245, July 23, 2001.
67 Abdel Halim Khaddam, *Agence France-Presse*, July 25, 2001.
68 *Financial Times*, April 25, 2001.
69 *Reuters*, May 16, 2001.

It was the return of the old PLO slogan "Revolution until Victory," which had guided the organization through so many defeats, miscalculations, and setbacks.[70] As Muhammad Dahlan, a young favorite of Arafat who commanded the Preventive Security force in Gaza and represented the next generation of Palestinian leadership, explained in October 2000, "The release of some Hamas people [imprisoned for past terror attacks against Israel] is an ordinary, natural, and simple step, compared to the steps we are going to take in the future. . . . The Intifada will continue until victory."[71] Similarly, a communiqué published that same month by the Supreme Supervisory Committee of the Nationalist and Islamist Forces, signed by twelve groups including Arafat's Fatah, proclaimed, "The Intifada will continue until the aggression is repelled and the realization of all its goals." The committee called for a united struggle that would by force "disarm the settlers, expel them, and destroy the settlements."[72]

Yet not one settlement was dismantled, nor a single settler expelled. By December 2001, Arafat was forced to announce, though he did nothing to implement, an unconditional cease-fire. One of the few public critics of the *intifada* strategy was Salah Abdel Jawad, chairman of the Political Science Department at Bir Zeit University. No Palestinian newspaper would publish his op-ed piece, which warned that the Palestinians were unprepared for such a military confrontation, that there was an enormous gap between the two sides' capabilities, and that Palestinian leaders simply did not understand the situation.[73]

Younger Palestinian militants, who did not remember the 1960s, 1970s, or 1980s, repeated their father's mistakes. Muhammad Dhamrah, deputy commander of Arafat's bodyguard corps, Force 17, echoed such assertions. The Arabs must "force Israel to end its occupation of the Arab lands, without the smallest [Arab] concession on any right whatsoever." The proper method was to fight relentlessly: "Kill your

---

70 Barry Rubin, *Revolution until Victory: The Politics and History of the PLO* (Cambridge, MA, 1993).

71 *Al-Jazeera*, October 12, 2000; *al-Ayyam*, October 12, 2000. Translation in MEMRI No. 135, October 13, 2000.

72 *Al-Ayyam*, October 12, 2000. Translation in MEMRI No. 135, October 13, 2000.

73 Saleh Abdel Jawad (head of the Department of Political Science at Birzeit University), "The Intifada's Military Lessons," *Palestine Report*, October 25, 2000.

enemies wherever you may find them. This is a life and death conflict between you and them." Independence would be achieved "through sacrificing. We have prepared thousands, tens of thousands, martyrs in order to regain our land and for the return of the refugees. . . . I am not worried. I am very optimistic that victory will come."[74]

There was no limit to the Palestinians' military capacity:

> I promise that the number of shootings at the occupation will increase to 500 to 1,000 [incidents] per day. . . . The Palestinians have trained themselves to attack the Israeli tanks and explode their bodies that will be loaded with a belt of explosives. . . . The Palestinians have nothing to lose, while the Israelis have a lot to lose. We can live on olives and za'tar [thyme] and continue our struggle until the liberation of our land.[75]

One episode illustrating this gap between theory and practice occurred after a brief incursion by Israeli forces into Jenin in August 2001. After the Israeli army pulled back, Palestinian media reports and discussion revolved around how the "heroic resistance" of armed Palestinian fighters had forced the Israeli tanks to retreat. Tayeb Adbel-Rahim, Arafat's top aide, stated that the Israeli forces had seized seventy collaborators who were being held prisoner and had killed two or three Palestinians. In fact, no one had died, no one had been freed from the local prison, and the Israelis had left when they completed their mission. The police had fled when the Israeli troops arrived. "Of course, I ran," said a police lieutenant. "I have nothing with which to oppose them. . . . We're not afraid of them, but we don't have the means. We don't have the weapons."[76] This was the kind of thing that happened when misjudgment led leaders of the weaker side to launch a war based on inflated claims of superiority and inevitable victory.

Remarkably, the statements of Arab leaders and writers during and after 2000 – including those of the younger generation of Palestinian activists – were often identical to explanations of strategy made thirty years earlier, which had of course proven wrong. In

---

74 Muhammad Dhamrah (Abu Awdh, deputy commander of Force 17), interview with *Al-Hayat*, August 17, 2001. Translation in MEMRI No. 260, August 22, 2001.
75 Ibid.
76 Clyde Haberman, "City Israel Raided Is Oddly Jubilant," *New York Times*, August 15, 2001.

1970, for example, Arafat had explained, "The Israelis have one great fear, the fear of casualties." He intended to exploit the contradictions within Israeli society. Killing enough Israelis would force the country's collapse, or at least its surrender to Palestinian demands, or – the new aspect of the argument during the more recent period – its unilateral withdrawal from the West Bank and Gaza. A PLO official in 1970 said that the Jews could not long survive under so much tension and threat: "Zionist efforts to transform them into a homogeneous, cohesive nation have failed," so they would run away or give up. "Any objective study of the enemy will reveal that his potential for endurance, except where a brief engagement is concerned, is limited." The 1968 Palestine National Council meeting concluded that wearing down Israel "will inevitably provide the opportunity for a decisive confrontation in which the entire Arab nation can take part and emerge victorious."[77]

The goal of Palestinian violence, Arafat said in 1968, was to destroy tourism, prevent immigration, and weaken the Israeli economy, "[t]o create and maintain an atmosphere of strain and anxiety that will force the Zionists to realize that it is impossible for them to live in Israel." Every Israeli, said the PLO's magazine in 1970, would come to feel "isolated and defenseless" against Arab forces, which would be everywhere. The Jew would then be bound to value more highly "the life of stability and repose that he enjoyed in his former country" compared to "the life of confusion and anxiety he finds in the land of Palestine. This is bound to motivate him towards reverse immigration." In the 1980s, too, similar themes were expressed in PLO documents. The enemy's "greatest weakness is his small population." Attacks against civilians in the streets would demoralize the Israelis.[78]

Even in December 2001, Faruq Qaddumi, head of the PLO's political department, explained why Israel was heading toward collapse. Israeli Prime Minister Ariel "Sharon is the last bullet in the Israeli rifle. If

77 "Yassir Arafat," Third World Quarterly, Vol. 8, No. 2 (April 1986), and also South, January 1986, p. 18; al-Anwar symposium of March 8, 1970, cited in Y. Harkabi, The Palestinian Covenant and Its Meaning, (London, 1979), p. 12; Yassir Arafat, May 1969, in International Documents on Palestine 1969 (Beirut, 1970), pp. 691–2; International Documents on Palestine 1968 (Beirut 1969), p. 400.

78 Arafat interview, January 22, 1968, in International Documents on Palestine 1968 (Beirut, 1969), p. 300; Filastin al-Thawra, January 1970, p. 8; Raphael Israeli, PLO in Lebanon: Selected Documents (London, 1983), p. 31.

Sharon is defeated, the rapid countdown [to the end] of Israel will begin, because that country was established through historical coercion and will find its end as the USSR and Yugoslavia did."[79]

Israel's ability to enter any part of the West Bank with its military and to besiege Arafat in the basement of his Ramallah headquarters in April 2002 had no effect on this analysis. Having learned all too little since 1965, the Palestinian movement's leaders still espoused the same basic concepts and expectations. Even if some of them personally recognized the need for a compromise, no basis had been laid for accepting real concessions or persuading their colleagues and the people that a new strategy was good and necessary.

No one had told younger Palestinians that these ideas had not worked before. Islamists especially took up the notion that their readiness to become martyrs would make the difference. The relatively recent immigration of most Israelis was no longer a factor, but now the Israeli withdrawal from Lebanon and the alleged decadence of Israeli society were supposed to explain why the Palestinians would win a war of attrition. Arguably, the first *intifada* of the late 1980s and early 1990s had been based on similar failed notions, though the enormous propaganda campaign waged around these events concealed the fact that the uprising had faded away and that Israel had actually won that round as well.

The case of Palestinian, and to some extent Arab, strategy was one of the greatest proofs of the dictum that those who do not remember history are doomed to repeat it. This was not a new pattern in Middle Eastern history. The Palestinians repeatedly, as a moderate Jordanian pointed out, missed opportunities and failed to learn the resulting lessons because their leaders feared "being accused of leniency and negligence [of Palestinian rights]." Since "the Arabs will never agree to be defeated, and the Jews will never allow the shattering of the State of Israel," the only way out was a pragmatic solution involving "mutual concessions from which both sides benefit."[80] Many Palestinian leaders understood this in private but would not speak out in public. At any rate, to whatever extent Arafat understood this reality, he did not act in the manner required to implement it.

79 Interview with *al-Hayat*, December 12, 2001. Translation in MEMRI No. 315, December 17, 2001.
80 Fahed al-Fanek in *al-Rai*, March 22, 2001. Translation in MEMRI No. 203, April 5, 2001.

In terms of domestic and inter-Arab politics, the Palestinian strategy might have been brilliant, but in dealing with Israel or the international situation it was disastrous. Those forces in society – political leaders, intellectuals, journalists – who were supposed to serve as a reality check instead led the march of folly. "It is proper that the call to hate Israel continue to be a medal worn on the chest of every Arab," wrote a Palestinian journalist. Such an attitude should serve "as a measurement of patriotism and as a certificate of greatness and nobility." Hating Israel, the theme of a hit song recently released in Egypt, signaled "the eruption of a volcano of hatred, abhorrence and bitterness that had been continuously accumulating for half a century."[81]

One Arab liberal horrified by these developments pointed out the remarkable indifference of such doctrines to the real world. The United States is extremely powerful, but "all over the Arab world voices are popping up calling for boycotting American merchandise, severing relations with Washington, and even launching war against the United States." The struggle for Palestinian rights has been turned "into an expression of hate and violence. Political emotions have taken the place of reason; the glory of suicide, killing, and the disrespect for human life has become prevalent. The Arab mentality has not realized that even imperfect peace agreements are preferable to war." What the Arab world really needs is "democracy, co-existence, development and modernization, things that the authoritarian Arab regimes are not ready for."[82]

Such burning hatred, history has shown, may more likely destroy its purveyors than their enemies. When a weaker party insists on sustaining a conflict against a stronger one, its situation is likely to worsen. In this case, the demand to continue the battle was a major factor in keeping the Arab world weak. But it was also a major factor in keeping the Arab regimes and the existing social order strong.

81 Fahmi Huwaidi in *al-Hayat al-Jadida*, May 16, 2001. Translation in *Palestinian Media Watch Bulletin*, May 17, 2001.
82 Amin al-Mahdi in *al-Hayat*, December 6, 2000. Translation in MEMRI No. 169, December 29, 2000.

9

THE TRUTH ABOUT U.S.
MIDDLE EASTERN POLICY

After the September 11, 2001, terrorist attack that killed more than 3,000 people in the United States, there was much discussion about what role U.S. Middle Eastern policy had played in motivating the terrorists and those who supported them or at least sought to justify their deeds. American policy was said to be responsible for profound grievances on the part of Arabs and Muslims that required an apology for past behavior and a change in future U.S. policy, and that somehow justified or explained the attack.

But this argument misrepresented the history and nature of U.S. Middle Eastern policy to the point that it became a caricature of reality. Equally, such distortions made it far more difficult to understand the terrorists' true motives and the reasons why many Arabs and Muslims seemed to support or sympathize with them.

This basic worldview is well represented in a 1981 speech by Syrian President Hafiz al-Asad: "The United States wants us to be puppets so it can manipulate us the way it wants. It wants us to be slaves so it can exploit us the way it wants. It wants to occupy our territory and exploit our masses. . . . It wants us to be parrots repeating what is said to us."[1] The part chosen by Arab nationalist and Islamist ideology for the United States to play is that of the nineteenth-century imperialist state, seeking to build a Middle Eastern empire in which Arabs and Muslims are colonial subjects. Actual U.S. behavior is largely irrelevant, as it will always be reinterpreted to fit into this mold, a distortion that well serves the needs of both regimes and revolutionary movements in the region.

---

1 Speech at graduation ceremony for paratroopers in Latakia, Syria, Damascus radio, October 1, 1981. Translation in *BBC Survey of World Broadcasts*, October 3, 1981.

Obviously, the United States, like all countries, seeks to make a foreign policy in accord with its interests. The important question, however, is how U.S. policymakers interpret those interests. If the United States saved Kuwait from annexation by a radical secularist regime in Iraq in 1991 because of its oil, for example, its policy was still in practice pro-Kuwait, pro-Muslim, and pro-Arab. After all, the United States could as easily have tried to seize oil assets for itself or demanded lower petroleum prices or benefits for American companies. What is important is that U.S. leaders usually defined American interests and set policies in a way that sought support from the largest number of Arabs and Muslims.

In fact, the main external influence on U.S. Middle Eastern policy has been the conflicts among Arab and Muslim states and factions, usually pitting radical Arab regimes and forces (often themselves militantly secularist and anti-Islam) or radical Islamist regimes and groups (which most Muslims held to be deviant if not heretical) against their moderate counterparts. This same factor played a key role in the background of the September 2001 attacks, another case of radical groups wishing to seize power by defining themselves as the only legitimate Muslims, against whom any resistance constitutes opposition to Islam itself.

During the 1940s and early 1950s, U.S. leaders wanted to play an anti-imperialist role in the Middle East. They tended to oppose continued British and French rule in the region and to voice support for reform movements.[2] When Gamal Abdel Nasser took power in Egypt in 1952, American policy makers welcomed his coup.[3] That same year, the United States also opposed British proposals to overthrow the nationalist government in Iran.[4]

The Cold War – the global U.S.-Soviet conflict that shaped U.S. foreign policy for many decades – altered this strategy. By the mid-1950s, U.S. leaders believed with good reason that this conflict was being extended into the Middle East, where local governments were also taking sides. The United States saw that Egyptian leader Gamal Abdel Nasser had decided to align with the Soviets. In some states, such

---

2 Regarding U.S. anti-imperialism, see Barry Rubin, *The Great Powers in the Middle East 1941–1947: The Road to Cold War* (London, 1981).

3 On U.S. relations with Nasser's coup and regime, see Barry Rubin, *The Arab States and the Palestine Conflict* (Syracuse, NY, 1982).

4 For a detailed account of these events, see Barry Rubin, *Paved with Good Intentions: The American Experience and Iran* (New York, 1980).

as Lebanon and Jordan, there was a wave of radical nationalist subversion; in others, such as Syria and Iraq, this turmoil led to coups and new regimes that also became friendly to Moscow. Fearing that the government of Iranian Prime Minister Muhammad Mossadegh was being taken over by Communist forces, the United States helped to overthrow it and returned the shah to power in 1953.

Even so, there was one last service that the United States rendered to radical Arab nationalism. In 1956, in an unusual break in its close relationship to England and France, the United States opposed their plot to overthrow Nasser during the Suez crisis, arguing that this action would antagonize the Arab world and increase Soviet influence. It threatened Britain and pressured Israel to withdraw from Egyptian territory. Thus, the United States saved Nasser, its biggest enemy in the region.

Basically, what U.S. policy did was to take sides in an inter-Arab conflict – Malcolm Kerr aptly called this the "Arab Cold War" – that had taken on global implications. Far from being anti-Arab, between the 1950s and 1980s the United States backed some Arab countries that were under assault by others that happened to be allied with the Soviet Union. This same fundamental factor, backing moderates against radicals, was the pattern prevailing in many circumstances down to the Kuwait crisis of 1990–91, as well as in U.S.-Israeli relations.

During most of this period, the United States became literally the political patron of Islam in the Middle East. After all, traditional Islam was a major bulwark against communism and radical Arab nationalism. Saudi Arabia, the stronghold for the doctrine of using Islam against radicalism, sought U.S. help to ensure that it survived the Nasserist and Ba'thist threats. Even in Iran, the U.S.-organized 1953 coup against the nationalists and in support of the shah met with the approval of most Muslim clerics.

Understandably, militant nationalists portrayed themselves as representing the only legitimate Arabs and claimed that moderate regimes – such as Morocco, Jordan, Saudi Arabia, and Lebanon, as well as post-Nasser Egypt – were merely stooges of the West, a claim later adapted by Islamists, who insisted that Muslims who opposed them were not proper Muslims. Yet while the moderate Arab regimes were not models of democracy or human rights, the radical states – such as Libya, Syria, Iraq, and Islamist Iran – were always far worse in these categories.

Consider a Cold War analogy. Soviet propaganda claimed that by opposing the triumph of communism in Western Europe, the United States foiled the wishes of the European masses. Equally, the United States fought Germany (which proposed a new order of a united Europe) in coalition with other European states and fought Japan, which promised to unite all Asia in prosperity, along with other Asian states.

Actually, the Cold War's existence and centrality in American strategy may have deterred the United States from taking even tougher stands against radical Arab forces. American policymakers reasoned that Arab regimes or groups too alienated by American actions might side with the Soviet Union. Thus, the United States pursued a careful course, always on the lookout for "winning away" those Arabs who were aligned with the Soviets and avoiding the "loss" of those who were not. Thus, the United States successfully wooed Egypt in the late 1970s, and that country became the second-largest recipient of U.S. aid in the world (with Israel in first place). The United States also did not attack or act too directly to counter Syria, whose control over Lebanon it accepted, or Iraq.

Even with the existence of an Arab-Israeli conflict, and despite the myth of Arab and Muslim unity, much of the region's turbulence, as well as most U.S. involvement there, resulted from conflicts among Muslim and Arab groups or states. America was dragged into crises when Muslim Iraq attacked Muslim Iran, when Arab Muslim Iraq seized Arab Muslim Kuwait, and when Arab Muslim but secularist Egypt threatened Arab Muslim Jordan and Saudi Arabia. Usama bin Ladin's anger was most provoked by the presence of U.S. troops in Saudi Arabia starting in 1990. Yet this action not only protected Saudi Arabia and freed Kuwait from an Iraqi threat, it was also sanctioned by the Arab League. The grievance most closely associated with bin Ladin's turn to an anti-American strategy and his September 11 attacks was clearly based on a U.S. action that was pro-Arab and pro-Muslim.

This situation also posed an insoluble dilemma for U.S. policy, one common to all great powers. If the United States supports and aids a government like Egypt or Saudi Arabia, it can be accused of sabotaging revolutionary movements seeking to overthrow that regime. But if the United States opposes any given Arab government, or presses it to be more democratic or tolerant of human rights, it can be accused of meddling in domestic affairs and thus of acting in an imperialist manner.

In fact, the United States played a very limited role in the internal conflicts pitting radical Islamist revolutionaries against Middle Eastern regimes during the 1980s and 1990s. Similarly, during Iran's Islamist revolution in 1978, the United States decided not to intervene and therefore in effect restrained the shah from taking tougher action to save his throne. Certainly, the U.S. government hoped that the shah would survive or that a moderate regime would emerge, but it nonetheless did little to prevent Ayatollah Ruhollah Khomeini's triumph.[5]

Once the revolution succeeded, President Jimmy Carter sought to conciliate the Islamist regime. It was indeed the growing contacts between the United States and moderate elements in the new government that led to the U.S. embassy's being seized in November 1979. The United States was such an immediate threat not because it tried to bring down Khomeini, but because it might influence the revolution to become less radical. While the United States did not want Iran to spread its revolution, it preferred to have the best possible relations with Tehran in order to minimize that country's cooperation with the USSR. During the mid-1980s, the Reagan administration was even ready to sell arms to Tehran in order to build an alliance with the Islamist regime there.

American "counterrevolutionary" involvement in the Arab world was equally limited. Arab regimes neither wanted nor needed U.S. help to fight and defeat Islamist insurgents. Even if the United States had totally ignored the Middle East during the 1980s and 1990s, it is doubtful that a single additional Islamist revolution would have succeeded. In Algeria, the United States maintained a neutral stance, despite the Algerian government's attempt to obtain its help. Similarly, the United States never took sides in Lebanon's civil war. At the same time, the most ruthless suppression of Islamist revolutions took place not with U.S. involvement but at the hands of two anti-American countries – Syria and Iraq.[6]

---

5 Ibid.

6 Compared to Europe, Latin America, and Asia, U.S. involvement in Middle Eastern domestic conflicts for the purpose of preserving existing regimes was positively minuscule. In Europe, the Marshall Plan and other policies did help to defeat communism in the late 1940s. In Latin America, there were periodic interventions and massive support for the local militaries, focusing on internal security efforts. In Asia, there were the Korean and Vietnam Wars along with other direct and active counterinsurgency and covert efforts, as well as the long-term presence of huge U.S. bases. Yet all these activities never inspired very much anti-American terrorism, except for a few limited acts in South America.

Ironically, the only real direct U.S. involvement in a battle between a regime and Islamists took place in Afghanistan, where the United States took the side of Islamist forces battling the Soviets. Bin Ladin, who would later claim that their victory proved the viability of radical Islamist revolution, forgot that U.S. arms, training, and financial help had played a central role in that triumph. Elsewhere, blaming the United States served as an excuse for radical Islamists as it had earlier for militant Arab nationalists, a way to explain away their own ineffective tactics and inability to win the support of the Muslim (or Arab) masses.

As Professor Fawaz Gerges accurately wrote: "Radical Islamists blame the United States for their defeat at the hands of the pro-U.S. Arab regimes. They claim that the West, particularly the United States, tipped the balance of power in favor of secular regimes by providing them with decisive political and logistical support."[7] This claim was untrue, but it became a central rationale for turning their guns against the American people.

Taken as a whole, then, U.S. policy in the Middle East was usually intended to win support from the great majority of Arabs and Muslims who were opposed to radical forces seeking to take power in the region through coup, revolution, or aggression. On many other occasions, the United States tried to win over enemies by proving its goodwill or ability to help them. Such occasions included:

• The United States saved Yasir Arafat in Beirut in 1982 by arranging safe passage for him out of Lebanon, where he had been besieged by the Israeli army. It initiated a dialogue with the PLO in 1988 and turned a blind eye to terrorism by PLO member groups until, in 1990, a blatant attack and the PLO's refusal to renounce it made this policy unsustainable. It became the Palestinians' patron between 1993 and 2000. The United States forgave Arafat for his past involvement in murdering American citizens, including U.S. diplomats. The United States worked hard to mobilize financial aid to the Palestinian Authority. Arafat was frequently invited to the White House. The United States almost always refrained from criticizing the PA. President Clinton went to Gaza and made a sympathetic speech to an audience of Palestinian leaders.

7 Fawaz Gerges, "The Tragedy of Arab-American Relations," *Christian Science Monitor*, September 18, 2001.

Finally, the United States tried to broker a peace agreement producing an independent Palestinian state, with its capital in East Jerusalem. After Arafat rejected the U.S. peace attempts and did not implement cease-fires that he had promised to the United States, American leaders did not treat him as an enemy. Despite this, some Arabs and Muslims supported or justified bin Ladin's attack by blaming Palestinian suffering on the United States.

- The United States proposed numerous détente efforts with Islamic. Iran – by Carter in 1979, by Reagan in the mid-1980s, and several initiatives by the Clinton administration. The United States did maintain sanctions on Iran in an attempt to change three specific Iranian policies (sponsoring terrorism, developing weapons of mass destruction, and opposing Arab-Israeli peace), but it also sought to find ways to end those sanctions through diplomatic compromise and never waged a serious campaign to overthrow that regime.

- The United States saved Afghanistan from the Soviets, Kuwait and Saudi Arabia from Iraq, and Bosnia and Kosovo from Yugoslavia. In the first case, the United States used covert means; in the other three instances U.S. troops were actually sent into combat situations. In short, the United States risked American lives to help Muslims. Despite this fact, bin Ladin and his apologists blamed the United States for Muslim suffering in Bosnia and Kosovo, while labeling it an aggressor and defiler of Islam because it deployed troops in Saudi Arabia.

- Year after year, administration after administration, U.S. governments were careful not to hurt Muslim sensibilities by any speech or policy. In every statement, distinctions were made between radical Islamist movements and Islam itself.

- The U.S. government supported Muslim Pakistan against India, though Congress put some sanctions on Pakistan because of its nuclear weapons program. The United States ignored Pakistan's sponsorship of terrorism against India.

- The U.S. government supported Turkey, a country with a Muslim population, against Greece in the Cyprus conflict.

- In Somalia, where no vital U.S. interests were at stake, the United States engaged in a humanitarian effort to help rescue a Muslim people from anarchy, civil war, and murderous warlords. When it became clear that the mission could not succeed, U.S. forces left. Bin Ladin and others portrayed U.S. involvement in Somalia as yet another grievance justifying the attacks, as an imperialist anti-Islamic aggression defeated by Islamist Somalis.

- The United States supported Arab Iraq against Iran during the latter part of the Iran-Iraq war. It took this step at the urging of such Arab allies as Saudi Arabia and Kuwait.

- When Iraqi President Saddam Hussein began to seek Arab leadership in 1989 and repeatedly denounced the United States, U.S. policy did not respond in a tough manner in order to avoid offending Arabs. The United States continued to provide Iraq with credits and other trade benefits even when it had evidence that the money Iraq obtained was being misused to buy arms. When Saddam Hussein directly threatened Kuwait, the United States hurried to assure him, through U.S. Ambassador April Glasspie, that America was not his enemy and was neutral in this dispute. Convinced that America would not intervene, Saddam then invaded Kuwait.

- When Saddam Hussein hid weapons of mass destruction and refused to cooperate with UN inspectors, the United States supported continued sanctions against the Iraqi regime. Had the Baghdad government kept its commitments, the sanctions would have ended years earlier. Moreover, Iraq's government inflicted suffering on its own people as a propaganda tool and continued to threaten its Arab and Muslim neighbors. Bin Ladin and his apologists portrayed American policy as a deliberate attempt to injure and kill the Iraqi people.

- For many years, the United States kept its military forces out of the Persian Gulf in order to avoid offending the Arab and Muslim peoples there. It went in only when requested, first to reflag Arab oil tankers and later to intervene against Iraq's invasion of Kuwait. Its forces never went where they were not invited and left whenever asked to do so by the local states. American forces also stayed away from Mecca and Medina in order to avoid giving offense to Islam. After Kuwait was liberated, the United States even advocated the concept of the Damascus agreement, in which Egypt and Syria would have played a primary role in protecting the Gulf. It was the Gulf Arab states who rejected implementing this idea. Nevertheless, bin Ladin, other Arabs, and Iran's government portrayed the U.S. presence as an imperialist plot to dominate the area and subjugate its people.

- The United States rescued Egypt at the end of the 1973 war by pressing Israel to stop advancing and by insisting on a cease-fire. The United States became Egypt's patron during the 1980s, after the Camp David peace agreement, providing large-scale arms supplies and other military and financial assistance and asking for little in return. Indeed, all of this help gave the United States no leverage over Egyptian policies, and no goodwill in the state-controlled Egyptian media or in the statements of that country's leaders. Bin Ladin and his allies, however, portrayed Egypt as a puppet of the United States.

Indeed, on twelve major issues where Muslims had a conflict with non-Muslims or secular forces, or where Arabs had a conflict with non-Arabs, the United States sided with the former groups on eleven of the twelve.

The United States backed Muslim versus non-Muslim states in six of seven conflicts: It supported Turkey over Greece, Bosnia and later Kosovo against Yugoslavia, Pakistan against India, the Afghans fighting the Soviets, and Azerbaijan against Armenia. The only exception to this pattern was U.S. support for Israel in the Arab-Israeli conflict.

When Muslims came into conflict with secular forces, the United States helped moderate Islamic-oriented states to oppose both Egyptian Nasserism and the Ba'thist regimes in Iraq and Syria, and it assisted Kuwait and Saudi Arabia in resisting Iraq. The only apparent exception to this rule was U.S. help for Iraq against Iran, but even this effort was an attempt to help conservative Muslim Gulf Arab regimes that were threatened by militant Islamist Iran. Given this aspect of the Iran-Iraq war, the United States helped Muslim against secularist governments in three out of three conflicts.

If one considers Arab versus non-Arab conflicts, the United States supported Arab Iraq against non-Arab Iran, and both the Arabs and Iran against the Soviet Union.[8]

Remarkably, then, the U.S. backing for Israel was the only significant case where the United States did not follow this pattern. No matter how much Arabs and Muslims are aggrieved at that particular U.S. policy – an issue discussed below at greater length – it seems strange that this single complaint should so totally overwhelm all of the points just mentioned and that none are seen as balancing factors. Indeed, for reasons to be analyzed later, virtually none of these events is even mentioned in Arab or Muslim discussions about the United States.

8 U.S. support for Israel is counted only once on this list. I have put this issue in the first category, but it could equally be placed in the last.

This pattern of U.S. attempts to maintain good relations with Arabs and Muslims was so strong that even after several thousand Americans were murdered in a massive terrorist attack, U.S. leaders spent much of their time urging that there be no retaliation against Muslims and Arabs in the United States. American policymakers repeated at every opportunity that they did not see Islam as the enemy and tried everything possible to gain Arab and Muslim support and sympathy for the U.S. effort.

Rather than seeking revenge against Afghanistan, whose safe haven for bin Ladin had helped to make the attacks on New York and Washington possible, President George W. Bush even asked American schoolchildren to send donations to help their counterparts in Afghanistan. The United States dropped food to the Afghan people, waged war to overthrow the Taliban while trying to minimize Afghan civilian casualties, eliminated the ferocious dictatorship ruling the country, turned power over to a broad-based new government, and organized large-scale aid for reconstruction there.

Again, the fact that many or even most Arabs and Muslims in the Middle East did not recognize this consistent thread in U.S. policy does not mean that it did not exist. But what it does demonstrate is that there were forces and factors within the region that had a stake in distorting American policy for their own purposes.

Just as the United States took many steps to help Arabs and Muslims – or at least to help moderates against radical ones – it is equally revealing to analyze what the United States did not do. This tally also undercuts the notion of overwhelming and justified Arab/Muslim grievances based on American misdeeds in the Middle East. If the United States wanted to carry out "anti-Arab" or "anti-Muslim" policies, as is charged, or even if it wanted to act as a traditional great power, it would have taken dozens of actions that could have been justified by events there. The fact that the United States did not do so reflects its goals, which include a serious desire to win support from Arabs and Muslims, for reasons ranging from the Cold War, to maintaining good trade relations, to avoiding conflict.

Clearly, a large part of the Arab/Muslim critique of U.S. policy is based on an expectation of what America wants and how it might behave. Whatever the failure of America and Americans in understanding the Middle East, the inability of Middle Easterners to understand the

United States seems to exceed it. Many in the Middle East view the United States as a projection of what their own leaders or movements would do if they were in control of the world's most powerful country. They would seek global hegemony and control over the Middle East, using force to do so and wiping out enemies without mercy or tolerance. Consequently, the United States is accused of thinking the same way, as aiming to subordinate the Arab world and to defeat or destroy Islam.

Consider what the United States did *not* do in past decades:

- It did not embark on an all-out effort to overthrow the Islamist regimes in Iran, Afghanistan, and Sudan, even though these regimes sponsored terrorism against the United States and unilaterally declared it to be an enemy. Nor did it attack Iran for its involvement in holding American hostages in Lebanon or in sponsoring terrorist attacks that cost American lives. The United States merely invoked economic sanctions in an effort to change certain specific policies of these states.

- Even when Iran held American diplomats as hostages, the United States publicly declared that it would avoid using force and sought diplomatic means to resolve the situation.

- It did not try to overthrow Saddam Hussein in 1991, partly because it accepted the argument that to do so would make the United States unpopular in the Arab world. Even when Kurdish and Shi'ite Iraqis rose up against the regime, the United States did not help them bring down its most hated enemy in the Middle East.

- It did not pressure or seek to subvert Syria, even when Damascus was involved in anti-American terrorism. It courted Syria for the Kuwait war and the peace process; the United States put no serious pressure on Damascus even when the Syrians walked out of the peace process. Rather than act as an imperialist power, the United States flattered and courted Damascus.

- It did not try to destroy Arafat and the PLO, even when they were responsible for anti-American terrorism and aligned with the USSR. It usually did not criticize or pressure them even when they broke agreements, rejected Clinton's two peace initiatives in 2000, and broke cease-fires promised to the United States in 2000 and 2001. The United States did not have an "anti-Palestinian" policy except in the sense that it opposed Palestinian efforts to destroy Israel's existence, while supporting efforts to find a compromise solution to the conflict that would help satisfy moderate Palestinian goals.

- It did not try to punish Egypt for its rapprochement with Iraq or its secret purchases of missiles from North Korea. It did not threaten Egypt with a cut-off of aid, even when Cairo refused to cooperate with the war against terrorism in 2001.
- It did not bully King Hussein of Jordan after his decision to follow the domestic radical forces' demand that he support Iraq, a country at war with America, during the Kuwait crisis. Afterward, Jordan suffered no U.S. retaliation. Indeed, it was Saudi Arabia and Kuwait who denied Jordan aid, while the United States tried to persuade them to forgive and help Amman.
- It dropped sanctions on Libya when Libya turned over for trial two intelligence officers and took no further action, even though the court case showed Libyan involvement in the bombing of a U.S. airliner that caused the deaths of many Americans. It bombed Libya on one occasion for its involvement in terrorism aimed at killing Americans – a bombing in West Berlin – but never used military force against Libya at any other time.
- When two U.S. embassies in East Africa were blown up, with immense loss of life, by Usama bin Ladin's group in 1998, it responded only with one cruise missile attack on a specific factory in Sudan, allegedly owned by bin Ladin and being used to make chemical weapons, and one similar attack on a terrorist training base in Afghanistan. If the United States was so bullying, imperialistic, and eager to hurt Islamist forces, it could have justifiably launched full-scale military assaults and other punishments on those hosting or helping bin Ladin.
- It did not go all-out in supporting Israel even when the peace process collapsed in 2000, but instead maintained a studious position of neutrality, probably spending more time criticizing Israel than it did the Palestinians, at least during the conflict's first twelve months.
- It did not use all of its assets and resources to force Arab states to support the peace process with Israel, but employed only very limited efforts at persuasion. When these efforts were almost always rebuffed, the United States did not retaliate.
- It did not use the occasion of an Iraqi attempt to assassinate former President George Bush to go to war with Iraq, sending only a one-day cruise missile attack on Iraqi intelligence headquarters. (And even that was done at night, in order to minimize casualties.)
- While the United States did bomb Iraq and fight to retain sanctions when Iraq broke its commitments on eliminating weapons of mass

destruction, the United States also made compromises in order to ease sanctions, tried to improve the humanitarian situation in Iraq, limited its use of force, and resisted proposals to go all-out in using the Iraqi opposition to overthrow Saddam.

- When U.S. oil companies' holdings were nationalized and oil prices were raised steeply, the United States did not try to overthrow regimes or force them to lower prices by using threats or force.
- The United States did not try to dominate the Gulf after 1990, despite its position of overwhelming military strength there; it did not over-throw or dominate the local governments, did not demand a huge payment for its help (as Iraq did after the Iran-Iraq war), or threaten to punish Gulf states unless they changed their policies (unlike the behavior of the radical Arab states and Iran), or insist that they transform their systems (unlike Iran and the radical movements).
- The United States did not at any time launch an anti-Islamist campaign in the region. It did not send military forces or special counterinsur-gency aid, or demand that Islamist groups be repressed, or do a host of other things it could have done in this regard.
- It did not take advantage of the USSR's disappearance as a super-power to impose anything on anybody, and certainly not to establish American domination in the region. Despite having won the Cold War, the United States did not seek to take revenge on regimes that had supported the losing side.

This list is far from complete, but it gives a sample of how the United States chose options that reflected the fact that it did not seek to domi-nate the region, destroy Islam, undermine Arabism, or take other ac-tions of which it has been accused. Whatever America has done or done wrong in the Middle East, it has used only a small portion of its poten-tial power, stopped far short of what it could have done, and avoided intervention whenever possible. If, for whatever reason, the United States has limited its actions in the region, then the alleged grievances against this restrained superpower should likewise be limited.

How can the real U.S. record be so disregarded in the Middle East, and why has this been done?

There are four ways that are being used to distort this history. The first is simply to ignore the truth about U.S. policy. For reasons to be discussed, Arab and Iranian media hardly ever say anything positive about the United States. Arab and Iranian leaders – even those who benefit from U.S. help – rarely praise America. Shut off from contrary information and constantly fed antagonistic views, it is hardly surprising that the masses are hostile to the United States. Those who would present a different view are discouraged by peer pressure, censorship, and fear of being labeled U.S. agents.

The second technique is to distort the record. For example, bin Ladin himself charged that the suffering of Muslims in Kosovo and Bosnia – whom the United States actually protected – or in places like East Timor, the Philippines, and Algeria – where the United States played no role – are America's fault. In other areas, American motives can be misrepresented. For instance, U.S. humanitarian efforts in Somalia are portrayed as an imperialistic, anti-Muslim campaign defeated by heroic local resistance. Again, the Arab media and leaders are complicit in this approach, having laid a foundation for it by their own presentation of the issues.

A third method is to ignore other threats to the region. An outstanding example here is the whitewashing of Iraqi President Saddam Hussein. After all, the Iraqi leader began two wars, killing hundreds of thousands of Muslims and Arabs; looted and vandalized Kuwait; threatened all of his neighbors and thus the holy cities of Mecca and Medina; tortured and repressed his own people, against some of whom he also used chemical weapons; fired missiles at Iran, Saudi Arabia, and Israel; and worked to develop nuclear arms with which he could seize power in the Gulf.

Yet now the Arab peoples are told that it is the United States, not Iraq, that threatens to dominate the Gulf and enslave its people. American-backed international sanctions against Iraq and the sporadic use of force to render Iraq less dangerous are cited as major reasons justifying the assault on America. The strange implicit alliance between bin Ladin and Saddam Hussein, a secularist who has killed many Muslim clerics (albeit mainly Shi'a ones) is one of the more bizarre elements of the situation.

Fourth, there has been an attempt to reduce all of American policy to a single issue, defined as "U.S. support for Israel," while at the same time distorting the nature and policies of Israel itself. This point will be discussed more fully later. For the moment, though, it can be said that to try to negate all that the United States has done for the Arab and Muslim world – and all that it has not done *to* the Arab and Muslim world – on the sole basis of US-Israel relations shows the flimsiness of the case against America.

Just because the United States has been accused of pursuing a policy hostile to Arabs and Muslims does not mean that these accusations are true, and certainly does not mean that American policy should be changed. Indeed, the reasons for this claim have far more to do with Middle Eastern politics than with U.S. policy. And when the purposes of this campaign are thoroughly examined, this anti-American effort actually reflects credit on American motives, choices, and strategies.

Before considering the real roots of anti-American views and behavior, however, the issue of the U.S.-Israeli relationship requires some separate consideration. Clearly, the United States has been Israel's main ally since the 1970s. But what does the concept that "the United States supports Israel" mean in the overall context of U.S. policy and the current spate of anti-Americanism?

Part of the problem here is how the Arab world and Islamists conceive of Israel itself. For those whose starting point is that Israel is some evil force seeking to dominate the Middle East, kill Arabs, and despoil Islam, it is not surprising that any U.S. help to Israel is viewed as a terrible deed. More accurately, the United States has helped Israel to survive the efforts of its Arab neighbors to remove it from the map. Moreover, during the entire period since the late 1960s, the U.S. goal has been to achieve a mutually acceptable compromise peace agreement between the Arabs and Israel that would ensure good American relations with both sides in the conflict. In addition, the U.S.-Israel alliance was created and reinforced because the Arab states took certain hostile steps, including aligning themselves with the USSR and using such tactics as sponsoring anti-American terrorism.

Radical forces in the Arab world objected to all aspects of the U.S. policy toward Israel because of their own objectives and interests. They wanted to eliminate Israel, and saw U.S. policy as blocking that effort. At the same time, they did not want a peaceful solution to the conflict because they rejected any outcome in which Israel survived. Equally important, a successful peace process would deny them the benefits of using the conflict to foment support for revolution and to justify their own rule. Finally, American success in achieving a resolution of the conflict would strengthen U.S. leverage in the region, making it better able to counter radical forces there.

From the 1970s on, the United States has repeatedly sought to seize opportunities to advance a negotiated solution of the Arab-Israeli conflict. During the 1993–2000 Oslo process, the United States tried to facilitate a deal on the Israeli-Palestinian and Israeli–Syrian fronts. While it is possible to critique the details and timing of specific American efforts, the overall goal was quite clear. The United States put such peacemaking at the top of its international agenda, with its highest officials devoting a considerable portion of their time to this issue. Over time, when convinced that forces on the Arab side were ready to make peace, the United States moved considerably closer to the Arab/Palestinian standpoint and urged Israel to do so as well. When the United States doubted the readiness of Arab leaders to resolve the issue, however, U.S. policy moved in the opposite direction.

Negotiating a compromise agreement was always in the U.S. interest precisely because it did want good relations with the Arab world. By resolving this passionate issue, the United States would be better able to promote regional stability, reduce the possibility of war, and ensure its own regional position. For these same reasons, Islamist radicals opposed this policy. U.S. efforts at peacemaking were more antithetical to their revolutionary goals than had the United States refrained from such activities. This is the reason why radical Islamist forces opposed the peace process altogether and staged many terrorist attacks in an effort to destroy it.

Their complaint was not that the diplomatic process moved too slowly, but rather that it might succeed at all. For Hamas and Islamic Jihad, the Palestinian Islamist groups, peace would make it difficult to gain power and continue their armed struggle. Ironically, if one Middle Eastern leader benefited from U.S. efforts to strengthen him against Islamist forces in the 1990s, it was Yasir Arafat. The fact that Arafat and the Palestinian Authority became virtual U.S. clients during that era only further dismayed the Islamist radicals.

Events demonstrate the accuracy of this analysis. Israel's withdrawal from Lebanon, urged and supported by the United States, was not seen as a step toward "ending occupation" or achieving peace, but as a sign that Israel was weak and a signal to escalate violence against it. Bin Ladin's ideological framework was laid down, and the September 11 attacks were being planned, at a time when the peace process seemed closest to success, even though the actual attack took place at a time when it had clearly failed.

It is strange that the height of anti-Americanism in the Middle East came at the height of U.S. proposals to support an independent Palestinian state with its capital in East Jerusalem. And even if the specific offers were judged inadequate by various Arabs due to their details or presentation (and often on the basis of misleading information about what was offered), this hardly explains or justifies claims that U.S. policy was brutal and hostile.

The attempt to reduce all of U.S. Middle East policy to the phrase "support for Israel" – and then to misrepresent that stance – was really an attempt to exploit xenophobia as a tool to justify radical groups and dictatorial regimes. The real complaint was that the United States had helped Israel to survive, then sought a diplomatic solution that would simultaneously undermine the case for Islamist revolution and the justification for the regimes' dictatorial rule. It was not "U.S. support for Israel," as such, that created anti-Americanism, but rather the distortion of what the United States was actually doing and the goals of various forces in the region that opposed these efforts.

Obviously, this is not necessarily the way that most Arabs and Muslims see – or at least publicly profess to see – America and its Middle Eastern policy. "For many Arabs, regardless of their politics, the United States has replaced colonial Europe as the embodiment of evil," Gerges wrote. "In their eyes, the United States is the source of the ills and misfortunes that befell their world in the second part of the past century. Today, to be politically conscious in the Arab world is to be highly suspicious of America, its policies, and its motives."[9] Why, then, is the perception so different?

Obviously, a difference of opinion in viewing events is rooted in a whole set of cultural and historical factors, questions of language and familiarity, interests and politics. Nevertheless, to attribute this outcome to simple misunderstandings or honest disagreements over the facts is insufficient. Only by examining such issues further can the reason for anti-Americanism, and especially its timing, be better understood.

The real basis of anti-Americanism in the Arab world is that it is a strategy that offers something for everyone, and at no significant cost:

- For radical oppositionists, anti-Americanism has been a way to muster mass support after their failure to do so for an anti-government

9 Gerges, "The Tragedy of Arab-American Relations."

revolutionary strategy. Given the inability of revolutionary Islamist movements to overthrow any Arab government using a variety of strategies, they desperately sought some new tactic. The masses overwhelmingly rejected the radical Islamists' claims that they represent true Islam, noting the many ways in which their views deviate from Islam as it has always been practiced. But this objection can be swept aside by clothing the Islamist cause in the attractive garments of xenophobia. It is an old trick of totalitarian movements, and one that works very well.

An added benefit for radical opposition movements is that anti-Americanism is a relatively safe strategy. Arab regimes that will quickly and brutally repress a challenge to themselves will do nothing against militants who only attack the United States. Indeed, it is precisely because the image of a bullying and anti-Arab America is a myth that verbally bashing the United States is such a profitable and secure enterprise.

The extremists' real goal is to delegitimize the moderate forces; to mobilize the masses, using the existing hatred for America and stirring up more; and to maintain the myth of Arab or Islamist unity against a foreign foe. Our enemy, they argue, cannot come from our own ranks but must be external and alien to our religion and culture. Our problems and suffering cannot in any way be attributed to our own actions or decisions but only to the meddling of evil foreigners and their local agents.

• For the regimes, anti-Americanism is a way to distract attention from their numerous failings. Instead of pressing for democracy, human rights, higher living standards, less corruption and incompetence, a change of leadership, or any number of other demands that would damage the interests of governments and rulers, the focus of attention is turned to shouting at the United States. This strategy defuses opposition and takes the pressure off the rulers.

By seizing control of the anti-Americanism card, regimes also defuse its use by the opposition and make it an element strengthening their own power. The Egyptian government can accept billions of dollars in U.S. aid, obtain American arms, use the United States to protect itself from an aggressive Iraq, and even carry out joint military maneuvers with U.S. forces. It can then push anti-Americanism in its own state-controlled media and official statements. Such a strategy appeases radicals, distracts its own citizens, and maintains its legitimacy as a politically correct Arab and Muslim power. Governments can even demand national unity (i.e., insist that no one criticize them or demand domestic change) in the face of this American "threat." They can simultaneously deflect Islamist anger from themselves, distance themselves from bin Ladin, and glean the benefits of alliance with the United States. Even if the Arab and Iranian governments do nothing, they know that the United States will eliminate the threat of bin Ladin for them.

For Iraq, anti-Americanism becomes a useful tool in its battle to escape sanctions and rebuild its military might. With America being charged with murdering defenseless Iraqis through sanctions, who can remember Iraq's seizure of Kuwait? Even the 1991 war is transformed from a U.S.-led liberation struggle to an example of anti-Muslim, anti-Arab American aggression.

For Iran, putting the emphasis on anti-Americanism provides an opportunity to get U.S. forces out of the Gulf and to make a trans-Muslim appeal that negates Iran's regional handicaps – those of being Shi'a, not Sunni, and Persian, not Arab. At the same time, the United States has eliminated Iran's troublesome neighbor, the Taliban government in Afghanistan (though Tehran does not want Afghanistan to become a U.S. client either).

For Syria, anti-Americanism is a substitute for the reform that President Bashar al-Asad promised and quickly squelched. For Palestinian leaders, anti-Americanism erases their own rejection of compromise peace offers and their resort to violence, while providing a good weapon to mobilize the Arab world and a lever to undermine Israel's international support and to demand that it give up even more. Claiming that U.S. support for Israel is the cause of anti-Americanism, Palestinians can even demand new American pressures on Israel.

Egypt can once again show itself to be the leading champion of Arab interests, with some additional Islamic credentials added to the government's portfolio. Cairo can expect that a refusal to cooperate with the American war against terrorism and also the anti-American hostility of the state-controlled Egyptian media will in no way jeopardize its two billion dollars in annual U.S. aid.

Arab governments can also use the crisis to demand more concessions from the West and hence material gains for themselves. They argue that they can do nothing because their hands are tied by the passion of public opinion (a factor which never stops them from tough action when their own interests are threatened). They insist that the United States must pressure Israel for unilateral concessions, end sanctions against Iraq, and meet their other demands – without any real reciprocal action on their part – as the only way to defuse the problem.

None of this means that any Arab government liked bin Ladin, endorsed his specific brand of Islamist ideology, or wanted him to succeed. But the Arab and Iranian regimes would exploit aspects of his ideas and deeds, adapting them to their own needs, and might attack such forces directly only if they were deemed to be a threat to internal stability. Unlike bin Ladin, they seek no real confrontation with the West or war with Christianity. They don't want to lose the trade, economic aid, or military defense arrangements they have with the United States. But they will play the militancy game at home for domestic benefit, reinforcing their own people's antagonism to the West and the United States and making a peaceful resolution of the Arab-Israeli dispute more difficult.

• For intellectuals and opinion makers, anti-Americanism permits them to vent their anger against a government-approved target, rather than risking their positions as the rulers' privileged courtiers by taking courageous stands against their own societies' injustices. In addition, they do not have to consider changing their own traditional militant ideologies. Anyone who differs from the prevailing view can be intimidated into silence by being accused of being anti-Arab, anti-Muslim, or an agent of America. Those who talk of domestic reform, democratization, privatization, and other changes can be shut up.

• For the masses, anti-Americanism falls in line with what they have been taught in school, told by the state-controlled media, heard preached at the mosque, and seen purveyed by their leaders, whether they be the nation's rulers or the Islamist oppositionists. Holding America responsible for everything wrong in their lives makes them feel better and provides an explanation of how the world works. The anti-American struggle makes them feel strong, giving them hope for a better future. It validates their pride in being virtuous Arabs and Muslims superior to their evil enemies.

Consider, for example, how Egypt – America's greatest ally in the Arab world – handled the Egypt Air crash of 1999. Official statements and the state-controlled media claimed that this tragedy was caused by a U.S.- or Israeli-orchestrated conspiracy. Suggestions that an Egyptian copilot might have deliberately caused the crash for political or personal reasons were rejected as a slander on Egypt and its people. In short, even the investigation of a plane crash was presented to the masses in inflammatory anti-American terms.[10]

Are there legitimate Arab and Muslim grievances against America? Of course there are. But there are legitimate American grievances against Arab states and Islamist opposition movements that are equally impressive. Moreover, one must assess the overall level of legitimate grievance and the legitimacy of a terrorist response. A good way to do so is to compare them to the grievances and responses of people in other countries and regions.

If one wants to assess relative grievances against America based on past U.S. policies, the Arabs and Muslims of the Middle East would be relatively far down the list. After all, one could far more easily find, justify, and see as significant the grievances of Native Americans and African-Americans; the Japanese and Germans, defeated and occupied after World War Two; Latin Americans, who faced U.S.-supported coups and military regimes that really did depend on U.S. backing, along with a high level of American economic domination; Filipinos and Puerto Ricans, who were ruled by the United States for decades; Cubans subject to U.S. sanctions; Russians and other ex–Soviet bloc citizens defeated in the Cold War; the Vietnamese and other peoples of Southeast Asia, who suffered hundreds of thousands of casualties through American carpet bombing, napalm, and deforestation; the Chinese, who dislike U.S. support for Taiwan; and sub-Saharan Africans, who deplored U.S. support for South Africa. Yet virtually none of these peoples evince significant anti-American sentiments, nor do they carry out or justify anti-American terrorism.

One grievance that has relatively little objective basis in the Middle East, while being paramount in other regions, is the issue of economic exploitation. The oil-producing states have a great deal of economic power and wealth, bossing around U.S. companies as they wish. Unlike the situation in Latin America and Asia, there is relatively little direct American investment in the Middle East. There is no U.S. control of the

10 See "Egypt Air Crash: The Hidden Hand Behind the Disaster," *al-Ahram*, April 2, 2000. http://www.albalagh.net/current_affairs/egypt_crash.shtml.

economy as there is in Latin America, sweatshops as there are in Asia, or ownership of raw materials as there is in Africa. In this respect, the Middle East has far less in the way of legitimate grievances than other regions. It is hard to argue that Arabs are poor because Americans are rich. And it cannot be claimed that Arab raw materials are sold at low prices in exchange for high-priced Western industrial goods, a situation quite different from that of countries having only cacao or tin to sell.

Another grievance that has little or no reality in the Middle East compared to other areas is the complaint that the United States makes or breaks governments there. Since the pro-shah Iranian coup of 1953, there is literally not a single case in which U.S. covert intervention can be credibly charged, much less proven, to have changed a Middle Eastern regime. Only regarding Iraq has the United States been even half-heartedly involved in trying to overthrow a government in recent memory.

Arguably, everyone in the world – including the Europeans – has an equal or better case for grievance against the United States than those in the Middle East. Yet only in that part of the world does this hatred take on such an intensive and popular form. Nowhere else is there popular and governmental support for terrorist attacks against the United States. Something is very peculiar in this situation, and clearly the problem does not stem from the extent of American misdeeds. Instead, the problem emerges from local forces using America as an excuse and as a tool for political manipulation and control.

In the Middle East, the case against America is often an attempt to justify the use of the United States as a handy target, employing the same technique that Nazi Germany, the Communist USSR, and other dictatorships have used in their time. It is a way to mobilize the masses, to excuse the shortcomings of local governments, and to carry ideological movements to victory. It is also a way to disparage a whole set of otherwise attractive ideas – political freedom, modernization, and so on – that are linked to America by slandering the perceived exemplar and sponsor of that way of life. "The United States exports evil, in terms of corruption and criminality," says Saddam Hussein, "not only to any place to which its armies travel, but also to any place where its movies go."[11]

Traditional Islam and aspects of Arab society are indeed under assault by Westernization and Americanization, modernization and

11 Saddam Hussein, Republic of Iraq television, September 12, 2001. Translation in FBIS.

globalization. But the same situation exists in every other part of the world, including Europe. In many places, this challenge is met by rejecting some aspects of these things and adapting others. Nowhere else in the world, however, is resistance as uncompromising and thoroughgoing as it is (at least in rhetorical terms) in the Arab and Muslim world. Anti-Americanism is also a specific element in this response.

A subtlety of labeling is very revealing on this point. Starting with the Iranian revolutionary leader Ayatollah Ruhollah Khomeini in the 1970s, it has become commonplace to call the United States the "Great Satan" (and Israel the "Little Satan"). But Satan, in both the Christian and Muslim religions, is not an imperialist bully; rather, he is a tempter. He makes his wares seem so attractive that people willingly and voluntarily sell their souls to him.

Many of the extremist Islamists, including most of the September 11 suicide terrorists, have had a great deal of personal contact with the West, as did many of the militant Iranian students who supported Khomeini and seized the U.S. embassy in Tehran in 1979. They were people who came close to yielding to the "temptation," who came to define their Islam not as most typical Muslims do – as a body of belief in which their faith is secure – but as a way of maintaining personal identity against America and the West, precisely because they feared their own desire to join Western society. This basic attitude, to a greater or lesser extent, is common among Arabs, especially among the class of people who govern and who dominate the media. In short, anti-Americanism in this respect arises not from the ugliness of U.S. policy but from the attractiveness of American society.

A saying has it that patriotism is the last refuge of scoundrels. In a real sense, anti-Americanism is a last refuge of failed political systems and movements in the Middle East. Hatred of America justifies a great deal that is bad in the Arab world and helps to keep it politically dominated by dictatorships, socially unfree, and economically underdeveloped. Blaming national shortcomings on America means that the Arab debate does not deal with the internal problems and weaknesses that are the real and main cause of these countries' problems. It justifies the view that the only barrier to complete success, prosperity, and justice for the Arab (and Islamic) world is the United States.

Instead of dealing with privatization, women's equality, democracy, civil society, freedom of speech, due process of law, and twenty other issues that the Arab world needs to address, attention can be focused on – or rather, diverted to – the conjuring of an American conspiracy. Fixing blame for the Arab world's problems on Israel's existence is a regional staple. Yet no matter how emotional the charge against Israel, its salience is truly overwhelming only for the Palestinians. The advantage of anti-Americanism is that there is something to everyone's advantage in this argument, and any Arab or Muslim can adapt it to his own list of priorities. The solution to the dilemma of the Arab world and of the hard-liners in Iran was not peace but the stirring up of a new wave of hysteria against external enemies.

While bin Ladin's role has been particularly important in helping to destroy the best chance in modern history for Arab and Muslim societies to rethink their past mistakes and to change course, the role he is playing is hardly new. In Islamic thought there is the idea of a "century reformer," a charismatic individual who appears at the end of each century to revitalize Islam.

Bin Ladin might more accurately be called a "decade challenger." In every decade, a leader has arisen to issue a call for the Arab or Islamic world to rise up against the West. This was the role played by Nasser in the 1950s and 1960s, by Palestinian and other revolutionary movements in the 1970s, by Khomeini in the 1980s, and by Saddam Hussein in the 1990s. Each has mustered a broad range of support, and for a historical moment has held center stage. Each has promised to be the savior solving the Arabs' problems, defeating their enemies, and ushering in a new age in which the Arabs (or Muslims, or Iranians) would be powerful, happy, rich, and restored to their rightful, leading place in the world.

Each also failed. But after a period of disappointment, a new hero and magic idea has been grasped. Islam rejects the use of alcohol, but the ideology of utopian expectation has proven to be an equally dangerous intoxicant.

Enter bin Ladin. After so many defeats, the September 11 attacks on America could be judged a great success. Anti-Americanism was the new, and badly needed, doctrine. It made sense. What was being rejected, after all, was an "American" paradigm for modernization and change, so why not hit directly at the source of the despised program of moderation, peace, democracy, compromise, private enterprise, secularization, Westernization, the rule of law, open media, pragmatism, and so on? If America is the example you don't want to follow and want to discourage people from accepting, then it must be bad, all bad. If America is the temptation that seems so appealing it must be made repugnant, then anyone who accepts that paradigm and the paradigm itself must be discredited. Bin Ladin's ideas will not lead Islamists to victory over either their own governments or America. But they are very useful in stopping the kinds of rethinking and social and political change that would most benefit the Arab and Middle Eastern Muslim worlds.

One of the most fascinating aspects of anti-Americanism is the contradiction between seeing the United States as an arrogant bully whose mistreatment of the Arabs and Muslims merits punishment, and as a cowardly weakling that is impotent to punish those who criticize or even attack it. There are two slight variations in how this problem is addressed, though the difference between them is not so important. It could be claimed that America has always been cowardly, and that the heroic revolutionaries are only exposing that fact, or that the United States is made cowardly by the revolutionaries' own heroism and their clever strategy of attacking America directly.

While the radicals must portray America as a bully in order to provoke outrage against it, they must also portray America as weak in order to encourage Arabs and Muslims to fight against it and believe they can win. After all, the revolutionaries and radical states are frustrated by the fact that too many Arabs and Muslims are already afraid of the United States, or at least see its friendship as an asset that they don't want to lose. The revolutionaries have an uphill battle in solving this problem. How can they explain why people don't listen to them and thus rise up against their rulers and U.S. influence? Why don't regimes all go to war against Israel at once, and why don't Muslims by the thousands become suicide bombers? Why aren't U.S. interests attacked everywhere and American "ideas" rejected outright?

An obvious reason for this situation is that various people and governments are worried that they will lose this war because they are afraid of the United States. Of course, one by-product of building up America as the Great Satan is to make it seem even more frightening, giving it additional leverage in the region. As has often been shown in Middle Eastern history, many politicians and others – whatever they may proclaim in public – want such a powerful force on their side.

Practical experience also challenges the notion that the United States is a pitiful, helpless giant. Iran's revolution and the hostage crisis of 1979–81 were followed by a successful U.S. military intervention against Tehran's war effort in the Gulf during the mid-1980s. Iraq's invasion of Kuwait in 1990 was followed by the U.S.-led defeat of Baghdad in 1991. The September 11, 2001, terrorist attack on America was followed by the U.S. destruction of the Taliban government and al-Qaida's main base there in December 2001. But these lessons never seemed to have a lasting effect. The cycle began again, because the basic ideology did not shift. No doubt, in some next round of confrontation, an "unprovoked" U.S. "aggression" and "mass murder" in Afghanistan will figure on the list of anti-American grievances.

So the revolutionaries must persuade the masses and leaders that America is simultaneously horrible and helpless: that the United States cannot do anything if it is attacked, ridiculed, and disregarded. Powerless against their own dictators, against defeats, against regime corruption, against restrictions on their religion or the restrictions of their religion, and against poverty, any Arab or Muslim may feel it possible at least to spit on the United States and get away with it.

Consequently, the truth is the exact opposite of the complaint. Anti-Americanism was encouraged not by a real belief that the United States is too tough, but by the idea that it is weak and meek and vulnerable. Far from attacking America because it is really a big bully, extremists past and present have launched assaults in order to prove their belief that the United States is a paper tiger. Such sentiments were voiced by Khomeini, Saddam Hussein, and many others. An Egyptian Islamist writes that the Americans are cowards, while the Muslims are brave: "The believers do not fear the enemy. . . . Yet their enemies protect [their] lives like a miser protects his money. They . . . do not enter into battles seeking martyrdom. . . . This is the secret of the believers' victory over their enemies."[12] Bin Ladin himself explained, "[Those] God guides will never lose. . . . America [is] filled with fear from the north to south and east to west. . . . [Now there will be] two camps: the camp of belief and of disbelief. So every Muslim shall . . . support his religion."[13]

12 Abdallah Al-Najjar, *al-Gumhuriya*, October 7, 2001. Translation in MEMRI No. 289, October 19, 2001.
13 Usama bin Laden, al-Jazira television, October 7, 2001.

Middle Eastern leaders who complained of America's alleged hostility always made it clear that power – not popularity – was the most important factor in gaining influence and advancing one's interests. Bashar al-Asad noted that "it is important to gain respect, rather than sympathy."[14] Then Iraqi Deputy Foreign Minister Nizar Hamdoon wrote in similar terms: "Aggressors thrive on appeasement. The world learned that at tremendous cost from the Munich agreement of 1938.... How could the German generals oppose Hitler once he had proven himself successful? Indeed, aggressors are usually clever at putting their demands in a way that seems reasonable."[15]

Far from being a bully, the United States was too soft to merit respect. After the United States did not respond forcefully to the many terrorist attacks against its citizens, stood by impotently while Americans were seized as hostages in Iran and Lebanon, led Saddam Hussein to think he could invade Kuwait without American opposition, then let him stay in power after letting the shah fall, pressured its friends and courted its enemies, allowed its prized peace process to be trashed with barely a word of criticism for those responsible, and acted so often in this same manner, why should others respect its interests or fear its wrath?

Many Iranians were fearful of pushing the revolution too far in 1978 and 1979, convinced that America would step in and destroy them. This was in tune with a classic part of the Iranian worldview, which saw their country as a pawn of stronger foreigners and their conspiracies. Now Khomeini proclaimed that everything would be different. If the United States, with all its power and satanic determination, could not free its own diplomats from captivity, how could it destroy Iran's revolution? "Our youth should be confident that America cannot do a damn thing," Khomeini said repeatedly. The United States was too weak to interfere by direct military force, and, if necessary, Iran could defeat such a move by mobilizing its own people, who were willing to become martyrs.[16]

Iranian leaders continued to stress this theme. Almost a decade later, Planning and Budget Minister Mas'ud Zanjani, ridiculing U.S.

14 Interview in *al-Safir*, July 16, 2001. Translation in MEMRI No. 244, July 20, 2001.
15 Iraqi Deputy Foreign Minister Nizar Hamdoon, "The U.S–Iran Arms Deal: An Iraqi Critique," *Middle East Review*, Summer 1982.
16 See, for example, his speech of November 7, 1979. Text in FBIS, November 8, 1979.

intervention to defend Gulf shipping from Iranian attacks in 1987, explained that the United States would never fight in the Gulf: Its forces were too vulnerable, the American people and their European allies would oppose intervention, and the Americans would quickly retreat if they suffered casualties.[17]

In 1998, after another decade, Ayatollah Ali Khamenei, Khomeini's successor as supreme guardian of the Islamic Republic of Iran and leader of the hard-line faction, insisted that there was no need to negotiate with the United States. After all, he proclaimed, Iran had demolished the American superpower's myth of invincibility by standing up to its threats and not bowing to its demands. Following Iran's example, Muslims all over the world had started fighting and expressing their Islamic feelings. Khamenei posited a struggle during the previous twenty years between two competing camps on the world political scene – the camp of arrogance led by America, and the Islamic camp led by the Islamic Republic of Iran. The Islamic camp had advanced and gained victories, with Islamic movements coming to power in various states.

Saddam Hussein did not agree with Khomeini about much, but he did agree that the man who would lead the Middle East in attacking America must convince Arabs and Muslims that America was weak. And, like Khomeini, he was assisted by U.S. policies that seemed to prove his point. In response to Saddam's actions and threats in the late 1980s, Washington sent signals of weakness to Baghdad. Saddam interpreted attempts to avoid conflict as proof that America feared confrontation with him. Each act of appeasement only increased Iraq's boldness without persuading Baghdad that the United States wanted to be its friend. The Americans "are out to hurt Iraq," one of that country's top leaders claimed. The problem was not that U.S. actions had alienated Iraq, but that the nature of Iraq's regime inevitably made it antagonistic to the United States.

After evincing no strong reaction to Iraq's use of chemical weapons against the Kurds, its threats against Israel, outspoken anti-Americanism, or the ultimatum to Kuwait, the United States had helped to convince Saddam that he could get away with occupying and annexing his neighbor. By seeking to avoid any trouble with Iraq, U.S. policy had helped to precipitate a much larger crisis in August 1990.

17 *Kayhan*, October 20, 1987. Text in FBIS, November 4, 1987, p. 54.

Saddam told visiting Assistant Secretary of State John Kelly in February 1990 that America was the only outside power that counted in the Middle East. He assumed that the United States would use its overwhelming power as he would in its place: to eliminate the radical regimes and seize control of the region. If the United States would not act, Saddam would fill the vacuum. But the Iraqi leader knew that America was objectively strong and could presumably dictate changes in policy and behavior to Arab regimes. What could the Arabs do to save themselves from America? Two weeks after meeting with Kelly, Saddam openly launched Iraq's new radical phase in one of the most important speeches of his career, on February 24, 1990.[18]

Saddam suggested that the Arabs had three choices. They could wait until a new balance of power was restored – which might allow them to play off the Europeans against the Americans – but by then it could be too late. Or the Arabs could give up, arguing that there was "no choice but to submit" to America. This second alternative would require the Arabs to give up forever the hope of destroying Israel or of uniting themselves.

There was, however, a third possibility. Rather than revising their own thinking, the Arabs might change the situation. Saddam claimed that Arab pessimism, not Arab nationalism, was the delusion. If the Arabs united behind a strong leader they could still defeat the United States and Israel, or at least hold their ground against the alleged U.S. and Zionist conspiracies to destroy them. Saddam's unconventional weapons would make Iraq the Arab superpower, replacing the lost Soviet nuclear umbrella.

The United States, he insisted, was far weaker than it seemed because it feared military confrontation and losses. America had shown "signs of fatigue, frustration, and hesitation" in Vietnam and Iran and had quickly run away from Lebanon "when some Marines were killed" by terrorist suicide bombers there in 1983. He believed that if Iraq acted boldly, America would not dare confront him. Had not this been his experience with the United States during the previous two years?

These declarations were not only a challenge to the United States, they were also a dare to the Arab world. Would the Arab leaders and

---

18 Speech at Arab Cooperation Council, Royal Cultural Center in Amman, February 24, 1990. Text in FBIS, February 27, 1990.

peoples remember the unpleasant lessons of recent history – the cycle of war, failure, and wasted resources – or would the old ideas and patterns of behavior overwhelm common sense and carry them into another adventure?

The result was just as Saddam had hoped: The Arab masses cheered, and the Arab governments – whatever their private contempt for or fear of Iraq – jumped on his bandwagon. The United States stayed out of his way. Of course, Saddam was wrong in thinking that he could take over Kuwait and that America would stand by and do nothing. But he was right enough about the United States that he remained in power many years after making that miscalculation.

Bin Ladin himself, and Islamist writers like the Egyptian Najjar (both quoted earlier), similarly concluded that America would not respond effectively after the September 11 attacks. A Hizballah leader in Lebanon, Shaykh Nabil Qaook, remarked that America had been loud and dominating in the past but now, "when the balance of power leans the other way, we hear them scream."[19]

A member of Hamas exulted over the anthrax attacks:

You have entered the . . . White House and they left it like horrified mice. . . . The Pentagon was a monster before you entered its corridors. . . . And behold, it now transpires that its men are of paper and its commanders are of cardboard, and they hasten to flee as soon as they see . . . chalk dust! . . . You make the United States appease us, and hint to us at a rosy future and a life of ease.

He suggested that terrorism was a good way to obtain concessions from the United States without giving anything in return, though he made clear that even such a surrender would be insufficient.[20]

These anti-American voices attributed U.S. behavior to cowardice, arguing that striking against America was a reasonable, practical, and successful way of getting what they wanted. They were wrong in their reading of U.S. motives. But if America had acted in this same manner out of a desire to prove to Arabs and Muslims that America was a friend, to win their support through kindness, the result might well have been the same. The exercise of American good intentions could

19 *New York Times*, November 8, 2001.
20 Atallah Abu Al-Subh in *al-Risala*, November 1, 2001. Translated in MEMRI No. 297, November 7, 2001.

be just as costly to the United States in the Middle East as the wrongly alleged sins of bullying and cowardice.

By the same token, the United States will not persuade its adversaries and critics that anti-Americanism is a mistake or a misunderstanding. Even if the United States were to pressure Israel, end sanctions on Iraq, pull its troops out of the Persian Gulf, and take other such steps, the Arab media, opposition groups, and even the regimes would not praise America as a wonderful friend and noble example. Instead, these acts could well be taken as signals of fear and weakness, encouraging even more contempt and making a campaign of anti-American terrorism seem irresistible. And if the root cause of this wave of anti-Americanism is internal, it is dependent on those needs and forces rather than on anything the United States actually does. Indeed, the quick U.S. defeat of the Taliban in Afghanistan in December 2001 did more to silence sympathy for bin Ladin than any words could have achieved.

Finally, the ferocity of anti-Americanism, in word and deed, will inflict the most lasting damage on the Arab world itself. The blaming of external forces blocks any serious effort by Arabs to deal with their own very serious internal problems and shortcomings, which are the real causes of continuing dictatorship, violence, and instability, relatively slow economic and social development, and other problems.

Like so many totalitarians of earlier times – past dictators in Japan, Germany, and the USSR, current dictators in Iran, Iraq, and elsewhere – those who have declared war on America are playing the dangerous game of exaggerating outside menaces in order to justify incompetence at home and aggressiveness abroad. They deliberately misunderstand American policy and society, and successfully soil them in the eyes of others. At least one might hope that the United States would not join in this slander. For that would be a betrayal not only of American interests and ideals, but also of those in the Arab world and Iran who have been fighting against the decadent order there, fighting for a truly better and freer life for their peoples.

THE UNCIVIL SOCIETY
AND THE WALL OF LIES

Winston Churchill once said, "Dictators ride to and fro upon tigers which they dare not dismount. And the tigers are getting hungry."[1] This image fits the Middle East remarkably well. The region's dictatorships – that is, virtually all of its governments – ride upon a system based on the four legs of demagoguery, ideology, populism, and the external conflict. The tigers are satiated on a rich diet of distracting wars and crises, misinformation and ideas permitting no contradiction, rewards and punishments, the manipulation of nationalism and religion, the cultivation of hatred and deflection of blame onto others, the promotion of paranoid fear, and hopes for utopia. In this case, the tigers do not consume their riders but instead devour the potentialities of those countries and peoples, all the while striding back and forth in their confining cage, getting nowhere.

In the 1990s, more than in any previous decade, this system faced serious challenges. At the time, these factors seemed capable of overturning the existing orders, though later, in retrospect, this belief appears to have been exaggerated. How could one have been so mistaken? Certainly wishful thinking played a role. More important, perhaps, was the difficulty in believing that historical experience could be so disregarded – though perhaps it was merely interpreted differently – and that the modern Middle East could be so different from other places and other times.

To pick one example of such expectations among many, U.S. National Security Advisor Sandy Berger said, "The Middle East is in

---

1 Sir Winston Churchill, November 11, 1937, in a letter later published in Winston S. Churchill, *While England Slept* (New York, 1938).

the midst of a transition unlike anything we have witnessed in living memory. From North Africa to the West Bank, the region is changing in ways small and large that will affect every single aspect of people's lives." If this transition did not take place, he warned, allowing "a climate in which reformers can take charge, tomorrow's Middle East could be a region of exploding demographics and imploding econo- mies; of overpopulation and underperforming educational systems."[2]

The seemingly inescapable dire consequences of such a failure seemed all the more reason for local rulers to choose reform as the only way to survive. In the end, though, it was reasonably logical for them to conclude that domestic change actually constituted a far greater risk than the status quo. This struggle's outcome can be better understood by seeing how completely authoritarian ideas and information monopolized the field and reinforced the existing system.

Given the Arab regimes' pervasive controls and ideological power, mass media offer one of the few potential ways for alternative informa- tion and ideas to reach their citizens. But rather than representing a window onto the rest of the world, the media usually – with rare exceptions and slight variations – act as a wall, reinforcing near- unanimity, shutting out the kind of discourse that has become dominant almost everywhere else in the world. Within each Arab country, radio and television are tightly controlled by the state. In this hothouse of fundamental consensus, failed policies and problems are analyzed only in the reigning framework's context of ideas, which excludes the kind of new thinking needed to find a better way.

One of the most candid assessments of the Arab media came from the veteran Lebanese journalist and editor Jihad Khazen. Its assigned task has largely been to "deny the news, or praise the ruler. . . . A critic is seen as a traitor to his tribe. If he writes in English for a foreign audience, he is ostracized as a traitor to the nation." This does not mean that dissent does not exist, and there have always been courageous journalists who sometimes paid for their integrity with their lives.[3]

2 Sandy Berger, transcript of a lecture to the Israel Policy Forum, October 20, 1999.
3 Jihad Khazen, "Censorship and State Control of the Press in the Arab World," *Harvard International Journal of Press Politics,* Vol. 4, No. 3 (1999), p. 87. http://jhupress.jhu.edu/journals/harvard_international_journal_of_press_politics/v004/4.3khazen.html.

Khazen explained how the system works. "The most prevalent form of censorship is self-censorship. Sitting at my desk, I feel at times that I'm not so much covering the news as covering it up." Editors will risk angering some Arab governments but must consider the cost in each case: "We can afford to be banned in Sudan, where the currency is almost worthless, but if we are banned in Saudi Arabia, we stand to lose tens of thousands of dollars in advertising revenue. Consequently, we are more careful with Saudi news; it is a matter of economics, even of survival." *Al-Hayat* was temporarily banned in various Arab states sixty times in 1994, thirty-five times in 1995, twenty times in 1996, and twenty times again in 1997.[4]

"Each country has its own sensitive story that might get us banned," Khazen recounts.

In Saudi Arabia, there are many sensitive stories, especially those concerning religion, women, and the military. In Bahrain and Qatar, the prohibited story is their border dispute. And so forth. In all Arab countries, perhaps with one or two exceptions, criticism of the head of state and his immediate family is taboo. In some cases, it is tantamount to signing one's own death warrant.[5]

If we write about fundamentalist groups in London, we risk being banned in Algeria and Tunisia; if we write about women's right to drive vehicles, we risk the wrath of the Saudi censor. Even the peace process is not always a safe topic. *Al-Hayat* was the first Arab newspaper to interview Israeli government leaders and to publish articles by Israeli writers. But as the Syrians became edgy over their stalemated negotiations with Israel, *al-Hayat* suddenly came under attack in Lebanon "for dealing with the enemy," and we had to reconsider our position.[6]

In general, though, Israel is the one country on which journalists can take out their frustrations, attacking it without risk. No statement, regardless of how inflammatory, and no claim, no matter how contrary to facts, will ever be checked or criticized. Usually this same rule also applies to criticizing the United States, and it is a key factor in the Arab media's anti-Americanism.

Within Arab states, much or all of the media is owned or closely controlled by the government. Arab newspapers publishing outside the

4 Ibid., p. 87.
5 Ibid., pp. 87–8.
6 Ibid.

Arab world may be owned by supporters of a particular government – usually wealthy Saudis connected to the royal family – or are able to exist mostly due to subsidies. *Al-Hayat* and *al-Sharq al-Awsat* are Saudi-backed; Iraq supported *al-Quds al-Arabi*. A relative of the Saudi royal family owned the Middle East Broadcasting Center, perhaps the most popular Arab satellite station; Saudis also controlled another station that went out of business when their heavy-handed demand for censorship made its BBC partner pull out.

Khazen points out that Arab advertising revenue is minimal (and some of the main agencies are also owned by regime-connected Saudis), and small circulations also keep down revenues. In 1997, the *New York Times* and *Los Angeles Times* earned $2 billion in advertising revenue, compared to about $40.5 million, including government subsidies, for a leading Saudi newspaper.[7]

Control over the media during the late 1990s was further tightened in almost every Arab state. Civil rights activists confirmed that "the timid democratization that began in some corners of the Arab and Moslem world at the turn of the 1990s is in retreat."[8] There was one apparent bright spot in this pattern: the highly touted Qatar-based satellite news channel, al-Jazira. But while al-Jazira was exceptional in doing stories that some regimes did not like, it also reported them in a way that reinforced rather than undermined the existing system of ideas. Paradoxically, the station used "free speech" as one of the most effective forces combating the possibility of real free speech or democratic reform.

Al-Jazira's own employees were effusive in their praise of its virtues. It was "the best news station in the Arab world," said one of them. "Al-Jazira is complete freedom." Another explained that "al-Jazira provides a space of freedom to the Arab viewer. . . . When you talk about things considered taboo in the past, it encourages people to be more open-minded and courageous about issues." The station did face some retribution from regimes. Its Kuwait bureau was shut down after an Iraqi on a call-in show insulted Kuwait's ruler; and Saudi Arabia didn't admit its reporters at all.[9]

---

7 Ibid.
8 Reuters, July 30, 1998.
9 "Tiny Qatar Beams Big Signal to Arab World," *Arabia Weekender*, August 12, 1999.

Yet al-Jazira's outrage was usually pointed in only one direction, a slant reflecting the reporters' own radical Pan-Arab nationalist or Islamist views that regimes were not applying those ideologies consistently or militantly enough. By not challenging the states' dominant anti-democratic ideologies, but only their hypocrisy in not implementing them thoroughly enough, the station actually ended up reinforcing the power of the existing system and even of the regimes themselves.

In addition, al-Jazira was in many ways simply the vehicle for one state in particular – its sponsor, Qatar. Saudi Arabia and Egypt were often targeted for attack because Qatar's ruler disliked them, while Iraq and Iran received favorable coverage for the same reason. And, of course, there was no serious coverage of Qatar's own government or internal affairs. When a Palestinian called on the air for Egyptians to overthrow Mubarak, for example, it was not in order to enhance human rights in Egypt but to install a government ready to fight Israel and the West. The same person claimed Jews use Arab blood in observing the Passover holiday. An Egyptian newspaper responded by publishing cartoons giving al-Jazira program hosts Jewish names and showing them wearing Jewish religious garb.[10] In the Arab world, any criticism whatsoever can be discredited simply by being branded as Jewish or Zionist in origin.

"Day in and day out, al-Jazira deliberately fans the flames of Muslim outrage," notes the Lebanese-American scholar Fouad Ajami. That it evinced strong support for and gave extensive coverage to the Palestinian *intifada* in 2001 could be taken for granted. What was perhaps significant and different from other Arab media in this respect, however, was symbolized by the station's frequently shown photo montage on the conflict, which ends with a Palestinian boy holding a banner proclaiming shame that the Arab world doesn't do more. The station's clear intention was to provoke intensified militancy in the Arab-Israeli struggle – not exactly an original notion in Arab politics, and a long-time excuse of regimes for rejecting domestic reform and human rights in their own countries.

The same pattern holds for al-Jazira's stance toward the United States and the West, again reinforcing the rejection of the Western

---

10 Simon Henderson, "The 'Al-Jazeera Effect': Arab Satellite Television and Public Opinion," *Policywatch*, December 8, 2000.

model – or such allegedly exclusively Western ideas of democracy, civil liberties, and pluralism – that was a mainstay of the old system and its leaders. Al-Jazira was particularly conspicuous in its favorable view of bin Ladin, both before and after the September 11, 2001, attacks on America. As Ajami wrote, bin Ladin was clearly the channel's star, romanticized in words and pictures. A large poster of him hung at the back of the main studio stage. As Ajami puts it, "al-Jazira's reporters see themselves as 'anti-imperialists' . . . convinced that the rulers of the Arab world have given in to American might; these are broadcasters who play to an Arab gallery whose political bitterness they share – and feed." Coverage was clearly supportive of the Taliban, suggesting that it would defeat the United States in Afghanistan, maintaining that all the Afghan people supported this extremist Islamist government, and accusing the Americans of engaging in deliberate brutality in the war to overthrow it.[11]

On the station's interview and religious programs, Islamist guests and callers vastly outnumbered traditionalists. This would seem to be an example of refreshing independence, since conservative clerics are often backed by governments and support them. Yet the result was a constant condemnation of Arab regimes as already too Westernized, not pious enough, and excessively tolerant. In short, the views represented on al-Jazira had popular support and were certainly those most loudly expressed in the Middle East, but they reflected an arguably minority interpretation of Islam and represented a strongly anti-democratic political stance. The guests and callers might be critical of the incumbent dictators, but they wanted to replace them with even more extreme dictatorial regimes.

For example, on one popular show, Shaykh Muhammad Ibrahim Hassan, a young Egyptian preacher, offered an interpretation of Islam virtually identical to that of bin Ladin, without challenge from the program's host. He declared, in an argument paralleling bin-Ladin's almost word for word, that Muslims are under threat by the West everywhere in the world. He saw the September 11 attacks as a defensive retaliation:

Oppression always leads to an explosion. . . . Under the cover of the new world order, Muslims in Chechnya and Iraq have been brutalized. . . . Any

11 Fouad Ajami in the *New York Times*, November 18, 2001.

Muslim on the face of the earth who bears faith in God and his Prophet feels oppression today. . . . We saw things – horrors – in Bosnia that would make young people turn old. . . . Where were the big powers and the coalitions and the international organizations then? Where are they now, given what is going on in Palestine?[12]

Although al-Jazira journalists had no hesitation about attacking guests who expressed moderate opinions, they almost never interrupted or challenged radical ones. Thus, no one pointed out to the audience that the United States had sent troops and campaigned diplomatically to help Bosnian Muslims, or that the U.S. pressure on Iraq was to stop it from attacking its neighbors, including Qatar itself. Similarly, there was no mention of strenuous and protracted U.S. attempts to broker a compromise solution that would have created a Palestinian state, had the Arab side agreed, thereby avoiding the subsequent Palestinian casualties in the war they started in 2000.

Not only were the guests often extremists, so were those who called in. Since the calls were screened, this might well be the result of a deliberate choice by the al-Jazira staff. They echoed Hassan's themes: Arab states were too friendly to America; Arab rulers should go to war against the slaughter of Muslims; Arab governments should be overthrown and replaced by radical Islamist states; and America was the real enemy.

As one caller put it, "America considers Islam as the sole obstacle to its hegemony over the Islamic world. . . . Muslims should unite their countries in one Islamic state. Islam is the only challenge to world capitalism, the only hope after a black capitalist century."

Hassan responded, "The Jews are the ones responsible for spreading this hostile view of Islam. The Jews dominate the Western media, and they feed the decision-makers this distorted view of Islam. No sooner did the attacks in America take place, the Jews came forth accusing the Muslims, without evidence, without proof."[13] Yet actually it was al-Jazira and people like Hassan who were themselves distorting normative Islam to present precisely the type of ideology that would provoke hostility to the West and be perceived as hostile by the West.

One al-Jazira program was focused around the theme of whether bin Ladin represented the Arab world or whether this idea was just a

12 Ibid.
13 Ibid.

Western invention. The irony was that bin Ladin did not represent the majority views of Muslims or Arabs, but al-Jazira – and large sectors of the Arab media – wanted to prove otherwise and promote his ideas. On this occasion, the Palestinian writer Fayez Rashid praised bin Ladin as "a celebrated resister" who was "an Arab symbol of the fight against American [and Israeli] oppression." The United States had exaggerated his threat in order to have an excuse to strike against the Arabs. The second guest, Hafez Karmi, director of an Islamic center in London, also considered bin Ladin a "struggler in the path of God," simply a man who cared about Muslim rights. The real reason for the September 11 attacks, Karmi said, was that the United States was invading the Arab world, precisely the formula bin Ladin used to justify them.

Shafeeq Ghabra, a liberal Kuwaiti political scientist, disagreed, making the obvious and logical point that "bin Laden has not come forth bearing a democratic project, or a new project to improve the condition of women, or to repair our educational system. What he proposes is a Talibanist project, which would be a calamity for the Arab people." Only then did anchorwoman Montaha al-Ramhi spring into action, inter- rupting him: "'Someone has to say to the United States, this is a [limit]," she shouted. "Here and no more, in Palestine and Iraq, in other Arab realms!"

Coincidentally, all but one of the average people questioned in the street interviews chosen for broadcast by al-Jazira agreed with Ramhi. "Any young Muslim would be proud to be Usama bin Ladin," one young man said. "America is the maker of terrorism," another asserted, "and it is now tasting its own medicine." Only one person interviewed expressed the traditional opinion on the issue: "I am a good Muslim," he said, "and Islam does not permit the killing of noncombatants. Islam could never countenance the killing of civilians."[14] No one could ever guess that this standpoint – even if abused in practice – was the view that had been endorsed by the overwhelming majority of Islamist clerics and scholars for many centuries.

The point is that inasmuch as a public debate took place during the 1990s, it was mainly between those who supported the existing regimes and their system, on the one hand, and those who wanted an intensification of the existing doctrine and its more faithful

14 Ibid.

implementation on the other. Although a larger number of liberal views were heard than previously – especially in Kuwait and Jordan – those advocating political and economic reforms or democracy remained a distinct minority and were often shouted down. And, caught in the middle, even they had little choice. As Ghabra noted on the aforementioned al-Jazira program, if forced to choose between bin Ladin's vision and Saudi King Fahd, most would choose the king. Similarly, Algerian liberals had to prefer the military regime over the Islamists, and their Palestinian counterparts stuck with Arafat rather than risk the alternative of Hamas.

It would be easy to maintain that the two main lines of argument – those supporting the regimes and those criticizing the regimes as too moderate – truly represented the real feelings of the Arab masses. But what are the true feelings of the Arab masses? No one knows. There are, however, three reasonable suppositions in this regard that raise questions about the genuineness of their enthusiasm for their leaders.

First, it seems reasonable to assume that if any given Arab regime fell from power, the leader and his regime would not be heroes to their people a week later. The new government would be adored in the media and celebrated in all public utterances. In other words, the love for the existing regimes is largely a function of their control, demagoguery, and ability to close out other options.

Second, however Arabs feel about their rulers, religion, and culture, there is not much reason to believe that they are so totally different from all other nations, religions, and cultures in the world. There are the cycles of life – young people want education, jobs, and a chance to better their lives. There are needs for survival – people crave sufficient food, housing, shelter, and clothing. There are ways the changing environment – urbanization, faster communication and transport – and the possession of or having knowledge of material goods affect the way people think and act. Moreover, there is the phenomenon of globalization, whose attractive, though not necessarily better, ideas and commodities are desired by more and more people throughout the world.

Finally, there is the fact that a government's failure to fulfill citizens' needs usually turns people against them, and the inability of ideologies to fulfill their promises brings rejection of those ideologies. In modern times, it has been hard for dictatorships to continue for more than a few decades. Even in Iran, where enthusiasm for the newly established revolutionary regime seemed to reach the highest possible level, within fifteen years they had fallen so far that the majority could be said to hate their rulers. The adored, all-knowing revolutionary hero, Khomeini, could not pass this status on to his successors. In the Arab world, the continuity of the same basic system of dictatorship and popular belief in twenty countries over forty or fifty years is a truly remarkable phenomenon.

There are clearly, though, factors that preserve this system that would otherwise decay, just as formaldehyde preserves a corpse that might otherwise naturally turn to dust. There is a wall of lies erected to preserve a discourse at variance with the realities of the region and with the basic worldview accepted almost everywhere else in the world. In most other places, intellectuals, journalists, students, and other groups challenge dictatorships, expose their shortcomings, and campaign for democracy. In the Middle East, these same groups tend – not always, of course – to defend dictatorships (though not *necessarily* the one existing at the moment), extolling those features of policy and ideology that are its greatest shortcomings. More often than not, the Arab media campaign on behalf of even more hatred and extremism than already exists. The regimes have, in effect, nationalized the usual democracy-manufacturing sectors and closed down production.

In every Arab country, there is an intense atmosphere of intimidation, a bizarre juxtaposition of rigid official doctrine and tendrils of freedom perhaps best described in this passage from the London-based journalist Hazem Saghiya:

> Let's portray some of the characteristics of this surrealistic picture: Egypt's Islamists prate between two poles: [assassinating] people on the one hand, and controlling the cultural and even social [public] space, on the other hand. Egypt's intellectuals swing between Emanuel Kant on the one hand, and Saladin on the back of a horse in the battle of Hittin [against the Crusaders], on the other. The popular desire is war, but Egypt was the first Arab country to accept peace. An overwhelming majority of Egyptians prefer the severing of relations with the United States, but American aid to Egypt has reached $50 billion since Camp David in 1979.[15]

As Saghiya shows, it is Egypt, a relatively more open country, where these contradictions are most sharply visible. Periodic confrontations in

---

15 *Al-Hayat*, July 29, 2001. Translation in MEMRI No. 257, August 17, 2000.

which specific intellectuals were accused of political or religious heresy kept up the pressure for conformity and self-censorship. The novelist Salman Rushdie, condemned to death by Iran, allegedly for libeling Islam's founder – but more likely for ridiculing Khomeini – is internationally the best-known case, but there have been many others. When a fifteen-year-old novel by the Syrian author Haider Haider was suddenly declared by several clerics as defamatory of Islam after being reprinted, Egypt's Ministry of Culture quickly ordered that it be withdrawn. But student protest riots took place in Cairo anyway.[16]

A terribly symbolic scene took place at al-Azhar University, as students who had not read the book battled riot troops. Trying to explain the reasons for the protest, one student told a reporter: "First, the conditions here are very bad. The food – " Another demonstrator interrupted him angrily, "What? You're saying we're doing this because of food?" "No! No!" the first student shouted back defensively. "We can tolerate anything. Bad food. Bad drink. No freedom. We can take anything but an insult to Islam!" [17] Other students applauded loudly.

True, students mentioned other grievances – "There is no democracy, no human rights, no freedom of expression," shouted one demonstrator – but the alleged defense of Islam (or, at other times and places, Arab nationalism) would always trump any other issue. No food and no freedom, a lack of material goods and human rights, were less important to the masses (at least in their public expression – their private sentiments were often the opposite) than Arabism and Islam. Thus they would always be sacrificed on behalf of these ideologies. Normally, the reporter wrote, student demonstrations were not allowed to go on for so long. But since the students "claim to be protesting state-sponsored blasphemy," the government could not easily suppress them without appearing to be siding with heresy against Islam.

The government and the Islamists were basically on the same side. Few paid attention to the novel's author, who complained that his words had been taken out of context, or to the Egyptian Organization

16 *Cairo Times*, http://www.cairotimes.com/news/azhriots.html. On book banning by al-Azhar, see also *Cairo Times*, September 4, 1997. In Lebanon, a well-known singer was accused but later aquitted of blasphemy for using Quranic verses in a song. See *Middle East Intelligence Bulletin*, http://www.meib.org/articles/0006_ld.htm.
17 *Cairo Times*, September 4, 1997.

for Human Rights' condemnation of "cultural violence" and "campaigns that label writers and artists as apostates." Their voices were drowned out by the Islamists, intent on forcing government to be more repressive, and by the regime itself, comfortable with an opportunity simultaneously to prove its piety and to rationalize its control over all aspects of society.

The economy as well as politics and culture were mortgaged to such trump issues and demagoguery. Egypt's government tried hard to encourage foreign investment, and one of its rare successes was the decision of Sainsbury, Britain's second-largest supermarket chain, to open there in April 1999. Its 100 stores provided 2,500 jobs in a country with massive unemployment, and it planned to create more, making Egypt its base for exporting goods throughout the region. But Egyptian customs blocked its import of goods, competing small retailers convinced Islamic clerics to put a religious ban on shopping in its stores, and militants spread false rumors that the company's owner was Jewish and had given huge donations to Jewish West Bank settlements.

This campaign resulted in organized shopping boycotts, mob attacks on its stores, destruction of its signs, and assaults on its employees. Sainbury responded with ads saying that it had nothing to do with Israel and decorated its stores with Quranic verses. The government did nothing to help. And so, after big financial losses, the company left Egypt only two years after arriving there with ambitious plans. The anti-Israel boycott groups rejoiced at still another victory over the alleged forces of Zionism and imperialism – and also defeated any chance of improving Egypt's job supply, economic efficiency, and living standards.[18]

By contrast, the government did not seek to appease those espousing free speech, as it did with Islamist and other protestors. A critical event signaling the end of hopes for reform in Egypt was the state persecution of Saad ed-Din Ibrahim and twenty-seven colleagues. Ibrahim, one of the Arab world's best social scientists, known for his critical work on the motives of Islamist radicals, headed Cairo's Ibn Khaldun Center, a think tank that examined such issues as the fairness of Egypt's elections

18 See *Al-Ahram Weekly*, April 26–May 2, 2001, http://www.ahram.org.eg/weekly/2001/ 531/eg7.htm; Menas Associates, "Sainsbury's Scales Back Local Presence," December 2000, http://www.menas.co.uk/Egfa0004.html.

and the treatment of the Coptic Christian minority. The center was closed, and Ibrahim and his staff were arrested in June 2000. They were charged with embezzlement, receiving foreign funds illegally, defaming Egypt's reputation, and bribery. In May 2001, Cairo's Supreme State Security Court found them all guilty, gave twenty-two defendants suspended sentences, but sentenced Ibrahim to seven years' hard labor for "harming society's interests, values and laws." In February 2002, Ibrahim was granted a new trial by the court of appeals.

While the case was criticized in the Western media and by some governments, coverage within Egypt was overwhelmingly hostile and abusive toward the defendants. Six Egyptian human rights groups saw the issue as "a continuation of the state's hostile policies against civil society institutions in Egypt, aiming at the silencing of all institutions that try to participate effectively in public issues." But the editor of *al-Usbaa* declared, "Those who ally themselves with foreign quarters to harm Egypt's national security . . . should be executed in a public square." Mahfuz al-Ansari, chief editor of the official Middle East News Agency, asked why the United States complained about human rights violations by Egypt but not by Israel, sarcastically claiming that "the quickest reaction to the verdict came from Jewish and Zionist circles."[19]

When the Syrian regime wanted to frighten its own intellectuals into silence, it threatened them with Ibrahim's fate.[20] Following the arrest and trial, some groups shifted from domestic human rights to "safer" issues, such as supporting the Palestinian *intifada* and criticizing the suffering of the Iraqi people allegedly because of U.S. sanctions.[21] In other words, those groups that might otherwise criticize the governance of their own country and demand change were co-opted into being allies of the regime, thereby furthering its trump issues and foreign policy agenda.

The Ibrahim case paralleled the Haider case. In these and other instances, a trump issue – Islamism, anti-Zionism, anti-Americanism, xenophobia – was effectively used to silence the type of minimal dissent routine in all but the most totalitarian societies. In both cases, too, groups and institutions that elsewhere would have demanded freedom –

19 *Al-Ahram*, May 25, 2001; *al-Akhbar*, May 27, 2001.
20 See Chapter 4 of this volume.
21 *Cairo Times*, May 31–June 6, 2001.

such as students, professors, universities, and the press – instead endorsed repression. Even the masses seemed to be persuaded by demagoguery into applauding the restriction of their own rights and material welfare. Dissent was to be channeled into safe, permissible areas – supporting the Palestinians, attacking Israel, criticizing America, upholding Islam – that did not threaten the system. The government then showed that it sided with these grievances, indeed was the leader in expressing them.

Liberals and reformers faced tremendous intimidation from both governments and Islamists. Not only did this discourage them directly, but the passion of their opponents also drowned out their rational arguments and kept others from joining them. When the Moroccan writer Saleh Boualid argued on al-Jazira television in July 2001 that the Arabs should renew negotiations with Israel, several callers threatened him personally. One, a Moroccan Islamist, expressed "the rage of our nation" against Boualid. "This might be the worst day in the life of that illiterate. It is an honor for me to sow terror in the hearts of the enemies of Allah, such as [Boualid], because this brings me closer to Allah." Another added, "Scum like [Boualid], who want to bind the hands of the people – they can go to hell." A third remarked, "We say to all those people [like Boualid]: Just wait. . . . I think that he is actually a Jew. . . ."[22]

Challenging the system was blocked by the power of its taboos, constantly enforced and reinforced by governments, journalists, and intellectuals. When one sees how effective a verbal assault mounted by a fearless writer could be, it is easy to understand why such strong defenses were needed.

For example, the Kuwaiti university professor Ahmad al-Baghdadi, who himself had been briefly imprisoned on heresy charges, cleverly manipulated one of the main trump issues to turn it against the regimes in an article entitled "Sharon Is a Terrorist – and You?" Israeli Prime Minister Ariel Sharon, he claimed, was a terrorist, but at least Sharon didn't inflict terrorism on the people of his own country or imprison its intellectuals and writers. Unlike him, Arab prime ministers had never won office in democratic elections. Their regimes killed Islamists, tried intellectuals for heresy, and threw writers in prison. Iraq's treatment of

22 Al-Jazira television, May 23, 2001. Translation in MEMRI No. 245, July 23, 2001.

its own citizens and neighbors was especially terrible. Baghdadi asked, wasn't all this behavior terrorism? "The Arabs and the Muslims claim that their religion is a religion of tolerance, but they show no tolerance for those who oppose their opinions." These things did not happen in the West or in the "Zionist entity."[23]

To Egypt's credit, such ideas were sometimes permitted in its state-controlled press. Abd al-Mun'im Sa'id, head of the al-Ahram Research Center, warned of the dangers of relying on conspiracy theories, such as the blaming of the Egypt Air plane crash on a U.S. or Israeli plot. Conspiracy theories "keep us not only from the truth but also from confronting our faults and problems. This way of thinking relates any given problem to external elements, and thus does not [lead] to a rational policy to confront the problem. He who speaks of ghosts [as a problem's cause] can do nothing to solve it."[24]

The region's real problems, however, were neither these ghosts nor the concerns identified by the four trump issues. The system had been able to push aside the real concerns for many decades, but rising pressures might not let this go on indefinitely. In social development, economic progress, democratization, and even regional cooperation, the Middle East lags near the bottom of the list among all the world's regions. As the region slips behind others, it becomes harder to catch up. Only in the area of population growth does it take first place, putting even more pressure on the system. The situation should be alarming, yet the trump issues continue to overwhelm any serious response to these challenges.

A long chain of events had once seemed capable of changing the pattern. These included the Arab defeats of 1948, 1967, and 1973; the inter-Arab conflicts and coups of the 1950s and 1960s; and the Arab civil wars of the 1970s and 1980s. There was the Gulf turmoil of the 1980s and Iraq's defeated invasion of Kuwait in the 1990s. There had been the rise of new threats, such as Islamic radicalism, and the Soviet Union's collapse. Was it possible that Arab leaders would realize that their survival depended on reform? For a while, it seemed as if the regional political system might be transformed. Rather than dictating what was permissible and intimidating any dissent, the militants found themselves isolated and on the defensive.

23 *Akhbar Al-Youm*, November 3, 2001. Translation in MEMRI No. 302, November 20, 2001.
24 Ibid.

Between the 1940s and the 1990s, the Arab world suffered numerous disappointments, defeats, and failures. It was unable to unite, to destroy Israel, to achieve rapid economic development, to create representative political structures, to banish violence, or to significantly improve the people's living standards. The development of large-scale oil and gas resources in a handful of countries was virtually the sole exception to this situation. And even this was a frustration for many, since it strengthened the most traditional societies and their influence.

Generally speaking, Arab ideologies and strategies led to disaster. Pan-Arab nationalism divided the Arab world instead of uniting it. Unnecessary wars sacrificed scarce resources. Development lagged; dictatorships proliferated. The PLO went from one defeat to another. Lebanon and Algeria experienced destructive civil wars. Islamism, presenting itself as an alternative utopian plan to Arab nationalism, provoked more disorder and violence without being able to take power outside Iran. The Iran-Iraq war and the Iraqi invasion of Kuwait cost hundreds of thousands of lives and wasted billions of dollars for no good purpose.

One group or ideology after another promised to solve these problems – Nasserism, Ba'thism, Marxism, national liberationism, Saddam Hussein, Khomeini, Islamism, and others. All failed, usually in a way that inflicted heavy costs on the people and set Arab countries and societies back still further. Neither military coups, nor mass uprisings, nor terrorism, nor grassroots social organization, nor participating in electoral systems, nor guerrilla warfare brought the desired outcomes.

By the 1990s, this mountain of failure could no longer be concealed. The Arab world had appeared to reach rock bottom. Even in Iran, the Islamic revolution was being harshly criticized by the majority of the population. Having run out of old ideas, many Iranians were willing to consider such extreme innovations as moderation, privatization, democratization, modernization, civil society, peace with Israel, and friendship with the United States. There was a serious debate over choosing a different path.

In the end, though, many judged these proposed solutions to be too dangerous, despite the ample benefits that would have been possible. There were real and rational reasons for this concern. For example, democracy implied a loss of power for existing regimes. Modernization could mean more Western influence and secular trends. Peace with Israel required the abandonment of treasured ideas and expectations. Rather than being outraged by the failure of the Arab-Israeli peace process, Arab leaders, radical oppositionists, and intellectuals worried that it might succeed, and that they would thus lose this issue as an excuse for keeping the Arab world frozen in time. After all, with few real exceptions, the Arab states had ruling systems remarkably close to those that had prevailed in the 1970s and 1980s.

If, indeed, peace with Israel and other big changes actually occurred, virtually every regime would be in serious trouble. What excuse would they have for continued dictatorship? What rationale would they have for high military spending? How could they continue to stem the rising tide of demands for better living standards, more democracy, social change, and economic reform? Without the specter of conflict, it would also be harder to stem globalization, with its implied Westernization and challenges to tradition.

For the regimes, democratization and human rights could mean their defeat. In the West, the fall of the Soviet bloc was greeted as a great victory for democracy and international peace. In the Arab world, however, rulers had not only lost an ally but wondered whether the collapse of these regimes was a precedent for their own demise. They noted how democracy movements and pressure for greater civil liberties had led to the total overthrow of dictatorial regimes in the past, and might well have wondered whether there would be a firing squad in their future. Those individuals who had become wealthy through their government connections had to worry that they would be displaced by a real market and competition. Officers had to wonder whether their high military budgets would be sustained. Islamist and radical nationalist oppositionists might well assume that they would be swept aside as liberal, democratic opposition movements came to power. Islamic clerics knew that an opening of society could lead to a decline and dilution of piety. And lapdog intellectuals understood that if their ideological slogans – the only product they had to purvey – became unfashionable, they might actually have to work for a living.

This is an all-too-brief presentation of a complex historical era. Yet dozens of examples could be cited to justify each aspect of this argument. The bottom line is this: By the end of the 1990s, huge sectors of Arab and Iranian society were looking for some new leader, doctrine, or strategy to save them from becoming obsolete – both politically and perhaps physically dead.

Elements of this counterrevolution by the status quo had clearly emerged by 2000. The Palestinian leadership and Syria refused to make a compromise peace with Israel, not because they were appalled by one percent of the proposed deal or because their feelings were hurt, but because such an outcome seemed extraordinarily dangerous to their interests. Syria's new president, Bashar al-Asad, had moved to destroy incipient reform movements. Months before the attack on New York, Syria's government had discredited civil society and democracy by denouncing them as Western imports. Iranian hard-liners blocked the reformers despite the fact that the latter had won all the elections, in part by accusing their rivals of being American agents. Saddam Hussein was close to extricating himself from the sanctions regime without having to make a single compromise, in part by persuading much of the world that America was persecuting and murdering his people.

But the great "accomplishment" of September 11, 2001, was a defining moment in fashioning a new strategy, a doctrine to justify scuttling any major change in the region. In America, the toppling of the World Trade Center killed several thousand people; in the Middle East, it perhaps killed any hope of attaining a breakthrough for peace, democracy, greater freedom, or a more productive economic system. Without its advocates winning a single victory, the revitalization of anti-Western and anti-American sentiment, along with a new version of jihad-directed Islamism, seems to have further ensured the continued reign of demagoguery, extremism, and violence in the region.

The great challenge for modern Arab politics has been to find a way to escape a terrible situation of suffering, economic weakness, and foreign interference in order to achieve stability and progress. But while the solutions that the Arabs embraced – as they did once again at the end of the 1990s – may have saved the system, they also made matters worse. The prize was pride, authenticity, and a form of stability. The cost was a turbulent clash of doctrines, delayed development, arbitrary dictatorial rule, and mutual subversion among the Arabs themselves.

Few leaders or politicians – and not so many intellectuals or journalists – would publicly give up or reinterpret the trump ideas of victimization, the Palestinian cause, a hostile West, Arab nationalism, and the alleged defense of Islam. Militancy on these issues was demanded of all on the basis of justice and right. At the same time, though, this demand served as a tool to preserve dictatorship and crush opposition, to bully other Arab regimes, and to conceal domestic problems. More moderate regimes – knowing that these rules of the game were intended to disarm them for the plucking – played along, determined to display their political correctness by appeasing potential aggressors and proving their patriotic credentials for the domestic audience. Often knowing otherwise, they gave lip service to war and revolution, militancy and armed struggle, enmity toward the United States and statist economic policies.

By rejecting political transformation, economic reform, social openness, ideological pragmatism, and other changes, Middle Eastern regimes were also closing the door to solving their mounting problems. The experience of a half-century had remarkably little impact in encouraging a rethinking of policies, systems, and ideas that simply had not worked. On the contrary, it seemed that the only real advance was the rediscovery of the very ideas that had been tried and found wanting decades earlier.

Publicly, Middle Easterners still blame the West for most of what has gone wrong. But when Arabs discuss politics behind closed doors, they are fully aware of the crisis in leadership in the region. If Middle Eastern politics were directed by what was said in private rather than by leaders' speeches, state proclamations, and newspaper articles, it would be a very different story indeed.

Nevertheless, this is not how things worked out. The trump issues still ruled the day, and thus the struggle against those who supposedly wanted to destroy the Arabs and Muslims had to continue, whatever its cost in violence and dislocation. Violence and self-sacrifice were believed to work, even though they had never worked before. Construction had to be postponed until victory established the proper conditions. Many elements of modernization had to be rejected because they were alien imports.

The profound sense of victimization by the West coupled with fear of endless conspiracies from within, pervasive secrecy, and government control continues to poison public discussion and makes many thoughts impermissible. Saghiya writes, "When the facts do not reach [the public], rumors, exaggerations, fantasies, and fears develop.

History is not debated. . . . The main issues are not subject to [serious] discussion. . . . The state continues to be the boss, as it always has been. In view of this half-century old heritage, from where would a free man appear?"[25]

But indeed, in the Middle East of the 1990s a "free man" did appear. He was not afraid to challenge the strongest regimes in the region, to question Islam's principles, and to risk everything he had for his cause. Unfortunately, his name was Usama bin Ladin. He posed as the ultimate rebel and challenger of the system. But as was so typical of Middle Eastern history, his questions and proposed solutions offered the same old ideas and arguments, albeit in an intensified form.

In many respects, bin Ladin's rise and fall followed a typical pattern of Arab politics. A leader, movement, and strategy arises, claiming that it will unite Arabs or Muslims and lead them to total victory over the West and Israel, then create a new society solving all their problems. But each of these movements is based on a mistaken assessment of how the world in general, and the Middle East in particular, works. Consequently, it fails miserably and totally, bringing catastrophe on its adherents, who are nonetheless acclaimed as heroic. There follows a period of demoralization until the next cycle begins.

Bin Ladin's ideology, too – despite its distortions of mainstream Islam in declaring all Christians to be enemies and all Westerners targets – embodies many consensus Arab and Muslim ideas. Bin Ladin often sounded like Ayatollah Ruhollah Khomeini and his successors in Iran; Hamas and Hizballah; Presidents Gamal Abdel Nasser of Egypt, Saddam Hussein of Iraq, Hafiz al-Asad of Syria, and Muammar Qadhafi of Libya; Yasir Arafat, the Palestinian leader; and scores of leaders, intellectuals, and journalists throughout the Arab world.

Their common themes provide a good overview of the dominant doctrine in the Arab and Muslim Middle East from the mid twentieth century onward.

• The problems of the Muslims and Arabs are almost completely caused by Western and especially U.S. attempts to defeat, humiliate, injure, and subjugate them. This argument is made in many different styles, ranging from radical Islamist (Westerners as Crusaders) to secular Arab nationalist (the United States as an imperialist power in Marxist terms).

25 *Al-Hayat*, July 29, 2001. Translation in MEMRI No. 257, August 17, 2001.

- Since hostility toward the Arabs and Muslims underpins U.S. (or Western) policy, anyone who likes these enemies or defends them is suspect as a traitor. For an Arab regime to cooperate with the West is treasonous. Of course, Arab states do cooperate with the United States, but lip service to this principle must be maintained. There cannot be any openly competing doctrine. Saudi and Egyptian leaders don't make speeches to their people explaining why alliance with the United States is a good and necessary thing; the Saudi and Egyptian media don't run articles thanking the United States for saving them from Iraq, expressing gratitude for aid, or extolling America as a role model.
- Israel is an extremely evil state that seeks to conquer much or all of the Middle East. It is simultaneously the West's tool and master. Even if one makes peace with Israel, this can never be justified in doctrinal terms. At any rate, Israel will eventually disappear, because it is not a real country and future control of the Middle East inevitably belongs to Arabs or Muslims. This is one more reason why peace with Israel is unnecessary and why concessions are mistaken. Thus, all pragmatic explanations for compromise are illegitimate. Arab leaders cannot say anything positive about Israel or acknowledge its efforts toward peace; the Arab media will not present favorable information about Israel or explain its point of view.
- Since Muslims and Arabs are in perpetual conflict with the West and Israel, such things as democracy, human rights, economic reform, and civil society are dangerous distractions from this struggle and might weaken the Muslims (or Arabs).
- Because Western culture and its ideas are so innately hostile and subversive to the Arab and Muslim way of life, they cannot be adapted by these societies. Democracy, civil liberties, women's rights, economic reform, and other features of the West are poisoned gifts. Of course, in practice many such things are absorbed into the Arab world, but again ideology considers this process to be illegitimate, slowing its pace, limiting its extent, and ensuring a good reception when radicals denounce such things.
- Islam itself is under attack and must be defended from secularism and liberal-oriented reinterpretation. Even Arab nationalists insist that they are champions protecting Islam. If Islam is threatened by Westernization and modernization, this is another reason to reject reforming it or adjusting it to modern times.

- Since the West follows a deliberate policy of persecuting and destroying Arabs or Muslims, its victims should unite to combat it. The conflicts and differences among true Arabs or Muslims are of no importance, merely creations of the West or of its local agents. In practice, this means that moderates must avoid antagonizing radicals and must be careful about seeking Western help to defend themselves from their threats.
- Once Arabs or Muslims unite, they cannot be defeated no matter what the balance of power. Suicide bombing is an example of how a small group of Muslims (or Arabs) can erase the West's (or Israel's) apparent strength and shows how easy victory can be.
- No matter how difficult the struggle, it is better to continue in order to leave the door open for future success. Nonetheless, victory is far closer than it seems. The power of America or Israel is illusory. Unity, the proper ideology, a good strategy, and innovative tactics will bring enemies to their knees. They lack the Arabs' and Muslims' steadfastness, readiness to suffer, and willingness to sacrifice themselves.

After making these arguments, however, the paths of rulers and revolutionaries diverge.

On one hand, Arab rulers usually deal with this worldview from a cynical perspective. Most, but by no means all, of the time they are not eager to fight the West or do anything that would endanger their regimes. For them, such propaganda is a tool, a way of ensuring control at home and leverage over other Arab states. They are like a coachman who whips the horses to go faster but keeps tight control of the reins.

On the other hand, the revolutionaries – who are often the loudest voices in the public debate – keep asking reasonable questions. If all of these ideas are true, why don't the hypocritical leaders practice what they preach? How could they even consider making peace with Israel instead of going to war, especially when they could win? How can they allow U.S. troops on their soil to save them from Saddam? Why don't they all unite?

Since leaders never openly reject the belief system, it remains unchallenged even when it becomes obvious how erroneous its concepts and prescriptions really are. That's one reason why the main opposition in every Arab country is radical Islamist, and why liberal Arabs remain a tiny minority. Yet this doctrine's obvious deviation from reality and experience explains why many Arabs ridicule it in private, though they don't dare speak up in public.

And so it is only logical that about every ten years some alchemist blows up the Middle East in an experiment trying to prove that these ideas work. There was Nasser losing the 1967 war; Khomeini urging revolution in 1979 and bringing on Iraq's attack; Saddam Hussein seizing Kuwait in 1990 and suffering a crushing military defeat; bin Ladin and the Taliban in 2001 showing how easily America could be defeated, because God was on their side, but being chased down in Afghanistan; and the whole history of the Palestinian movement's repeated miscalculations and self-inflicted setbacks.

How does the system survive the effects of its massive failures? After all, the Arab world is a mess, falling behind every other region in almost every category of social and economic progress. From Algeria in the west to Iran in the east, there are dead bodies in the streets. And yet people are not yelling from the rooftops and proclaiming daily that their ideology is bankrupt, their leaders incompetent, and the radical Islamist opposition even worse.

Repression is part of the answer, but it is only a small part of the overall control mechanism. The broader answer is the strength of the ideological system. Each element in it provides a trump idea that can be used to block, delegitimize, and destroy any truly alternative view. If someone demands democracy, the response is that the Arab-Israeli conflict (or the Islamist threat) doesn't permit this luxury. When anyone criticizes the government's human rights record, he is chided for not complaining about Israel instead. When anyone raises questions about economic mismanagement, he is insulted for covering up the fact that it is really the fault of the United States. To demand the rule of laws passed by a freely elected parliament would mean being branded a threat to Islam and its legislation, which is made only by God.

It is this doctrine and the regimes it protects that contribute most to keeping the Arab world weak, backward, and ultimately alienated from the West. Those claiming to be the Arabs' great champions are the ones really ensuring that their people remain in chains and causing most of their suffering. The first step in changing these tragic circumstances is to recognize that they exist.

INDEX

Islamic Revolutionary Guards Corps
(IRGC), 127, 128, 129
Islamic Salvation Front (Algeria), 184
Islamism: and al-Jazira, 263; as dominant
ideology of Middle East from 1950s to
1990s, 13–32, 49–50; and political
systems of Arab world, 77, 168–92;
and Syria, 113–14; and terrorism, 167;
and violence in politics of Middle East,
139–40. *See also* ideology
Israel: agreement with PLO in 1993, 37;
Arab-Israeli conflict and politics of
Middle East, 3–4, 193–226; and Arab
military forces, 147; GDP per capita in
2000, 7; and ideologies of Arab
nationalism and Islamism, 21, 23–4, 44;
and nationalism, 40n7; and power
projection, 148; and Syria, 98, 99–104,
112, 115; and U.S. Middle Eastern
policy, 235, 238, 240–3. *See also* Zionism
Iyad, Abu, 196

Jawad, Salah Abdel, 222
al-Jazira (television), 213, 261–6, 271
Jordan: ethnicity and military of, 144;
and Islamism, 173, 181; military
expenditures, 142; and Palestine
Liberation Organization, 43; and peace
with Israel, 46; population growth, 53;
and reactionary monarchies, 42; and
Syria, 98; and terrorism, 157–8; and
U.S. Middle Eastern policy, 238.
See also Abdallah, King
Jumblatt, Kemal, 157

Kadda, Sulayman, 114
Kamil, Hussein, 86, 88
Karmi, Hafez, 265
Kelly, John, 255
Kemalism, and Turkey, 12
Kenya, terrorist attack on U.S. embassy in
(1998), 166, 191
Kerr, Malcolm, 229
Khaddam, Abd Halim, 113, 114, 115, 221
Khadir, Hasan, 32
Khamenei, Ayatollah Ali, 123–4, 128–9,
129–30, 134–5, 254
Kharrazi, Kamal, 134
Khatami, Muhammad: and foreign policy,
130–1, 134; and Islamism, 174; and
nuclear weapons program, 136; and
reform in Iran, 6, 119, 120–3, 125, 128,
129, 133; and student demonstrations,
127
Khazen, Jihad, 259–60
Khobar Towers, terrorist attack on (1999),
134

Khomeini, Ayatollah Ruhollah: and
anti-Americanism, 21, 135, 231, 249,
253; and Arab nationalism, 118; and
Iran-Iraq War, 94; Islam and theocratic
rule, 124–5; Khamenei as successor to,
129; and revolution in Iran, 122; and
terrorism, 191
Khouri, Rami, 26–7, 31
Kikhia, Mansur, 165
Kilburn, Peter, 164
Kinkel, Klaus, 132
Kosovo: and Arab-Israeli conflict, 217; and
U.S. Middle Eastern policy, 233
Kramer, Martin, 34n1
Kurds, in Iraq, 77–8, 80, 93, 144, 162
Kuwait: Iraq and annexation of, 36, 39,
79, 133, 199; Islamism and liberalism in,
185–6; and terrorism, 160, 162; and
U.S. Middle Eastern policy, 228, 234.
See also Gulf War

Lahoud, Emile, 17
Lake, Tony, 38, 202
Laroui, Abdallah, 203
Latin America: economic growth in 1990s,
51; and U.S. foreign policy, 231n6; and
Western model of civilization, 62.
See also South America
al-Lawzi, Salim, 157
Lebanon: civil war of 1970s and 1980s,
19; and Islamism, 180–1; and Israel,
196, 202–3, 210–11; military, 143; Syria
and control of, 17, 98, 99, 106, 111,
147; and terrorism, 153–4, 156–7, 160
liberalism: and Arab-Israeli conflict, 207;
and Islamism, 184–7. *See also* reform
Libya: military coup, 140; and terrorism,
47, 163–5; and U.S. Middle Eastern
policy, 238
life expectancy, increase in Middle East of
1990s, 55
literacy, and social development in Middle
East of 1990s, 54
Lockerbie, Scotland, terrorist attack over
(1988), 47, 164
Los Angeles Times, 261

Madrid conference (1991), 38
Mahbak, Ahmad Ziyad, 113
al-Mahdi, Amin, 207
Makiya, Kenan, 80n6, 162n45
al-Masri, Zafir, 158
Meaning of the Disaster, The (Zurayk), 217
media: and public opinion and politics in
Middle East, 260–6; state control of, in
Middle East, 72. See also *al-Hayat*;
al-Jazira